ASP.NET MVC 1.0 Test I

ASP.NET MVC 1.0 Test Driven Development

ASP.NET MVC 1.0 Test Driven Development

Problem – Design – Solution

Emad Ibrahim

Wiley Publishing, Inc.

ASP.NET MVC 1.0 Test Driven Development
Problem – Design – Solution

Published by
Wiley Publishing, Inc.
10475 Crosspoint Boulevard
Indianapolis, IN 46256
www.wiley.com

This book is dedicated to my beautiful soon-to-be-wife, Laura, for her unconditional love and support. I love you. Te amo mucho. Ana Bahebyk.

About the Author

Emad Ibrahim hates to talk about himself because he doesn't know what to say and how to label himself. He is a programmer, an entrepreneur, a thinker, a dreamer, and a humanist. He is all that and none of that. He is clearly conflicted.

He graduated from Virginia Tech in 1999 without honors and has since worked in small and large companies, in small and large teams. He has written code in coffee shops, libraries, skyscrapers, and basements. He has managed teams across the room, across the country, and across the world.

He was born in Egypt, graduated kindergarten and met Santa Claus for the first time in Jordan, graduated high school in Zambia, and graduated college in the USA. He has lived in Virginia for more than 14 years and now claims it as his home and final destination.

Emad programs in VB, C#, Objective-C, and Ruby. He programs for Windows, the Web, mobile devices, and the iPhone. Legend has it that after a few beers he once said, "I wish I had my computer. I feel like coding."

Credits

Acknowledgments

Many people contributed directly and indirectly to this effort. I am grateful for their thoughtful insights. I thank Adaobi Obi Tulton and Jim Minatel for their incredible patience, understanding, and support throughout the writing process. They have made the writing process so much easier.

By the time this book is published, I will be married to Laura — my fiancée of two years and the love of my life. I am looking forward to spending the rest of my life with you. Thank you for your love, support, encouragement, and your belief in me.

I want to acknowledge my dad for teaching me to dream big, encouraging and supporting me in everything I do. When I was a kid, I used to tell people I wanted to win the Nobel Peace Prize when I grew up. Needless to say, everyone thought it was funny except my parents, and specifically except for my dad. No dream was ever too big for him. Of course, I have not won the Nobel Peace Prize, but the fact that I am writing this acknowledgement means that one of my dreams did come true — to write a book.

I also want to acknowledge the best mom in the world. She is the best listener, and the most compassionate and loving mother. Thanks for unconditionally listening to all that I have to say even when none of it made sense. She is also a fantastic cook. One day we will create a cookbook together.

Last but not least, I want to acknowledge my "little" sister, Caroline. Thank you for being there when I need you. You are a great sister and friend. I can't believe you will be a doctor in a few months. Don't expect me to address you as "Doctor," though.

Oh, I almost forgot. I want to thank my puppy, Mac, for keeping me company during the writing process, for taking me on walks at convenient times, and for forcing me to take a break from work by chewing my laptop cable. Good boy Mac.

Contents

Contents

Introduction

Dear reader, thank you for picking up this book, and welcome to the exciting world of Test Driven Development (TDD) and ASP.NET MVC. Sometime in 2008, I quit my job and decided to start my own company. Naturally, my startup was web-based. At the time, I was already very familiar with the Microsoft web development platform, a natural choice for my website. I hesitated to use it because I wanted to learn something new and I wanted to use TDD. Several of the web startups at the time were written in Ruby on Rails (RoR), and I seriously considered going that route. I played around with RoR and became familiar with it. I liked its approach to development, the ease of testing, and the control I had over HTML and JavaScript. There are several things that I didn't like, however, especially the Integrated Development Environment (IDE). Nothing came close to Visual Studio. Luckily, around that time Microsoft introduced ASP.NET MVC, which made the decision very easy for me.

Even though ASP.NET MVC was still in early alpha, I went ahead and built my startup on top of it (talk about taking risks). It was a great experience for me and turned out to be a good decision. I instantly fell in love with the MVC way of doing things. I enjoyed the control I had over the generated HTML and scripts. I loved the clean and friendly URLs. I can't imagine living without the unit tests that I could easily run when I make a change, to verify that I haven't broken anything. I can go on and on about why I love ASP.NET MVC and TDD and how much more enjoyable they make programming.

Don't get me wrong, though; it's not all sunshine. There is a learning curve. You can't just drag-and-drop a control and instantly have a grid. You can't drag-and-drop a few controls, set a couple properties, and instantly have form validation. ASP.NET MVC requires some manual work. The upside is that there is no more magic, so you will actually *know* what is happening on your page, what gets rendered, and how it gets there. Best of all, you will not see anything that you didn't put on the page. No more hidden fields, strange scripts, or magical events — just straight up HTTP requests.

Who This Book Is For

Do you love programming? I don't mean "like" or "enjoy," I mean *love*. If you are like me, then you probably do, and if you do, then you owe it to yourself to learn ASP.NET MVC and to get into Test Driven Development. They will make something that you already love so much more enjoyable.

With that said, let me state up front that this isn't a book for completely novice programmers, or for experienced developers who have never touched ASP.NET and the .NET Framework in general. This book teaches how to write a real-world website from scratch to deployment, and as such, it can't explain every single detail of the technology, but must concentrate on designing and writing actual solutions. To read this book comfortably, you should already have had some experience with ASP.NET 2.0, even if not advanced solutions. You're not required to know ASP.NET MVC, as each chapter will introduce the new concepts and features that you'll use in that chapter, providing enough background information to implement the solution. If you then want to go deeper and learn everything you can about a feature, you can refer to the MSDN official documentation or to another reference book such as *Professional ASP. NET MVC 1.0* by Rob Conery, Scott Hanselman, Phil Haack, and Scott Guthrie (Wrox, 2009).

This book is not a crash course in ASP.NET MVC, and it's also not an advanced ASP.NET MVC or TDD book. I don't do a lot of handholding, and I don't delve into all the intricacies of the framework or theories of TDD. I wanted this book to be practical and as close to real-world development as possible. I wanted to create an application, show and explain my decisions, make mistakes, and fix them.

Think of this book as a documentary. I try to develop a web application from scratch and document the process. I make mistakes. I correct them. I (and hopefully you) learn from them. I intentionally kept the mistakes I made in earlier chapters and addressed them in later chapters because I wanted to show the flexibility, power, and usefulness of Test Driven Development. Do you know the feeling when you make a change to the code and cross your fingers hoping that you didn't break something somewhere else in the application? This problem, and the risks associated with it, is greatly diminished when you use TDD. Imagine making a change, running your tests, and instantly finding out that you just broke six different tests. This immediate knowledge is very comforting. It also allows you to make changes more frequently, fix bugs easily, and feel confident that your changes didn't break anything.

What This Book Covers

This book is basically a documentary of creating a web application using Test Driven Development. This book leads the reader through the development of an ASP.NET MVC 1.0 website that has most of the features users expect to find in a modern site.

The one thing that sets this book apart is its practicality. You will not find many (if any) theoretical explanations that span multiple pages. This book covers practical decisions and concepts, such as:

- Unit testing frameworks and tools
- Inversion of Control and Dependency Injection
- Code coverage
- Mocking
- JavaScript libraries and AJAX

I will also use the following .NET 3.5 features that were added in C# 3.0:

- LINQ
- LINQ-to-SQL
- Extension methods
- Anonymous methods

In addition, you will learn how these new features and concepts integrate with standard ASP.NET 2.0 features, such as:

- Master pages
- Membership and profile modules

Not only does this book cover the new features of ASP.NET MVC 1.0, it also demonstrates how to integrate all of them together in order to develop a single full-featured site. After reading this book, you will know many of the best practices for web development using TDD.

How This Book Is Structured

This books starts at the beginning of building a web application using TDD. It starts with a high-level description of the project I am building and then goes into the initial setup and tool selection. Then I start working my way through the actual development of the application.

There are many steps that are common to each chapter. These steps are explained in detail the first time, and from then on they are briefly mentioned.

If you want to build the application and follow along, then it will be more useful to read the book in order. Otherwise, you should be able to open any chapter and learn something new.

Each chapter has three major sections:

❑ **Problem** — This defines the problem or problems to be addressed in the chapter: What do you want to do in this chapter? What features do you want to add to the site and why are they important? What restrictions or other factors need to be taken into account?

❑ **Design** — After the problem is defined adequately, this section describes what features are needed to solve the problem. This will give you a broad idea of how the solution will work.

❑ **Solution** — After establishing what I am going to accomplish and why (and how that solves the problem defined earlier), I will produce and discuss the code and any other material that will realize the design and solve the problem laid out at the beginning of the chapter. Just as the book as a whole focuses primarily on the solution, so does each chapter. This is where you will get hands-on practice and create the code.

What You Need to Use This Book

All you need to follow along in this book is Visual Studio 2008 and ASP.NET MVC 1.0, as well as the tools, frameworks, and libraries mentioned in the first two chapters. Other than Visual Studio, all the tools used in the book are free and/or Open Source. There are one or two commercial tools, but they are only suggested, not required.

Conventions

To help you get the most from the text and keep track of what's happening, we've used several conventions throughout the book.

> **Boxes like this one hold important, not-to-be forgotten information that is directly relevant to the surrounding text.**

Notes, tips, hints, tricks, and asides to the current discussion are offset and placed in italics like this.

As for styles in the text:

❑   We show filenames, URLs, and code within the text like so: `persistence.properties`.

❑   We present code in two different ways:

```
We use a monofont type with no highlighting for most code examples.
We use gray highlighting to emphasize code that's particularly important in the
present context.
```

Source Code

As you work through the examples in this book, you may choose either to type in all the code manually or to use the source code files that accompany the book. All of the source code used in this book is available for download at `www.wrox.com`. Once at the site, simply locate the book's title (either by using the Search box or by using one of the title lists) and click on the "Download Code" link on the book's detail page to obtain all the source code for the book.

Because many books have similar titles, you may find it easiest to search by ISBN; this book's ISBN is 978-0-470-44762-8.

Once you download the code, just decompress it with your favorite compression tool. Alternatively, you can go to the main Wrox code download page at `www.wrox.com/dynamic/books/download.aspx` to see the code available for this book and all other Wrox books.

Errata

We make every effort to ensure that there are no errors in the text or in the code. However, no one is perfect, and mistakes do occur. If you find an error in one of our books, like a spelling mistake or faulty piece of code, we would be very grateful for your feedback. By sending in errata you may save another reader hours of frustration, and at the same time you will be helping us provide even higher quality information.

To find the errata page for this book, go to `www.wrox.com` and locate the title using the Search box or one of the title lists. Then, on the Book Search Results page, click on the Errata link. On this page, you can view all errata that has been submitted for this book and posted by Wrox editors.

A complete book list including links to errata is also available at `www.wrox.com/misc-pages/booklist.shtml`.

If you don't spot "your" error on the Errata page, click on the Errata Form link and complete the form to send us the error you have found. We'll check the information and, if appropriate, post a message to the book's errata page and fix the problem in subsequent editions of the book.

p2p.wrox.com

For author and peer discussion, join the P2P forums at `p2p.wrox.com`. The forums are a web-based system for you to post messages relating to Wrox books and related technologies and interact with other readers and technology users. The forums offer a subscription feature to email you topics of interest of your choosing when new posts are made to the forums. Wrox authors, editors, other industry experts, and your fellow readers are present on these forums.

At `http://p2p.wrox.com` you will find a number of different forums that will help you not only as you read this book, but also as you develop your own applications. To join the forums, just follow these steps:

1. Go to `p2p.wrox.com` and click on the Register link.

2. Read the terms of use and click Agree.

3. Complete the required information to join as well as any optional information you wish to provide and click Submit.

4. You will receive an email with information describing how to verify your account and complete the joining process.

> *You can read messages in the forums without joining P2P, but in order to post your own messages, you must join.*

Once you join, you can post new messages and respond to messages other users post. You can read messages at any time on the Web. If you would like to have new messages from a particular forum emailed to you, click on the "Subscribe to this Forum" icon by the forum name in the forum listing.

For more information about how to use the Wrox P2P, be sure to read the P2P FAQs for answers to questions about how the forum software works as well as many common questions specific to P2P and Wrox books. To read the FAQs, click on the FAQ link on any P2P page.

ASP.NET MVC 1.0 Test Driven Development

1

Requirements

Since in this book, we will create a fully functional web application, it makes sense to start by defining the requirements and what the application is. Keep in mind that we want to keep things simple and not create a hundred-page requirements document.

This book will document the development process of creating a web application using Test Driven Development (TDD) with ASP.NET MVC. We will develop a bulk email/newsletter distribution web application called EvenContact. In a nutshell, the application will allow users to manage and communicate to contacts using email messages.

Instead of delving into too much theory and in the process boring you, we will actually walk you through the development process using real tests and code. We will make mistakes on the way and correct them as we go — just as in real life. Fixing bugs and correcting mistakes is where TDD really shines, as it adds an extra safety net to ensure that the one line of code you added to fix a minor bug didn't unintentionally create five new critical bugs.

Problem

We have all received tons of email newsletters from all sorts of senders. A sender creates these newsletters and sends them out to a mailing list. The sender probably wants to track and report on the progress of their email campaign. They probably also want to manage their subscriber lists and give the subscribers the options to opt in and opt out. We will be creating a web-based email newsletter distribution application that will allow the sender to perform these tasks, and we shall call it EvenContact.

Design

There are three major and specific components in this application:

1. Message management (create, send, etc.)

2. Contact management (create, import, lists, etc.)

3. Reporting

The preceding list doesn't include generic and cross-cutting components such as membership, logging, billing, and so on.

Let's break each of these into smaller pieces that we can use as our requirements and to set the direction of the application.

> Message *refers to the email message or newsletter that the user of the application will create and distribute to their recipients.*

> A contact *is simply an email recipient or in its most basic form, an email address.*

Message Management

Our web application will need to allow us to manage messages. Management includes all actions related to this task, including creating, editing, displaying, deleting, and sending messages. The user interface for the application should be intuitive and easy to use, and the screen flow should fit with use cases for the system. For example, the user might want to send a message after creating it or might save it for later.

Create Message

The user needs the ability to create a message from scratch by going to a page that lets him compose the message and give each message a unique name. They need to be able to create a simple text message and a rich HTML message. The HTML message could contain images, tables, and standard HTML formatting such as bold, italic, and so on. HTML messages need to be created in a What You See Is What You Get (WYSIWYG) editor as well as provide the ability to edit the markup. The HTML message editor will provide functions to upload and use an image or link to an existing one.

Message Templates

The user can select from a list of predefined templates to jump start the message creation. Once a template is selected, the user will be directed to the message composition page with the message editor prefilled with the HTML from the template, where they can customize the message.

List Messages

The user can view a list of all their previously created messages. They should be able to perform actions on a selected message. Actions can be edit, delete, duplicate, and so on. The list should be in a grid format and support paging and sorting. The user can sort by date sent, date created, or message name. Only one message can be acted on at once, that is, no multiple selection.

Edit Message

The user can open a message and make changes to it. The most common scenario will be for the user to click the edit action in the message list to edit the message. Editing will provide a similar interface to the message creation view. Editing a text message will display the simple editor and editing an HTML message will display the WYSIWIG editor.

Save Message

The user can save a message without sending it. If a message has already been sent then a copy is created. The save action will be available from the edit and create screens. While in edit mode, saving will overwrite the existing message unless it has been sent before. In that case, a copy is created. The user will be prompted to name the copy.

Duplicate Message

The user can duplicate a message from a previously created message. This will create an exact copy of the message, and the user will be prompted to name the newly created message. The message name must be unique. Once a duplicate is created, it will have no relationship or association with the original message.

Send Message

The user will be able to send a message. Once a message is sent, it cannot be edited or deleted. The user is required to name the campaign before sending it. The user will have the option to send it right then or schedule a later delivery.

> *Campaign refers to an instance of sending a message. So when a user creates a message and sends it, they have created a campaign. For example, when a user creates and sends a message called "November Newsletter" to a recipient or group of recipients, that is a campaign.*

Delete Message

The user cannot delete a message that has already been sent. If a message has not been sent, then it can be deleted. Deleting a message completely removes it from the database. A delete action cannot be undone. The user must confirm the delete action.

Search Messages

The user can search their messages. The search should look into message content and metadata. Search results should display in a grid format that supports paging. Since this is a simple search and the results contain no weights, the results will be sorted by date in descending order (newest message on top).

Contact Management

Contacts are a centerpiece of this application, and the ability to manage these contacts is fundamental to the application. The user needs to create, modify, and delete contacts as well as group them in lists and target them in mailing campaigns.

Create Contact

The user can create a contact. All contacts are stored in the user's global "address book." An email address is the only required element for a contact and works as a logical unique identifier for a contact. This means that no two contacts can have the same email address.

> *The global address book is a list of all the contacts that the user owns. This is synonymous with global list, and the terms will be used interchangeably.*

There are several ways for a user to create a contact:

1. Enter one contact at a time
2. Enter multiple contacts in a multiline text field. One contact should be entered per line.
3. Import contacts from a text file. The text file will be comma delimited and contain one contact per line.

Edit/View Contact

The user can make changes to a contact. The email field cannot be changed (since it is the unique identifier for a contact). All other fields can be changed or cleared. Edit and View are identical except that when viewing, everything is read-only and cannot be changed.

List Contacts

The user can view all contacts and perform actions on the selected contacts. This will display the list of contacts in a grid format that can be paged and sorted. Actions will include edit, delete and view. The grid can be sorted by email, first name or last name. The user can select multiple contacts. The only action available when multiple contacts are selected is the delete action.

Delete Contact

The user can delete a contact. Deleting a contact that was used as a recipient of a previously sent message should not delete the actual record but mark it as archived. This is needed to preserve the accuracy of historical stats and to maintain the state of sent messages.

Search Contacts

This provides a way for users to search for a contact. The search will look through all contact metadata (email, name, description, etc.). The search results will be displayed in a grid format that is similar to the list of contacts and has the same features.

Create Contact List

The user can create a contact list to organize their contacts. A list can contain some or all of the user's contacts.

Think of a contact list as a mailing list. It allows the user to group contacts together to better target, segment, and organize their contacts. A user can create a contact list for Valued Customers, New Customers, and so on.

Edit/View Contact List

The user can edit a contact list. They can edit its metadata (name, description, etc.) and add/remove users to/from the contact list. Deleting a contact from a contact list only removes the contact from that list but doesn't actually delete the contact from the "global" list of contacts. Viewing is identical to editing except that nothing can be changed.

Add Contact to Contact List

The user can add contacts to the list in two ways:

1. Using the same workflow to create a contact as mentioned previously. If a contact already exists, it will be added to the list. If a contact is new, it will be created then added to the list.

2. By selecting contacts from a list. These can come from a previously created list or the global list.

Delete Contact List

The user can delete a contact list. Deleting a contact list does not delete its contacts by default. The user will have the option to also delete the contacts. When deleting a contact the same rules apply.

Reports and Stats

The user will be able to view reports and stats on users, campaigns, and so on.

There are a ton of reports that can be created to analyze the data and give users more insight into their customers, but for the sake of simplicity we will focus on basic reports.

Campaign Report

- ❑ Number of recipients
- ❑ Number of views (i.e., people who opened the email message). This only works for HTML messages
- ❑ Total number of clicks
- ❑ Links clicked and click count
- ❑ Number of unsubscribes

User Report

- ❑ Total number of emails sent to user
- ❑ Total click count
- ❑ Total view count
- ❑ Campaigns targeting user
    - ❑ Viewed?
    - ❑ Click count
    - ❑ Links clicked and click count

Miscellaneous Requirements

Here is a list of some miscellaneous requirements:

1. Emails sent must have a link to unsubscribe.

2. Users need an HTML/JavaScript snippet to provide a subscription form.

3. Accounts are free to create.

4. Users will be charged based on the number of emails sent.

5. There will be different payment plans, including a pay-per-use plan.

Solution

So far, the problem is that we need a website to manage email distribution and the design is a set of requirements that must be met to address the problem. In the solution section, I want to talk about the technology, tools, and methodology that we will be using to envision our solution.

Model-View-Controller

The Model-View-Controller (MVC) is a common architectural/design pattern that is used to isolate the business logic from the user interface. This results in a loose coupling between the two that allows us to easily modify the visual presentation (the view) or the underlying business layer independently without affecting each other. In MVC, the model represents data, the view represents the user interface, and the controller manages the communication between the user's actions on the view and the model.

ASP.NET MVC

The ASP.NET MVC framework — as the name implies — is the Model-View-Controller framework for ASP.NET. It is different than the ASP.NET WebForms model that we have been accustomed to for the past several years. In the WebForms world, we have *PostBacks, ViewStates, server-side event handling, server controls*, and so on. In MVC, we don't get any of that. Some might think, "What? I can't live without these things!" and others might think "It's about time." Microsoft has gone to great lengths to emphasize the fact that the MVC framework does not and will not replace WebForms. It is simply an alternative to it.

You might ask yourself, "Which one should I use?" The short answer is, "It depends." If you want to use Test Driven Development, then MVC is a much better-suited candidate. That doesn't mean you can't do TDD with WebForms, but it is so much easier with MVC. If you are creating a prototype or a simple data-driven website (an internal site, for example), then I would say WebForms is better suited for this. There is just no faster way to create a grid that is pageable, sortable, and editable than by using a grid view in a WebForms application with ASP.NET Dynamic Data.

MVC Strengths

- ❑ Absolute control over rendered HTML

- ❑ No ViewState

- ❑ No PostBack

- ❑ Clean separation of responsibility (model, view, controller)

- ❑ Better suited for TDD

WebForms Strengths

- ❏ Better suited for Rapid Application Development (RAD)
- ❏ A plethora of third-party controls and tools
- ❏ Better integration with the IDE (Visual Studio 2008)
- ❏ Abstraction of low-level technologies (HTML, CSS, JavaScript)

Some of the advantages of WebForms will eventually disappear as the MVC framework matures. For example, third-party support and IDE integration will eventually be comparable on both platforms. At the end of the day, it will be a matter of preference and personal style.

In the following pages, I want to explain some important concepts that are central and in some cases new to the ASP.NET MVC framework.

Model

The model is a domain-specific representation of the information. These are the classes that represent your entities; for example, `User`, `Customer`, `Account`, and so on. There are many ways to create a model; you can use a DataSet, LINQ to SQL, or the ADO.NET Entity Data Model. You can also use your preferred Object-Relational Mapping (ORM) tool to generate your model classes or you can just create your own POCO classes.

> *POCO stands for Plain Old CLR Object, and it came over from the Java world where it is called POJO (the J stands for Java; the CLR stands for Common Language Runtime). It is used to indicate that the object is a standard object and not a complex or special object to be used for a specific framework or component. For example, the DataTable, WebForm, and UserControl are non-POCO, while the following class is a POCO:*

```
public class User
{
    public string FirstName { get; set; }
    public string LastName { get; set; }
    public DateTime DateOfBirth { get; set; }
}
```

View

If you use ASP.NET MVC out of the box, then your views will either be a `ViewPage` or a `ViewUserControl`. These are the counterparts to a `Page` and `UserControl` in the WebForm world. Usually a `ViewUserControl` is used for partial views. Just as in WebForms a `ViewPage` can inherit from a master page, in MVC you inherit from `ViewMasterPage`.

Controller

The controller is the liaison between the view and the model. The controller is made up of actions that are invoked by the view. An action performs a specific task, which most likely involves dealing with the model, and then renders the next view to show its results. Think of a scenario when a user clicks the submit button on a form (the view). The framework will route the button click (or more specifically the HTML form submit) to a specific action in a controller that receives the form data and acts on it and then returns back the results by rendering a new view. Figure 1-1 shows the relationship between the model, view, and controller and is pretty much the standard diagram you will see whenever the model-view-controller pattern is discussed.

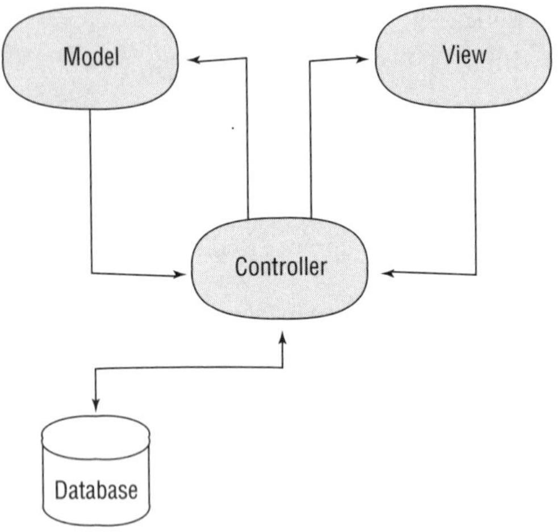

Figure 1-1

Routing

The ASP.NET MVC framework includes a flexible URL routing system that allows us to define mapping rules. The routing system maps an incoming URL to the appropriate controller and action. For example, if we use the default route definition, a URL like `/user/edit/2` will be mapped by the routing system to the Edit action in the User controller and will be passed 2 as an ID parameter. The mapping system also constructs outgoing URLs, which we use in our views to submit forms and create links and so on.

The routing system is pretty flexible and gives us the ability to change routes without changing code. So if we decide to change the URL from `/user` to `/customer`, then we just change it in our route definition in the application startup logic.

ViewData

You are probably wondering how the controller sends data to the view. For example, if you are editing a customer record, the controller needs to grab that data from our data store and send it to the view. This is done using the `ViewData` property in the controller. `ViewData` is of type `ViewDataDictionary`, and you can set/get values to/from it by either using the dictionary (e.g., `ViewData["title"] = "Edit Customer"`) or setting the `ViewData`'s Model property to an instance of your model class that you want sent to the view — or you can do both. Here is an example:

```
var model = Repository.GetCustomer(2);
ViewData.Model = model;
ViewData["title"] = "Edit Customer";
```

The view will be able to retrieve the data sent to it by accessing its own `ViewData` property. You can get the page title set above like this:

```
<title><%= Html.Encode(ViewData["Title"]) %></title>
```

And you can access the model mentioned above like this:

```
<%= Html.TextBox("firstname", Html.Encode(ViewData.Model.FirstName))%>
```

This will generate the following HTML:

```
<input id="firstname" type="text" value='Firstname' />
```

HTML Helpers

You might have noticed that, in some of the previous examples, I used the `Html` helper class. This class contains several helper methods that allow you to generate HTML easily. Some people prefer to use them, while others don't. I am somewhere in between. The following two statements are identical in that they produce identical HTML:

```
<%= Html.TextBox("email")%>
```

and

```
<input id="email" type="text" />
```

Which one to use is really your choice, but in this book, you might see me mix them together. I do that because sometimes the helper method might be less efficient (or uglier) than just plain HTML, and in other instances it might be a significant time saver. The preceding example is too simple to illustrate the benefit of using the helpers.

Action Filters

Action filters are attributes that are used to decorate an action, a controller class, or even the entire assembly, that allow us to intercept the action(s) and perform some logic prior to or after execution. The framework comes with some predefined action filters out of the box. One such action filter is `Authorize`, which will prevent an unauthorized user from executing the action by directing them to the login page. Action filters can be used for tracing, exception handling, and logging, among other uses. To create an action filter, you inherit from `ActionFilterAttribute` and override the methods you need. Your class would look something like this:

```
public class TraceAttribute : ActionFilterAttribute
{
    public override void OnActionExecuting(ActionExecutingContext filterContext)
    {
        //write trace stuff before executing the action
    }
    public override void OnActionExecuted(ActionExecutedContext filterContext)
    {
        //write trace stuff after executing the action
    }
}
```

TempData

`TempData` is similar to `ViewData` in that it allows us to send data to the view. The fundamental difference between `TempData` and `ViewData` is that `TempData` is only available for the life of one request. That makes it ideal for storing temporary information that you only want to send to the view once. Good candidates to store in `TempData` are messages that are only relevant for that specific request. For example, if a record update was successful, you could say `TempData["msg"] = "Record updated successfully";`. The view can then retrieve this message and notify the user that the record was updated successfully. Once that is done, the message is not needed anymore, and there is no reason to persist it anywhere.

ModelState

The `ViewData` contains a property called `ModelState`. The `ModelState` is a collection of model states. Specifically it is of type `ModelStateDictionary` and contains a dictionary of `ModelState` objects accessible with a string key. This dictionary is used to pass the model state back to the view, which is very useful in validation scenarios. For example, one can add an item to the `ModelState` indicating that the login credentials were not correct and, by using helper methods, validation is greatly simplified. We will discuss this in more detail later, but here is a quick example of how you would add something to the `ModelState`:

```
ViewData.ModelState.AddModelError("password",
                password, "Password is incorrect.");
```

Methodology, Concepts, and Approach

In the next few pages, you will learn about the approach, methodology, and common patterns that we will use to create the application. These are pretty large topics and going into depth about some of them is beyond the scope of this book. Nonetheless, I want to briefly explain them, so that we have a common language to use. At the end, it should help you understand the book better.

Test Driven Development (TDD)

Test Driven Development, or TDD, is a software development technique that is made up of short iterations where tests are written first and then code is written to satisfy the test condition. To use a more concrete example, if we wanted to write a method to validate an email address, we would write the test first that covers this use case and then write the method to make the test pass.

The TDD cycle consists of the following sequence:

1. **Add a test.** Create a test to satisfy a requirement. In our example, we would create a test that calls the email validation method with an invalid email address.

2. **Run the tests.** Since we haven't written any code, the test should fail. This is an important step because it validates that the test won't always pass, which would make it worthless. Initially, you can't even run the tests because you will have compiler errors, since you haven't written the code your test is calling yet.

3. **Write code.** Write code to satisfy the test condition. In this case, you will create the `IsValidEmail` method to validate an email address.

4. **Run the tests.** The tests should now pass. If they fail, then repeat step 3 until they pass.

5. **Refactor.** Now that the requirement is met, we can refactor our code. Re-run the tests as you refactor the code to make sure that you have not broken anything.

The preceding cycle is repeated throughout the development process for each new feature that needs to be added.

If you examine the preceding cycle and think about it, you might realize its benefits. One immediate and apparent benefit is that we already have a unit test written. We have all worked on projects where we agreed to create unit tests one week before release and what ends up happening most of the time is that we are so busy trying to meet the deadline that we don't have time to create the tests.

Having a test in place is tremendously powerful and comforting. It allows us to change the code in the future, press the Run Tests button, and immediately find out if the two lines of code we just added introduced 20 new bugs.

Starting the iteration with a test means that we need to very clearly understand the requirements in order to satisfy them. Having a clear understanding of the requirements, use cases, and user stories will inevitably lead to better software and ultimately a satisfied customer.

We all know that the requirements will change a few weeks (or even days) into the project. Therefore, satisfying the requirement with tests allows us to easily change the code and verify the changes by running the tests (see Figure 1-2).

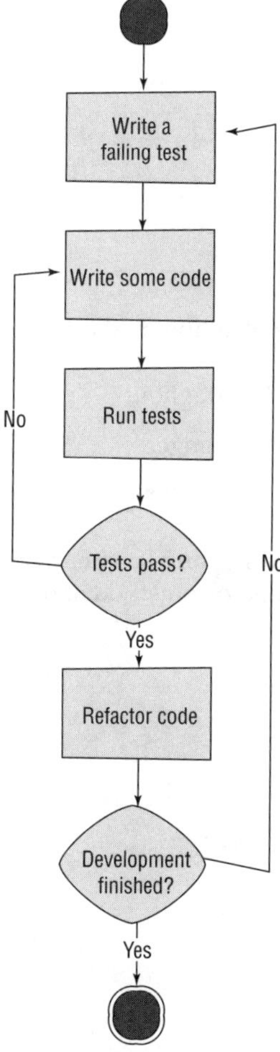

Figure 1-2

Aspect-Oriented Programming (AOP)

Aspect-oriented programming, or AOP, is a style of programming that increases code modularity, readability and reusability by allowing for the separation of cross-cutting concerns. A cross-cutting concern is a behavior that is common across your application layers and can be hard to express using traditional object-oriented techniques.

For example, a common aspect is logging. In order to log your application's actions, you have to sprinkle logging code throughout your code. However, most classes or methods that you want to log from don't (and shouldn't) really care about logging. For example, one can write a method like this:

```
public void AddFriend(string friendName)
{
    try
    {
        LogMessage("AddFriend Called");
        //code that adds a friend
    }
    catch (Exception ex)
    {
        LogException(ex);
        //handle exception
    }
    finally
    {
        LogMessage("AddFriend Ended");
    }
}
```

There are several problems with the preceding method:

- ❑ The logging code is dispersed throughout.

- ❑ The code is hard to maintain or change.

- ❑ The code has to be manually written for every method.

A better way to do this is to use aspects. Using PostSharp as our AOP framework, we can create a new aspect for logging that can be applied to our method above by simply applying an attribute. Our code might look like this:

```
[Log()]
public void AddFriend(string friendName)
{
    try
    {
        //code that adds a friend
    }
    catch (Exception ex)
    {
        //handle exception
    }
}
```

The `Log` aspect (attribute) will be able to log the appropriate messages at different points during the method invocation, for example on entry, on exit, on error, and so on.

Definitions

Aspect — A modularization of a cross-cutting concern — for example, logging, transaction management, tracing, exception handling, or authorization

Joinpoint — A point where the main program and the aspect meet during execution — for example, a method invocation or an exception being thrown

Advice — The action taken by the AOP framework at a joinpoint

---

Patterns

I want to briefly explain some design patterns that we will most likely use in this application. This is not a patterns book and there are people more qualified to delve into the details of each pattern; I simply want to briefly name and describe each pattern. Most of my pattern descriptions came from the canonical reference for software patterns — Martin Fowler's book *Patterns of Enterprise Application Architecture* (PoEAA; Addison-Wesley, 2002).

We have already explained the Model-View-Controller (MVC) pattern, so we will skip it in this section.

Strategy

This pattern is intended to define a family of algorithms, encapsulate each one, and make them interchangeable. Strategy lets the algorithm vary independently from clients that use it.

Definitions

Strategy — An interface declaration that is common to the algorithm

Concrete Strategy — An implementation of the strategy

Context — An object that is configured to use a concrete strategy

---

Conceptually, the strategy pattern is shown in Figure 1-3.

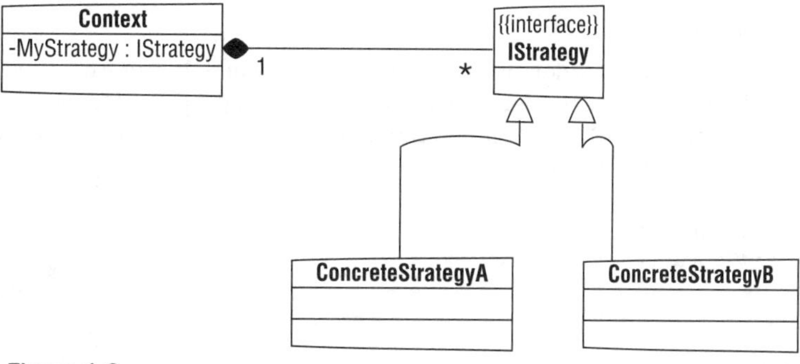

Figure 1-3

One example where the strategy pattern can be applied is in sorting. The class diagram could look
something like Figure 1-4.

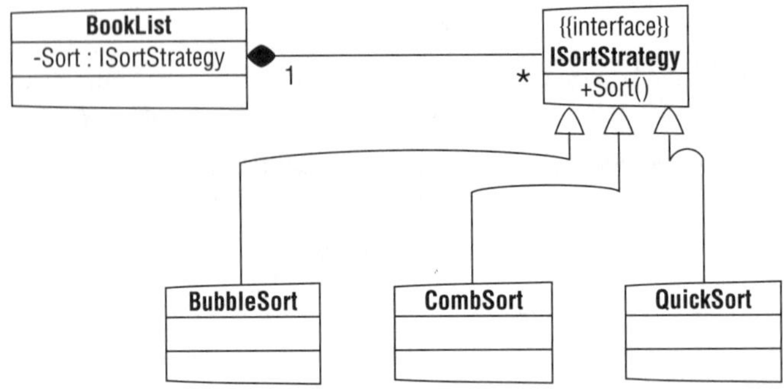

Figure 1-4

Null Object

A null object is an object designed to represent the absence of an object. If you invoke anything on a
null object in .NET, you will get a `NullReferenceException`. It is better to return an object instance
that represents the lack of an object. For example, if your customer doesn't have any orders and you try
to get their orders, using the null object pattern, you would do this:

```
public List<Orders> GetOrders(int customerId)
{
    //get orders from database
    //if no orders exist then return an empty list
    return new List<Orders>();
}
```

This is better than returning null because the consumers of your method won't have to perform null checks, and calling the `Count` property on the returned object won't throw a
`NullReferenceException`.

```
var orders = GetOrders(2);
//won't throw an exception
txtTotalOrders.Text = orders.Count;
```

Lazy Instantiation (aka Lazy Load)

This is the pattern where the creation of an object, calculation of value, or execution of an expensive
process is delayed until it is first needed. For example, here is a property that will return a user's contacts, but it is only computed when it is called the first time. So if it is never called, we never incur the
cost of retrieving the list of contacts.

```
private List<Contact> contacts;
public List<Contact> Contacts
{
    get
    {
        if(contacts == null)
```

```
        {
            contacts = GetContactsFromDatabase(userId);
        }
        return contacts;
    }
}
```

Repository

This pattern allows us to create a data access layer that is independent of the data store. This makes data access changes and TDD much easier. For example, we can create a contact repository by defining the following interface:

```
public interface IContactRepository
{
    IQueryable<Contact> GetContact(long id);
    IQueryable<Contact> GetContacts(long customerId);
    long Create(string email, string name, string description);
    bool Delete(long id);
    bool Update(Contact contact);
}
```

We can now implement this interface to talk to a SQL database in production, implement it to talk to an XML file during integration testing, or even implement it to talk to an in-memory database for unit-testing purposes.

Principles

The following is a list of software principles that I will apply throughout the book whenever and wherever possible. These principles are general and abstract and have wide applicability. They create a set of programming guidelines that can be used during software development regardless of the language. Actually, many of these principles are so generic that they can be applied to other fields unrelated to software development.

Open-Closed Principle

The open-closed principle states that a software entity (class, module, assembly, etc.) should be open for extension but closed for modification. This allows others to change the entity's behavior without changing its source code. This is usually achieved through inheritance. For example, if a class has a `Send` method that sends out a message, we can open it to extension by allowing derived classes to override the `Send` method and implement a different send functionality such as sending by instant messaging (IM) instead of Simple Mail Transfer Protocol (SMTP).

YAGNI

YAGNI is short for "you ain't gonna need it" and simply means that you should only add code/functionality when you need it and not when you foresee that you need it. Recently, I have become a big fan and advocate of the YAGNI approach. That is mainly because I remember all the code that I have written in the past that I *thought* I was going to need. We all know that every line of code adds complexity, and every new feature needs to be tested, debugged, fixed, documented, and supported.

So think very hard before you add new features. Do you really need it? Do you need it now? If you don't need it now then don't do it now. When the need arises (and it might never arise), then you go ahead and add it — by then it will probably be different than what you initially thought.

KISS

The KISS (keep it simple, stupid) principle states that things should be kept simple and complexity avoided. This principle can be applied to other disciplines and not just software development. But in the context of software development we should strive to keep things simple and avoid unnecessary complexity, so we don't end up with a Rube Goldberg machine. For example, if you know for a fact that you will only be using SQL server as your data store, then there is no need to add support for other database systems or to write database-agnostic code because you ain't gonna need it.

Everything should be made as simple as possible, but no simpler.

— Albert Einstein

DRY

DRY is acronym for "don't repeat yourself." The DRY principle is aimed at reducing duplication. Duplication decreases maintainability because it increases the difficulty of change. It might also lead to inconsistencies and ambiguity. During refactoring is a good time to look at code that you have been copying and pasting in multiple places and refactor it into a single and authoritative location. DRY is not only useful for application code but for test code as well.

Inversion of Control (IoC) and Dependency Injection (DI)

Inversion of Control (IoC) and Dependency Injection (DI) are two principles that allow us to create loosely coupled systems with fewer dependencies. Inversion of Control is the indirection of object instantiation so that objects do not directly create other objects. Instead, an IoC `Container` will inject the dependencies into an object through construct parameters or public properties.

Imagine a class that requires the use of an `EmailService` that encapsulates email functionalities. If we use constructor injection, we can define our class like this:

```
internal class MyClass
{
    public MyClass(IEmailService emailService)
    {
        this.EmailService = emailService;
    }
}
```

Then we would configure our IoC container to tell it how to instantiate an `IEmailService` and to inject the instantiated object into the above class. If this doesn't make sense or seems too vague and theoretical, don't worry; in the coming chapters, you will see better examples.

Single Responsibility

The single responsibility principle states that a class should have one responsibility. A responsibility is considered to be a reason to change. If there are two reasons to change for a class then it should be split into two classes. Take a look at the following class, which represents a `Customer`:

```
internal class Customer
{
    public long Id { get; set; }
    public string Name { get; set; }
```

```
    public Address ShippingAddress { get; set; }

    public void Save()
    {
        //code to save the customer
    }

    public void Delete()
    {
        //code to delete the customer
    }
}
```

At first glance, this class looks OK. The problem with the class is that it has two reasons to change. One reason is if the schema changes and you need to add new properties or change existing properties. The other reason is if the persistence changes. This could happen if you change your data store or if you normalize/denormalize your database and then you want to store `Customer` across multiple tables or one table. This class should be broken into two classes, one representing the model and another dealing with persistence.

Liskov Substitution Principle

This principle basically says that any derived class can be used to substitute for its base class without altering the correctness of the application. Look at the following classes; the Liskov substitution principle states that we can use `Airplane`, `Motorcycle`, or `Boat` wherever `Vehicle` can be used:

```
internal class Vehichle
{
}
internal class Airplane: Vehichle
{
}
internal class Motorcycle:Vehichle
{
}
internal class Boat: Vehichle
{
}
```

Convention Over Configuration

Convention Over Configuration is a design paradigm that emphasizes convention over configuration by reducing decisions (configurations) that the developer needs to make. You still have the ability to configure things and still maintain a level of flexibility, but by using the convention you gain simplicity and avoid any extra work. The ASP.NET MVC framework does a great job of applying this design paradigm throughout. Here are some examples of conventions that are used:

- ❑ All controllers are named `[something]Controller`.
- ❑ All views are in the `Views` folder.
- ❑ All public methods in a controller are considered actions.
- ❑ Form fields are mapped to action parameters with the same name.

These are just a few of the conventions; we will explore more of these conventions throughout the book, and they will be highlighted in sidebars.

Tools and Frameworks

So far we have talked about the problem, design, and solution. It is now time for us to choose the tools and frameworks that will help us implement the solution. I wanted my tool selection to be encompassing and open minded. I spent a lot of time researching the alternatives and trying to pick the one that fits my application needs. So don't think of this as an endorsement of one framework over another. Also, many of these tools are open source and are very rapidly changing so that one feature that is missing at the time of my research might be implemented by the time you read this book. I think the concepts are more important than the actual tools. One thing I have to admit is that it was extremely exciting and frustrating at the same time to be able to work with cutting-edge frameworks that aren't even in beta. The good news is that most of these tools are being actively developed and have great community support. Worst case scenario, I have access to the code and, if I don't like something, I can change it.

Unit-Testing Framework

If we are going to practice TDD, we are going to need a unit testing framework. Microsoft Visual Studio Team System 2008 Edition contains a unit testing framework usually referred to as MSTest. I decided not to use MSTest even though it was in my comfort zone. My decision was solely based on the fact that I didn't want to assume that you have a few thousand dollars to spare on a copy of Visual Studio. I looked into nUnit, MbUnit, and MSTest and decided to go with MbUnit. One of the reasons was the overwhelming and enthusiastic support of several influential developers. Personally, one feature that I really liked was Row Tests, which allows us to have a single test with multiple sets of data. For example, the test below will run three times to test three different invalid usernames:

```
[Test]
[Row("abc", Description = "Username is too short")]
[Row("1user", Description = "Username starts with non-alpha")]
[Row("user$abc", "Username contains invalid characters")]
public void Register_Should_Fail_For_Invalid_Usernames(string invalidUsername)
{
    //test registration process
}
```

MbUnit also works very well with ReSharper's test runner, which is well integrated into Visual Studio, and I can easily click on the marker next to every test to run or debug it, as shown in Figure 1-5.

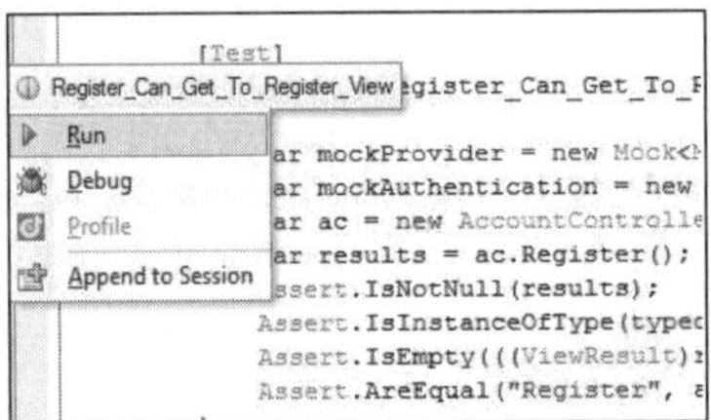

Figure 1-5

The test runner has a very good user interface that quickly pinpoints the status of the test(s) and points out failed tests as well as the reason for failure, as shown in Figure 1-6.

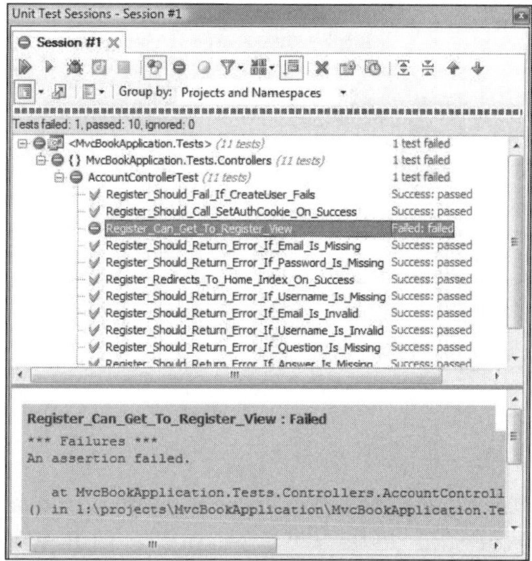

Figure 1-6

Code Coverage

Code coverage is an essential metric in Test Driven Development. It measures the degree to which the source code is tested, that is, covered. Using a code coverage tool, we can run our tests and look at our code coverage report. Ideally, you want to reach 100% code coverage. Most tools can help visually show you what is covered and what is not by highlighting code blocks in different colors. Figure 1-7 shows the code coverage window that is part of Visual Studio 2008.

Hierarchy	Not Covered (Blocks)	Not Covered (% Blocks)	Covered (Blocks)	Covered (% Blocks)
ResetPassword()	0	0.00 %	5	100.00 %
ResetPassword(string)	0	0.00 %	40	100.00 %
ResetPasswordQuestion(class MvcB...	0	0.00 %	15	100.00 %
ResetPasswordQuestionSubmit(class...	9	18.75 %	39	81.25 %
FormsAuthenticationWrapper	4	100.00 %	0	0.00 %
HomeController	12	100.00 %	0	0.00 %

Figure 1-7

Code coverage is only available in the Developer, Test, and Team Suite editions of Visual Studio Team System 2008.

You can see from Figure 1-7 that `ResetPasswordQuestionSubmit` method has nine blocks, or 18.75%, not covered. Double-clicking the item will display the method with the code highlighted in different colors to indicate blocks that have not been covered by the test. As shown in Figure 1-8, the first two `if` statements are never reached, which means my tests are not testing these conditions.

```
[AcceptVerbs("post")]
[ActionName("ResetPasswordQuestion")]
public ActionResult ResetPasswordQuestionSubmit([Model
{
    ViewData["Title"] = "Reset Password";
    if (string.IsNullOrEmpty(model.Username))
    {
        ViewData.ModelState.AddModelError("username", "
                                          "Username is
    }

    if (string.IsNullOrEmpty(model.Question))
    {
        ViewData.ModelState.AddModelError("question", "
                                          "Question is
    }

    if (string.IsNullOrEmpty(model.Answer))
    {
```

Figure 1-8

If you don't have code coverage in your Visual Studio edition, then you can use NCover, which is an excellent alternative.

JavaScript Library

We will need to use JavaScript and AJAX to enhance the usability and performance of the website. It is imperative that we use a JavaScript library that is fast, easy to learn, and easy to write. After reviewing several JavaScript libraries, I immediately fell in love with and have become a big fan of JQuery. JQuery allows you to do things in JavaScript that you either never thought were possible or are very hard to do. It has a very powerful and clean syntax and allows you to do things like this:

```
$(document).ready(function() {
    $("h2").addClass("red");
});
```

The preceding code will add the class "red" to any "h2" element. JQuery also has a huge community, good documentation, and a great repository of plug-ins and extensions.

With that said, I also really like YUI (Yahoo! User Interface Library); it has an excellent set of user interface controls/widgets. It is very well documented, has good support, and looks great. There are two components that I will use from YUI: the Rich Text Editor and the YUI Test Utility. The YUI Test Utility comes with a good test runner (shown in Figure 1-9) and has excellent documentation.

Figure 1-9

IoC Container

I wanted to use an IoC container to simplify my controllers and reduce their dependencies on other classes. This allows for vastly simplified test writing and a better design overall. There are several IoC containers out there, and they all looked very good and very powerful. But the majority had a very steep learning curve and a convoluted configuration process. I looked into the following:

- StructureMap
- Spring.Net
- Castle Windsor
- Autofac
- Ninject

Initially, I went with Autofac for its very fluent interface, highly discoverable API and very readable code. Here is a short Autofac example:

```
var builder = new ContainerBuilder();
builder.Register<Straight6TwinTurbo>().As<IEngine>();
```

After playing around with Autofac for a while, someone recommended that I check Ninject. It looked as good and as easy as Autofac, but it had better documentation and seemed slightly easier to learn. Ninject also had a very easy contextual binding syntax that lets you do this:

```
Bind<IService>().To<RedImpl>()
    .Only(When.Context
            .Target.HasAttribute<RedAttribute>());
Bind<IService>()
    .To<BlueImpl>()
    .Only(When.Context
            .Target.HasAttribute<BlueAttribute>());
```

In the following code `ConsumerA` will be injected with the `RedImpl` implementation of the `IService` interface, while `ConsumerB` will be injected with `BlueImpl` implementation.

```
class ConsumerA {
  public ConsumerA([Red] IService service) {
  }
}

class ConsumerB {
  public ConsumerB([Blue] IService service) {
  }
}
```

Choosing an IoC container was challenging and relatively subjective, but at the end of the day, I think if you choose any of these IoC containers, you will be fine.

One thing I love about ASP.NET MVC is the choices. You are not locked into using one vendor/product/framework and can pretty much plug in your vendor/product/framework of choice at every level of the framework. You can replace your controller factory, view engine, view rendering, route handler, and other extension points. It is very extensible.

Mocking

Mocking allows us to simulate the behavior of a complex object in unit tests. This is extremely valuable when using a real object is difficult or impossible to do. If you wanted to unit test the create user action, but don't want the code to create a record in the database, then you can mock the calls to the database. In the context of this test, we don't really care about the implementation of the database call; instead, we want to test the create user action's logic.

There are several very good mocking libraries, including:

- TypeMock
- NMock
- NMock2
- Rhino Mocks

In my opinion, none of them is as easy to use and as elegant as Moq. It is so easy to use that I was up and running in no time. Here is how easy it is to set up a mock:

```
var mockMembership = new Mock<MembershipProvider>();
mockMembership.Expect(p => p.MinRequiredPasswordLength).Returns(4);
```

In the preceding example, we created a mocked instance of `MembershipProvider` and told it that if `MinRequiredPasswordLength` is called, it should return 4. Now you can easily pass this mocked object to your controller constructor being tested without caring about the actual implementation of the `MembershipProvider`.

Moq as explained on its homepage "is the only mocking library for .NET developed from scratch to take full advantage of .NET 3.5 (i.e., Linq expression trees) and C# 3.0 features (i.e., lambda expressions) that make it the most productive, type-safe and refactoring-friendly mocking library available. And it supports mocking interfaces as well as classes. Its API is extremely simple and straightforward, and doesn't require any prior knowledge or experience with mocking concepts."

Why EvenContact?

I wanted to create a somewhat generic application that will benefit the readers with their real-world applications and help illustrate the power and flexibility of the ASP.NET MVC framework and the test-driven approach to development. I thought this would make a good application from a technical point of view. Plus, I also got tired of reading books, articles, and blog posts that use blog engines or some sort of content management system as the example to teach everything. The blog engine has become the "hello world" of today's programming book. Last, in order to kill two birds with one stone, I wanted to create a service that I can actually offer online and potentially generate revenue from. This has a two-fold advantage. I have to make sure I am creating something good that people will want to pay for, and by doing so, I am able to produce a better book and hopefully help others learn in the process.

Summary

Now that we have everything in place, we are ready to start coding. I want you to think of this book as a documentary. I am basically documenting my development process as I progress through it. I believe this will produce a more "real-life" experience of performing TDD with ASP.NET MVC. This means that I might make decisions in Chapter 2 that are changed in Chapter 4 because of new information or false assumptions. This should be an interesting experience for all of us and hopefully one that will highlight the benefits of TDD and good design.

2

High-Level Design

This chapter will talk about the high-level design of the application. We will discuss some screen flows as well as look at some draft screen layouts. The diagrams in this chapter were hand drawn to emphasize that this should not be a long and complicated process. We are basically trying to visualize the application to help us get some bearings on where to go next.

Problem

Now that we have the requirements, we need to create some high-level designs to direct our development. Remember that we are using a Test Driven Development/Design (TDD) approach, so we will not be creating detailed design documents. This is just high level enough to help us visualize the application, clarify some processes, and flesh out some potential gotchas along the way.

Design

We will start by designing some of the basic functions of the site that are common to almost any web application; then we will get into more topics specific to our application. I don't call them the basics because they are easier or simpler than the rest. All these features are still first-class citizens. They are basics because they are pretty much common to every application. Again, this will not be a detailed design, so let's talk about the major pieces and sketch some diagrams.

Membership

We need a membership system that allows us to manage our users and provide them with secure access to their account.

First, we start with the user registration (signup) process. The flow for registration is shown in Figure 2-1.

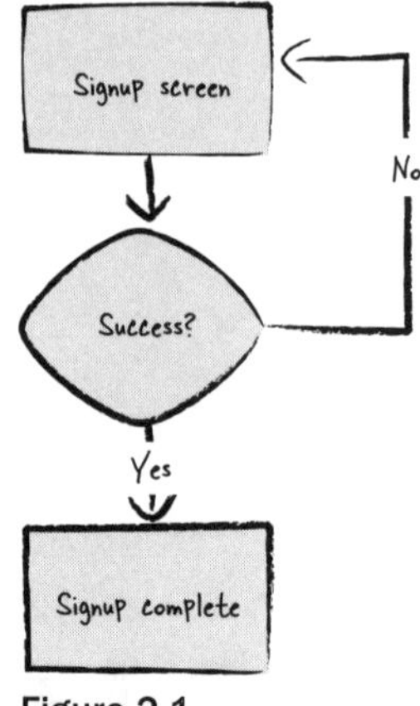

Figure 2-1

A screen layout will look something like Figure 2-2.

Figure 2-2

> ### Password Confirmation
>
> I sign up to hundreds of sites, and it amazes me that almost *all* of them force you to confirm your password. This doesn't make any sense to me. Most sites give you a way to reset your password, so what is the point of confirming it? If I forget it or had a typo in it (which is rare anyway), then I just reset my password. Personally, I feel that password confirmation is a waste of time and resources and is not very user-friendly.
>
> I know this seems like a small thing but this one, seemingly simple field is actually a significant amount of work. Here are some steps that would usually go into implementing it:
>
> 1. Write JavaScript to validate field.
> 2. Write server code to validate field.
> 3. Write unit tests to test the server validation.

Next is the login process, which is shown in Figure 2-3.

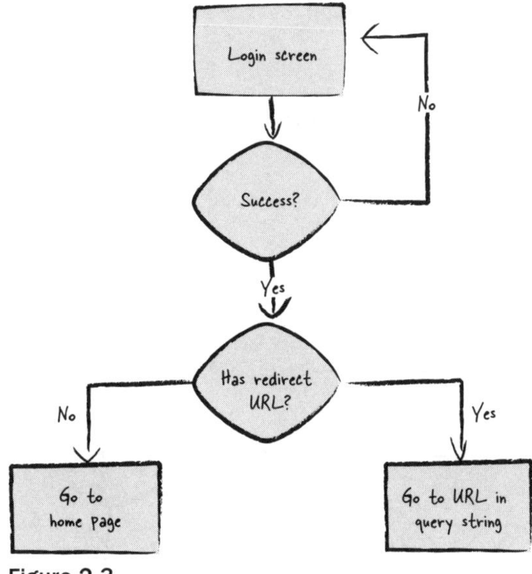

Figure 2-3

The screen layout would look something like Figure 2-4.

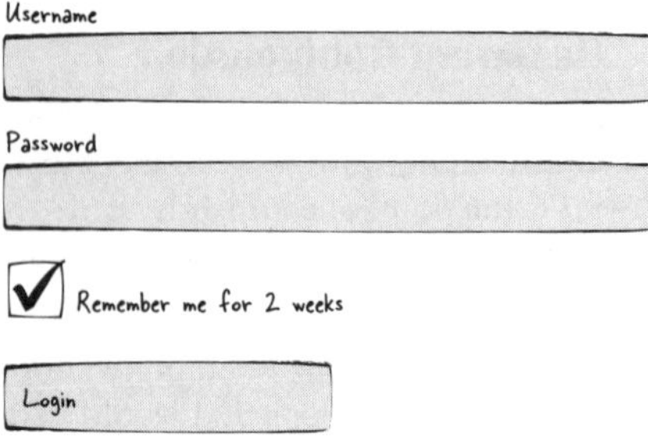

Figure 2-4

We also need a way for the user to reset their password. First of all, we don't want random people to just enter a username or email and allow them to reset the password for that account. We need to confirm that the legitimate account owner is requesting the reset. There are several ways to do this. One way is to send an email to the account owner and ask him to click on a link to initiate the reset process. But since we have a secret question and answer for the user, we can just ask the user the question and if the answer matches what we have on record, we reset the password and email the user their new password. This way, we eliminate the extra email and the hassles that come with that. The reset password process is shown in Figure 2-5.

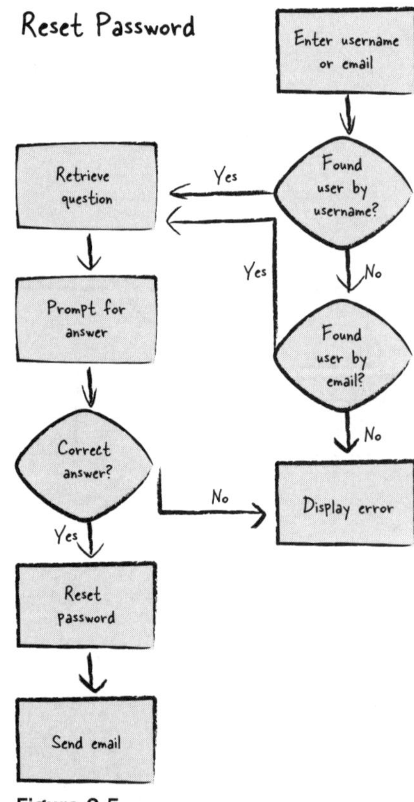

Figure 2-5

Figure 2-6 shows the reset password screen(s).

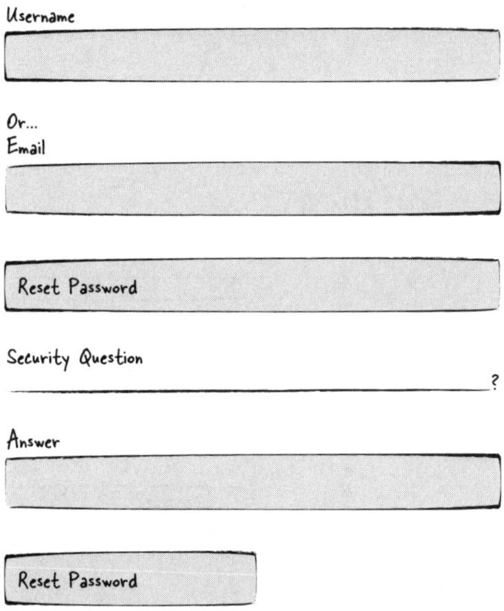

Figure 2-6

Account Management

Every member has an associated account. The account management component of the site allows the user to view their account as well as make changes to it. The account entity can be pretty large, and it makes sense to break it into smaller pieces. For example, billing information can be its own piece, even though it is part of the account. Let's say an account is made up of the following:

- ❏   Basic information (name, address, email, etc.)

- ❏   Billing information (payment method, credit cards, billing address, etc.)

- ❏   Subscription information (selected plan)

For the sake of this application, we will go with a very simple account entity and collect the least amount of data. All we really need is an email address, a PayPal account, and a subscription plan, which is illustrated in Figure 2-7. If we decide later to collect more information, we can break the account page into smaller sections as described.

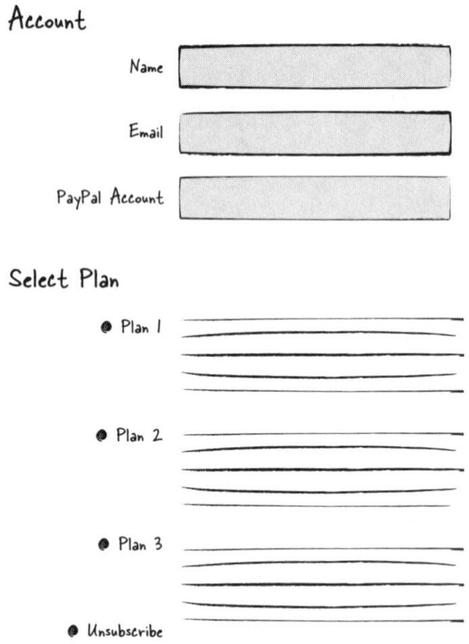

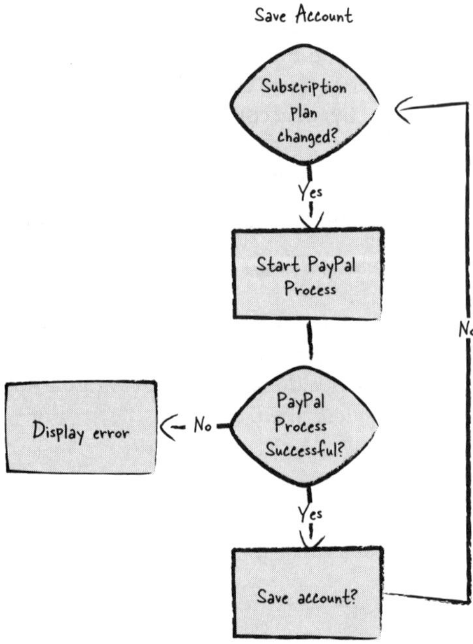

Figure 2-7

To further simplify billing, we will use PayPal as our payment processor, which supports subscriptions. Figure 2-8 shows our save account process.

Figure 2-8

Message Management

This is the part that deals with the messages. The first step would be to create a message; this is a really basic step, and if you have used any web-based email system, you are probably familiar with it. It is a basic form that takes a list of recipients and the message body at its most basic form. Let's look at the more interesting edit message process, shown in Figure 2-9.

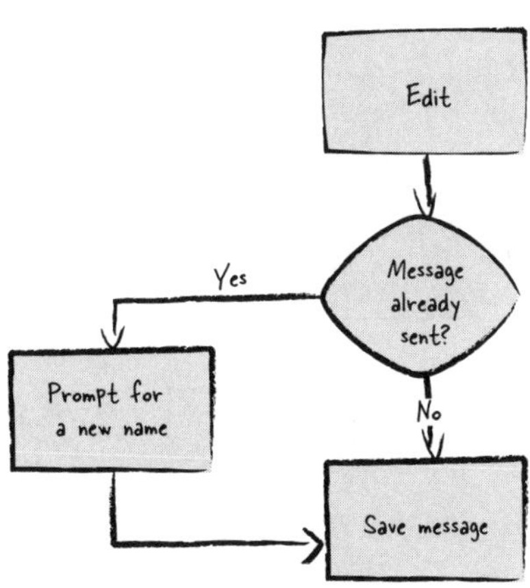

Figure 2-9

Sending a message involves several steps and needs to be asynchronous. Since the user might be sending to thousands of recipients, we do not expect to send thousands of emails synchronously. Instead, the emails are queued in a persistent queue (probably in the database). The queue can then be monitored by a Windows service. We will not discuss the queue-monitoring service, as it is out of the scope of this book. All we need to do is get the emails into the queue and assume that there is a service out there taking care of clearing the queue and doing the actual email send.

Message Queue

From the point of view of our web application, a record is added to the database to indicate that message X needs to be sent to recipient Y. The "queue-monitoring" piece can be a Windows service that runs in the background and polls the queue table in the database every 5 minutes (or whatever interval makes sense) and then sends the message to the recipient, deletes the record from the queue, and proceeds to the next one.

Another option is to create a SQL job that runs at a specific interval and performs the same functionality. Whichever method you choose will work as long as you can query the queue table, send email, and delete a record from the queue table.

Contact Management

Most of the contact and list management tasks are simple CRUD operations that I will just skip here. Instead, let's take a look at the overall process of creating a list and adding contacts to it. The diagram in Figure 2-10 shows this process.

> ## CRUD
>
> CRUD is an acronym for create, read, update and delete, which are the four basic operations of persistent storage. In SQL terms:
>
> > Create = INSERT
> >
> > Read = SELECT
> >
> > Update = UPDATE
> >
> > Delete = DELETE

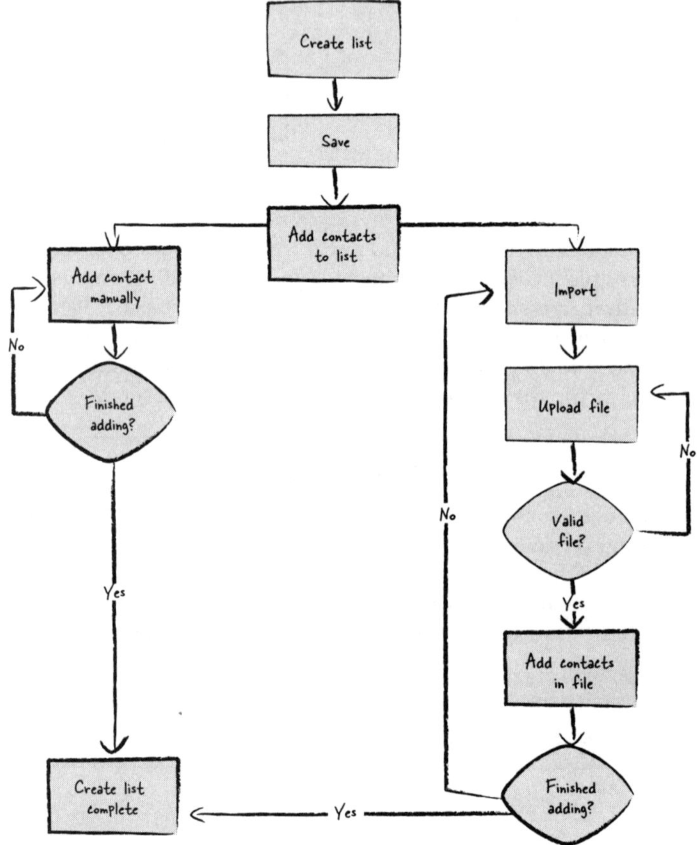

Figure 2-10

One thing to note about the create list process is that adding a contact to a list is not just creating a database record for the new contact. The contact might already exist in the user's global address book and should not be added again. We are also adding a reference to the contact in the list. This will let us edit contact information in one place and have all lists updated. The email address is the unique identifier of a contact, so if a contact with the same email exists, we should not add a new one but instead attempt to update values. For example, if the user already has a contact with the following information:

Name	Homer
Email	hsimpson@fox.com
DOB	(null)

and the new record being imported has the following:

Name	Homer Simpson
Email	hsimpson@fox.com
DOB	01/01/1955

then the process should update the existing record with the new date of birth because there is no conflict, but prompt the user to choose the correct name since there are two versions. Perhaps the flow diagram in Figure 2-11 will help.

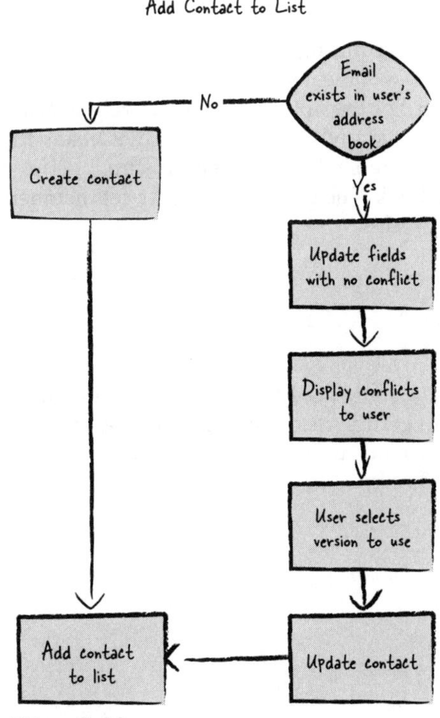

Figure 2-11

Solution

The solution for the design described in this chapter is really the rest of this book, but before we can start creating the application in the coming chapters, we have to set up our environment.

The following is required:

- Visual Studio 2008 with the latest service pack
- ASP.NET MVC framework (`http://asp.net/mvc`)
- Moq (`http://code.google.com/p/moq`)
- Ninject (`http://ninject.org`)
- JQuery (`http://jquery.com`)
- YUI (`http://developer.yahoo.com/yui`)
- MbUnit (`www.mbunit.com`)

I also highly recommend using ReSharper, a must-have productivity tool. ReSharper also includes a very good test runner that works with MbUnit. If you don't have ReSharper, you can use TestDriven.net (`http://www.testdriven.net`) which is a free test runner that also works with MbUnit.

I didn't mention version numbers because most of these libraries have a very short development cycle, and there is a new release almost every other week. I will be using the latest build that is available at the time of writing the book, which means that some of the code might change. Nonetheless, you should be able to get the concepts and easily modify the code to work with the latest version.

Once you get all the tools up and running, create a new "ASP.NET MVC Web Application" and an associated MbUnit test project. This will create a new web application for you that includes basic membership tasks — login and signup. For the sake of this book, we will assume that we are starting with a blank application that doesn't have anything. You can either delete the automatically created files or you can leave them and skip the chapters related to membership. I highly recommend that you get rid of them and follow along in the book. The goal is not to just get membership up and running but to do it using TDD, and learn in the process.

Summary

By now, you should be all excited and ready to write some code. In this chapter, we discussed some high-level designs and started getting ready to implement our solution by setting up our environment. We are now ready to hit the ground running and start cranking out some tests. Let the fun begin.

3

Membership

Where do we start? Since this application will require users to sign up and log in to use any of its features, it makes sense to start with the membership component of the site. In this chapter, we will go through the process of creating the registration (signup) functionality using a Test Driven Development (TDD) approach. The chapter starts with very elaborate and detailed steps, but as we progress, we will go over the common stuff pretty quickly.

Problem

We need to meet the membership requirements of allowing the user to:

1. Create an account (i.e., register, sign up).
2. Log in.
3. Reset password (we are using one-way password hash, so we cannot retrieve it and must reset it).
4. Update membership information (change email, security question, etc.).
5. Change password.

Design

Since we are using TDD, we can probably think of our tests as our design. We start by creating a test for a specific feature/requirement, and then we write the code needed to satisfy the test. In essence, we are designing our application by writing tests. For example, if we want to accept only usernames that contain only letters and that are three or more characters long, then we will write a test for that followed by code to satisfy the test.

As mentioned in the previous chapter, the registration process involves the following steps:

1. Collect name, email, password, security question and answer.

2. Ensure username is unique.

3. Ensure username is valid:

   ❑ It is 4 characters or more.

   ❑ It starts with a letter.

   ❑ It contains only letters, numbers, and underscore.

4. Ensure email is unique and valid.

5. Create the user account and log the user in.

Solution

Before we can start cranking out tests, we need to create a test class. Let's add a new test class for the `AccountController` and name it `AccountControllerTest`. In order for it to be a test class, you decorate it with MbUnit's `[TestFixture]` attribute. Here is the class:

```
[TestFixture]
class AccountControllerTest
{
}
```

> ### Convention
>
> Test classes will be named as follows: *[class name]Tests*. For example, if we are testing the `PayController` class, then the test fixture will be named `PayControllerTests`.
>
> Test methods will be named using clear and descriptive names that clearly identify the test and its outcome. You can separate the name either using uppercase letters or using underscores. For example: `CallbackShouldReturnNull` or `callback_should_return_null`.
>
> I personally prefer the underscore method, but there will be a mix of both in the code. I settle on using lowercases and underscores toward the end of the book.

There are two Register actions that we need to accommodate. One action just displays the view that would happen with a GET request, and the other will submit the form to the server to perform the registration that would happen with a POST request.

Let's ensure that the user can actually view the Register page. We start by creating a simple test that would simply need to show whether a user can navigate to the Register view, that is, `http://evencontact.com/account/register`.

I know you are twitching to write your first test. Simmer down and let's think about what we need to test. We want to make sure that:

❑ We can call the Register method with the correct arguments.

❑ The page title is set up correctly.

❑ We get a valid `ActionResult` as the return value.

Easy enough, but what constitutes a valid `ActionResult`? I know that when we go to the Register page we want to render the Register view, so let's take a first crack at the test:

```
[Test]
public void Register_Can_Get_To_Register_View ()
{
    var ac = new AccountController();
    var results = ac.Register();
    Assert.IsNotNull(results);
    Assert.IsInstanceOfType(typeof(ViewResult), results);
    Assert.IsEmpty(((ViewResult)results).ViewName);
    Assert.AreEqual("Register", ac.ViewData["Title"], "Page title is wrong");
}
```

Note how we decorate the method with the `[Test]` attribute. This tells the test framework that this is a test. You will notice that if you try to build this test, you will have a compiler error telling you that `AccountController` could not be found. This is our first test failure (red light).

Convention

Tests related to actions will be named in this format: `ActionName_[descriptive test name]`.

It's imperative to have a descriptive test name. *Register_Test* is not a good test name. It might sound OK now, but when you have 400 tests, it won't be very helpful.

Let's create the `AccountController` class and try to build; now we get an error that `AccountController` does not contain a definition for *Register*. So, let's create the Register action as follows:

```
[AcceptVerbs("GET")]
public ActionResult Register()
{
    return null;
}
```

> **Acceptable Verbs**
>
> The [AcceptVerbs] attribute tells the framework which HTML verbs the action can handle. This allows us to create two actions with the same name — that is, the same URL — and have each one handle a different HTML verb. For example:
>
> ```
> [AcceptVerbs("GET")]
> public ActionResult Login()
> ```
>
> will be called when the user navigates to http://mysite/login. And
>
> ```
> [AcceptVerbs("POST")]
> public ActionResult Login(string username, string password)
> ```
>
> will be called when the user posts a form to http://mysite/login.
>
> Both actions map to http://mysite/login, but one gets called for a GET and the other for a POST.

We have to return something for the project to compile, so let's just return null for now. The solution should now compile fine.

Let's run the test and make sure that it fails. Since we are returning null, the test will fail because the Assert.IsNotNull (results) fails. Let's change the Register action to:

```
[AcceptVerbs("GET")]
public ActionResult Register()
{
    return View();
}
```

This will return the Register view, and if we run the test now, we should get an error that the "Page title is wrong." Let's make one more change to the Register action:

```
[AcceptVerbs("GET")]
public ActionResult Register()
{
    ViewData["Title"] = "Register";
    return View();
}
```

Run the test. The test passes (green light). Woohoo!!! Our first test works.

This is a very simple action and test, so there isn't really much to refactor, at least for now.

Moving on, we need to write tests for the second Register action, the one that actually registers the user. We want to:

❏   Ensure that a Register action exists with the correct signature.

❏   Ensure that the user is registered.

❏   Ensure that we are redirected to the homepage after registration.

Here is our first test:

```csharp
[Test]
public void Register_Can_Successfully_Register_New_User()
{
    var ac = new AccountController();
    var results = ac.Register(username, email,
                               question, answer, password);
    Assert.IsNotNull(results);
    Assert.IsInstanceOfType(typeof(RedirectToRouteResult), results);
    var typedResults = results as RedirectToRouteResult;
    Assert.AreEqual("Index",
                    typedResults.Values["action"],
                    "Wrong action");
    Assert.AreEqual("Home",
                    typedResults.Values["controller"],
                    "Wrong controller");
}
```

In this test, we check that the returned value is not null and that it is of type `RedirectToRouteResult`. Then we make sure that it is redirecting to the correct destination, that is, /home/index. Then we check that the page title is correct.

The variables passed to the Register method are declared as fields at the class level in the `AccountControllerTest` *class because we are going to use them for the other tests.*

You are probably thinking, "Why do we need to check the page title if this is a POST action?" The reason we check is because we will need to validate the form at one point, and if there is a validation error (or any other error), we need to render the Register view again to display the errors.

Again, we won't be able to compile the project because no Register method with this signature exists. Let's create it:

```csharp
[AcceptVerbs("POST")]
public ActionResult Register(string username, string email,
                             string question, string answer,
                             string password)
{
    return null;
}
```

Run the test. It fails because we are returning null. Change the action to:

```csharp
[AcceptVerbs("POST")]
public ActionResult Register(string username, string email,
                             string question, string answer,
                             string password)
{
    return RedirectToAction("Index", "Home");
}
```

Run the test. It passes. You might think that this test is useless and doesn't prove anything. Although the test doesn't prove that we have successfully registered a user, it proves that the Register action exists and it has the correct signature. It also proves that the redirection to the Index action in the Home controller works.

It's time to refactor. It is now obvious that this test doesn't prove that we can successfully register a user. So the test name is misleading. I think `Register_Redirects_To_Home_Index_On_Success` will be a better name. Here is the new test:

```
[Test]
public void Register_Redirects_To_Home_Index_On_Success()
{
    var ac = new AccountController();
    var results = ac.Register(username, email,
                              question, answer, password);
    Assert.IsNotNull(results);
    Assert.IsInstanceOfType(typeof(RedirectToRouteResult), results);
    var typedResults = results as RedirectToRouteResult;
    Assert.AreEqual("Index",
                    typedResults.Values["action"],
                    "Wrong action");
    Assert.AreEqual("Home",
                    typedResults.Values["controller"],
                    "Wrong controller");
}
```

MembershipProvider

Unless I can make a better one, I don't like to reinvent the wheel. Hence, I am going to use ASP.NET Membership Provider.

To create a user using the Membership Provider, you simply call:

```
Membership.Provider.CreateUser(username, password, email,
                               question, answer, true, null,
                               out createStatus);
```

Things will start to get interesting now. When we run our test, it will create a user in the database. That's a bad idea because we will hit the database every time we run the test, which is not optimal; we want the test to be fast. We also have to write cleanup code to delete anything we create in the database; otherwise, subsequent tests will fail. For example, if we run the test and it creates the user *jdoe*, the next time we run the test it will fail because `jdoe` already exists. We can, of course, eliminate that by writing cleanup code to delete the records created, but that's too much work — too slow and irrelevant to our unit tests. We are not testing the database or the membership provider; we are testing the Register action.

If only there was a way to simulate the call to the membership provider! Of course, there is. That's where mocking comes into play. We want to mock the call to the `CreateUser` method, and here is how the test looks:

```
[Test]
public void Register_Can_Successfully_Create_User()
{
    //create mocks and set expectations
```

```csharp
    var mockProvider = new Mock<MembershipProvider>();
    mockProvider
        .Expect(p => p.CreateUser(username, password,
                                  email, question, answer, true,
                                  null, out createstatus))
        .Returns(new Mock<MembershipUser>().Object);

    //run tests
    var ac = new AccountController(mockProvider.Object);
    var results = ac.Register(username, email,
                              question, answer, password);

    //assert results
    Assert.IsNotNull(results);
    Assert.IsInstanceOfType(typeof(RedirectToRouteResult), results);
    var typedResults = results as RedirectToRouteResult;
    Assert.AreEqual("Index",
                typedResults.Values["action"],
                "Wrong action");
    Assert.AreEqual("Home",
                typedResults.Values["controller"],
                "Wrong controller");

    //verify mock expectations
    mockProvider.VerifyAll();
}
```

Mocking will be explained in more details in the next chapter.

I want to point out a few things in the above test. First of all, we need to add a reference to the Moq assembly. In the first line, we create a mock object of the `MembershipProvider`. Then we tell the mock object to expect a call to the `CreateUser` method, and when that call is made, it needs to return a mock `MembershipUser` object. Also, note that the `createstatus` variable is declared at the class level. The final step is to verify that the expectation was met after calling the Register method, and you do that by calling the `VerifyAll` on the mock provider.

The above test will not compile because the `AccountController` doesn't have a constructor that takes a `MembershipProvider` as an argument. We need to create an overloaded constructor to make this work. The only problem is that the MVC framework controller factory expects a parameter-less default constructor. One solution is to have two constructors like so:

```csharp
public AccountController()
    : this(null){}

public AccountController(MembershipProvider provider)
{
    Provider = provider ?? Membership.Provider;
}

public MembershipProvider Provider
{
    get;
    private set;
}
```

This way the MVC framework will call the default constructor, which will call the overloaded constructor and pass it null for the provider. The overloaded constructor will set the provider property to the passed provider, and if a null is passed, it will default to the `Membership.Provider` instance.

Run the test. It fails because the mock provider didn't meet the expectations. That means that the `CreateUser` method was not called from the Register action. Let's change the Register action:

```
[AcceptVerbs("POST")]
public ActionResult Register(string username, string email,
                            string question, string answer,
                            string password)
{
    // Attempt to register the user
    MembershipCreateStatus createStatus;
    var newUser = Provider.CreateUser(username, password, email,
                                      question, answer, true,
                                      null, out createStatus);
    return RedirectToAction("Index", "Home");
}
```

Run the test. It passes. Run all tests. They pass.

Let's add some more features. We need to add some validation to the registration method. First, we need to make sure that the username, email, password, security question, and security answer are not null; that is, they are required fields. We start off by creating a test for username:

```
[Test]
public void Register_Should_Return_Error_If_Username_Is_Missing()
{
    var ac = new AccountController();
    var results = ac.Register(string.Empty, email,
                        question, answer, password);
    Assert.IsNotNull(results);
    Assert.IsInstanceOfType(typeof(ViewResult), results);

    Assert.IsTrue(ac.ViewData.ModelState.ContainsKey("username"));
    Assert.AreEqual("Username is required",
            ac.ViewData.ModelState["username"].Errors[0].ErrorMessage);
}
```

In the above test, we call the Register action with an empty username. We expect the registration process to fail and display an error message that the username is required. With that in mind, we test the return type to be a `ViewResult` and test that the `ModelState` contains an item with the key `username` and that the error message associated with that item is correct. We also check that the `IsValid` property is set to `False`. I didn't bother to mock the membership provider because it won't be called. Now, we run the test and make sure it fails. Let's change the Register method to:

```
[AcceptVerbs("POST")]
public ActionResult Register(string username, string email,
                            string question, string answer,
                            string password)
{
```

```
//validate input
if (string.IsNullOrEmpty(username))
{
    ViewData.ModelState.AddModelError("username",
                                username,
                                "Username is required");
}

//if validation fails then return the view
if (!ViewData.ModelState.IsValid)
{
    return View();
}

// Attempt to register the user
MembershipCreateStatus createStatus;
var newUser = Provider.CreateUser(username, password, email,
                            question, answer, true,
                            null, out createStatus);
return RedirectToAction("Index", "Home");
}
```

We check if the username is empty; if it is, we add an error message to the ModelState collection. If the model state is invalid, then we return the view; otherwise, we proceed to create the user. Run the test to make sure that it passes.

We now repeat the same steps for each field:

1. Create a test.

2. Run it — it should fail.

3. Modify the Register method.

4. Run the test; if it fails, go back to Step 3.

After writing the remaining tests, I realized that there is a lot of repetition and I can refactor the code. The method to test for a missing email looks identical to the one for testing a missing username:

```
[Test]
public void Register_Should_Return_Error_If_Email_Is_Missing()
{
    var ac = new AccountController();
    var results = ac.Register(username, string.Empty,
                        question, answer, password);
    Assert.IsNotNull(results);
    Assert.IsInstanceOfType(typeof(ViewResult), results);

    Assert.IsTrue(ac.ViewData.ModelState.ContainsKey("email"));
    Assert.AreEqual("Email is required",
                ac.ViewData.ModelState["email"].Errors[0].ErrorMessage);
    Assert.IsFalse(ac.ViewData.ModelState.IsValid);
}
```

I can refactor the model state assertion into a method. I am probably going to need this in other tests, so I am going to create the method as an extension method and put it in a static class to house my model state assertions. Here is the class with our first method:

```
public static class ModelStateAssertions
{
    public static void AssertErrorMessage(this ModelStateDictionary modelState,
                                          string key, string errormessage)
    {
        Assert.IsTrue(modelState.ContainsKey(key));
        Assert.AreEqual(errormessage,
                        modelState[key].Errors[0].ErrorMessage);
        Assert.IsFalse(modelState.IsValid);
    }
}
```

Now, I can rewrite my tests to:

```
[Test]
public void Register_Should_Return_Error_If_Username_Is_Missing()
{
    var ac = new AccountController();
    var results = ac.Register(string.Empty, email,
                              question, answer, password);
    Assert.IsNotNull(results);
    Assert.IsInstanceOfType(typeof(ViewResult), results);
    ac.ViewData.ModelState.AssertErrorMessage("username", "Username is required");
}
```

That's much better. So far, I created the following tests:

- ❏   Register_Should_Return_Error_If_Username_Is_Missing
- ❏   Register_Should_Return_Error_If_Email_Is_Missing
- ❏   Register_Should_Return_Error_If_Password_Is_Missing
- ❏   Register_Should_Return_Error_If_Question_Is_Missing
- ❏   Register_Should_Return_Error_If_Answer_Is_Missing

And the Register method now looks like this:

```
[AcceptVerbs("POST")]
public ActionResult Register(string username, string email,
                            string question, string answer,
                            string password)
{
    //validate input
    if (string.IsNullOrEmpty(username))
        ViewData.ModelState.AddModelError("username",
                                          username,
                                          "Username is required");
    if(string.IsNullOrEmpty(email))
        ViewData.ModelState.AddModelError("email",
```

```
                                         email,
                                         "Email is required");
    if (string.IsNullOrEmpty(password))
        ViewData.ModelState.AddModelError("password",
                                         password,
                                         "Password is required");
    if (string.IsNullOrEmpty(question))
        ViewData.ModelState.AddModelError("question",
                                         question,
                                         "Question is required");
    if (string.IsNullOrEmpty(answer))
        ViewData.ModelState.AddModelError("answer",
                                         question,
                                         "Answer is required");
    //if validation fails then return the view
    if (!ViewData.ModelState.IsValid)
    {
        return View();
    }

    // Attempt to register the user
    MembershipCreateStatus createStatus;
    var newUser = Provider.CreateUser(username, password, email,
                                 question, answer, true,
                                 null, out createStatus);
    return RedirectToAction("Index", "Home");
}
```

Next, we need to validate that the email address is a valid address, and if it is not, then we should display an error message to the user and prevent the registration from taking place. As usual, we will start with a test:

```
[Test]
public void Register_Should_Return_Error_If_Email_Is_Invalid()
{
    var invalidEmail = "bad @ email .#.com";
    var ac = new AccountController();
    var results = ac.Register(username, invalidEmail,
                        question, answer, password);
    Assert.IsNotNull(results);
    Assert.IsInstanceOfType(typeof(ViewResult), results);
    ac.ViewData.ModelState.AssertErrorMessage("email", "Email is invalid");
}
```

We then make these changes to the Register method:

```
if (string.IsNullOrEmpty(email))
    ViewData.ModelState.AddModelError("email",
                                     email,
                                     "Email is required");
else if (!AppHelper.IsValidEmail(email))
    ViewData.ModelState.AddModelError("email",
                                     email,
                                     "Email is invalid");
```

Minor Interruption

This code will not compile because `AppHelper` and `IsValidEmail` don't exist. So we go through the same drill again:

1. Create the `AppHelperTest` class in the test project.
2. Create a test for the `IsValidEmail` method.
3. Create the `AppHelper` class in the web project.
4. Create the `IsValidEmail`.

There is a new twist to this test, though. In previous tests we usually tested a specific input value, for example, an empty string, but in this test we need to test for an infinite number of invalid emails. Of course, we can't really test every possibility, but we can come up with a list of invalid emails that would cover most cases. Lucky for us, MbUnit makes this very easy by using the `[Row]` attribute. Here is the test:

```
[Test]
[Row("test@test_test.com")]
[Row("sdfdf dsfsdf")]
[Row("sdfdf@.com")]
[Row("sdfdf@dfdfdf")]
[Row("sdfdf@fdfd. com")]
[Row("s&#dfdf@fdfd.com")]
[Row("sd@fdf@fdfd.com")]
public void IsValidEmail_Invalid_Emails_Should_Return_False(string invalidEmail)
{
    Assert.IsFalse(AppHelper.IsValidEmail(invalidEmail),
        "Email validation failed for " + invalidEmail);
}
```

The above test will run once for each row and pass the value as a parameter to the test method. We can add as many rows as we want, but I think this is a pretty comprehensive list.

The next step is to create the `AppHelper` class in the web project and then create the `IsValidEmail` method:

```
public static bool IsValidEmail(string email)
{
    var EmailExpression =
    new Regex(
        @"^([a-zA-Z0-9_\-\.]+)@((\[[0-9]{1,3}\.[0-9]{1,3}\.[0-9]{1,3}\.)|" +
        @"(([a-zA-Z0-9\-]+\.)+))([a-zA-Z]{2,4}|[0-9]{1,3})(\]?)$",
        RegexOptions.Compiled | RegexOptions.Singleline);
    return EmailExpression.IsMatch(email);
}
```

This is a pretty straightforward method and just uses a regular expression to test if a string is a valid email address and returns a Boolean. Let's run the test and make sure it passes. Then we should also test the condition where the string is a valid email, so here is another test that will check for valid email addresses:

```
[Test]
[Row("test@test.com")]
[Row("123@test.com")]
[Row("first_last@test.com")]
[Row("international@test.com.eg")]
[Row("someorg@test.org")]
[Row("somenet@test.net")]
public void IsValidEmail_Valid_Emails_Should_Return_True(string invalidEmail)
{
    Assert.IsTrue(AppHelper.IsValidEmail(invalidEmail),
        "Email validation failed for " + invalidEmail);
}
```

Back on Track

Let's get back to the registration process. We now run the test we previously created (`Register_Should_Return_Error_If_Email_Is_Invalid`) and make sure it works. I will add another validation to check that a username is valid. This will work pretty much the same way we validated emails except that I will use a different regular expression to validate the username.

A username is valid if:

❑   It is 4 characters or more.

❑   It starts with a letter.

❑   It contains only letters, numbers, and underscores.

Here is a quick playback of the steps:

1.   Create a test for one of the conditions:

```
[Test]
[Row("")]
[Row("a")]
[Row("ab")]
[Row("abc")]
public void Short_Username_Should_Return_False(string username)
{
    Assert.IsFalse(AppHelper.IsValidUsername(username),
            string.Format("username failed validation for {0}",
            username));
}
```

2.   Create the `IsValidUsername` to make the above test succeed:

```
public static bool IsValidUsername(string username)
{
    if (string.IsNullOrEmpty(username))
        return false;
```

```
        if (username.Length < 4)
            return false;

        return true;
}
```

3. Create another test to test for invalid characters and make changes to make it pass:

```
[Test]
[Row("user!")]
[Row("user@")]
[Row("user#")]
[Row("user$")]
public void Username_With_Invalid_Characters_Should_Return_False(
    string username)
{
    Assert.IsFalse(AppHelper.IsValidUsername(username),
        string.Format("username failed validation for {0}",
        username));
}
```

4. Create a test for usernames that start with a non-letter and make changes to make it pass:

```
[Test]
[Row("1user")]
[Row(" user")]
[Row("_user")]
public void Username_Starting_With_Non_Alpha_Should_Return_False(
    string username)
{
    Assert.IsFalse(AppHelper.IsValidUsername(username),
        string.Format("username failed validation for {0}",
        username));
}
```

5. Create a test for valid usernames and make changes to make it pass:

```
[Test]
[Row("user")]
[Row("user1")]
[Row("user_1")]
[Row("user_2_3")]
public void Valid_Usernames_Should_Return_True(string username)
{
    Assert.IsTrue(AppHelper.IsValidUsername(username),
                  string.Format("Username validation failed for {0}",
                  username));
}
```

The final version of IsValidUsername is as follows:

```
public static bool IsValidUsername(string username)
{
    if (string.IsNullOrEmpty(username))
        return false;
```

```
    if (username.Length < 4)
        return false;

    var UsernameExpression =
        new Regex(@"^[a-zA-Z][a-zA-Z0-9_]+$",
                    RegexOptions.Compiled |
                    RegexOptions.IgnoreCase |
                    RegexOptions.Singleline);
    var valid = UsernameExpression.IsMatch(username);

    return valid;
}
```

Our Register action is looking pretty good so far. It has very thorough validation, and all conditions are backed with unit tests. So I am feeling pretty confident, but it is not done yet. We are validating the input before we attempt the creation. The next thing we need to do is handle registration failures from the provider. When we call the `Provider.CreateUser` method, we pass it as an out parameter (`ByRef` in Visual Basic) of type `MembershipCreateStatus`. This parameter contains the results of the method and can tell us the reason for a failure — for example, duplicate username, duplicate email, and so on. The `CreateUser` method returns a null if it fails; otherwise, it returns an instance of `MembershipUser` for the newly created user. Because of a limitation in our mocking framework, we are unable to mock *out* parameters, so we cannot create a test for every possible value. Ideally, I would have liked to create a test like this:

```
[Test]
[Row(MembershipCreateStatus.DuplicateUserName, "Username already exists. " +
    "Please enter a different user name.",
    "Failed duplicate user name test")]
[Row(MembershipCreateStatus.DuplicateEmail,
    "A username for that e-mail address already exists. " +
    "Please enter a different e-mail address.",
    "Failed duplicate email test")]
[Row(MembershipCreateStatus.InvalidPassword,
    "The password provided is invalid. " +
    "Please enter a valid password value.",
    "Failed invalid password test")]
public void Register_Should_Fail_If_Provider_Create_Fails(
                        MembershipCreateStatus status, string errorMessage)
{

    //create mocks and set expectations
    var mockProvider = new Mock<MembershipProvider>();
    MembershipCreateStatus createstatus;
    mockProvider
        .Expect(p => p.CreateUser(username, password,
                                    email, question, answer, true,
                                    null, out createstatus))
        .Returns(null).SomehowSetOutParamaterValueTo(status);

    //run tests
    var ac = new AccountController(mockProvider.Object);
    var results = ac.Register(username, email,
                                question, answer, password);
    //assert that the error message is correct
    mockProvider.VerifyAll();
}
```

Unfortunately, I cannot mock the out parameter. Our other option is to create a fake membership provider that implements the MembershipProvider abstract class and set it up to simulate different values for the out parameter so that we can test all conditions. Let's see how we can do that. We start by writing the test:

```
[Test]
[Row(MembershipCreateStatus.DuplicateUserName, "Username already exists. " +
    "Please enter a different user name.",
    "Failed duplicate user name test")]
public void Register_Should_Fail_If_CreateUser_Fails(
                        MembershipCreateStatus status, string errorMessage)
{
    //create fake membership provider
    var fakeProvider = new FakeMembershipProvider();
    //tell the fake provider what status to return when CreateUser is called
    fakeProvider.SetFakeStatus(status);
    //run tests
    var ac = new AccountController(fakeProvider);
    var results = ac.Register(username, email,
                            question, answer, password);
    Assert.IsNotNull(results);
    Assert.IsInstanceOfType(typeof(ViewResult), results);
    ac.ViewData.ModelState.AssertErrorMessage("provider", errorMessage);
}
```

For brevity's sake, I omitted all the rows from the previous code sample. The actual test has a row for every possible value of the out parameter.

I don't need to implement all the MembershipProvider methods right now. I only need CreateUser and a helper method — SetFakeStatus — to allow me to fake the out parameter. Here is the part of the calls that is implemented:

```
internal class FakeMembershipProvider : MembershipProvider
{
    #region "Code to support unit testing"

    //default to success
    private MembershipCreateStatus _fakeStatus =
        MembershipCreateStatus.Success;

    public void SetFakeStatus(MembershipCreateStatus status)
    {
        _fakeStatus = status;
    }

    #endregion

    public override MembershipUser CreateUser(string username,
        string password, string email,
        string passwordQuestion, string passwordAnswer, bool isApproved,
        object providerUserKey, out MembershipCreateStatus status)
    {
        //set the out parameter
```

```
            status = _fakeStatus;
            //return null if a status other than success otherwise mock the call
            return _fakeStatus != MembershipCreateStatus.Success
                    ?
                        null
                    :
                        new Mock<MembershipUser>().Object;
        }
    }
```

The above implementation doesn't do anything other than set the `out` parameter and return null or a mocked `MembershipUser` object depending on the fake status. The `SetFakeStatus` method is for testing support and allows my unit test to set the status that should be returned when `CreateStatus` is called. Let's run the test above. It fails because we haven't written the code to set the error message. So I change the Register method last few lines from:

```
// Attempt to register the user
MembershipCreateStatus createStatus;
var newUser = Provider.CreateUser(username, password, email,
                                  question, answer, true,
                                  null, out createStatus);
return RedirectToAction("Index", "Home");
```

to the following:

```
// Attempt to register the user
MembershipCreateStatus createStatus;
var newUser = Provider.CreateUser(username, password, email,
                                  question, answer, true,
                                  null, out createStatus);
if (newUser != null)
{
    return RedirectToAction("Index", "Home");
}

ViewData.ModelState.AddModelError("provider",
    username,
    ErrorCodeToString(createStatus));
return View();
```

The `ErrorCodeToString` above is a helper method that takes in a `MembershipCreateStatus` and returns an error message. Run the test and make sure it passes. The `ErrorCodeToString` is as follows:

```
public static string ErrorCodeToString(MembershipCreateStatus createStatus)
{
    switch (createStatus)
    {
        case MembershipCreateStatus.DuplicateUserName:
            return "Username already exists. Please enter a different user name.";

        case MembershipCreateStatus.DuplicateEmail:
            return "A username for that e-mail address already exists. " +
                "Please enter a different e-mail address.";
```

```csharp
        case MembershipCreateStatus.InvalidPassword:
            return "The password provided is invalid. " +
                "Please enter a valid password value.";

        case MembershipCreateStatus.InvalidEmail:
            return "The e-mail address provided is invalid. " +
                "Please check the value and try again.";

        case MembershipCreateStatus.InvalidAnswer:
            return "The password retrieval answer provided is invalid. " +
                "Please check the value and try again.";

        case MembershipCreateStatus.InvalidQuestion:
            return "The password retrieval question provided is invalid. " +
                "Please check the value and try again.";

        case MembershipCreateStatus.InvalidUserName:
            return "The user name provided is invalid. " +
                "Please check the value and try again.";

        case MembershipCreateStatus.ProviderError:
            return
                "The authentication provider returned an error. " +
                "Please verify your entry and try again. " +
                "If the problem persists, " +
                "please contact your system administrator.";

        case MembershipCreateStatus.UserRejected:
            return
                "The user creation request has been canceled. " +
                "Please verify your entry and try again. " +
                "If the problem persists, " +
                "please contact your system administrator.";

        default:
            return
                "An unknown error occurred. " +
                "Please verify your entry and try again. " +
                "If the problem persists, " +
                "please contact your system administrator.";
    }
}
```

Now if you run all the tests you will notice that one of the first tests we wrote — `Register_Redirects_To_Home_Index_On_Success` — fails. If you recall, the test was as follows:

```csharp
[Test]
public void Register_Redirects_To_Home_Index_On_Success()
{
    var ac = new AccountController();
    var results = ac.Register(username, email,
                            question, answer, password);
    Assert.IsNotNull(results);
    Assert.IsInstanceOfType(typeof(RedirectToRouteResult), results);
```

```
        var typedResults = results as RedirectToRouteResult;
        Assert.AreEqual("Index",
                        typedResults.Values["action"],
                        "Wrong action");
        Assert.AreEqual("Home",
                        typedResults.Values["controller"],
                        "Wrong controller");
    }
```

The reason it is failing is because the code is trying to create a user but the call to `CreateUser` fails and returns a null `MembershipUser`, which causes the Register method to return a view with the errors instead of redirecting to the /home/index view. If you step through the code, you will realize that `CreateUser` fails because of duplicate usernames. That is because our test created an actual user in the database the first time it ran, and since we are using the same username, subsequent calls fail with the duplicate username error. Luckily, this is an easy fix: All we have to do is use a mock provider and mock the call to `CreateUser`. Here it is:

```
public void Register_Redirects_To_Home_Index_On_Success()
{
    //create mocks and set expectations
    var mockProvider = new Mock<MembershipProvider>();
    mockProvider
        .Expect(p => p.CreateUser(username, password,
                                  email, question, answer, true,
                                  null, out createstatus))
        .Returns(new Mock<MembershipUser>().Object);
    //run tests
    var ac = new AccountController(mockProvider.Object);
    var results = ac.Register(username, email,
                              question, answer, password);
    //assert results
    Assert.IsNotNull(results);
    Assert.IsInstanceOfType(typeof(RedirectToRouteResult), results);
    var typedResults = results as RedirectToRouteResult;
    Assert.AreEqual("Index",
                    typedResults.Values["action"],
                    "Wrong action");
    Assert.AreEqual("Home",
                    typedResults.Values["controller"],
                    "Wrong controller");
}
```

Now all tests should pass, but to make sure that this doesn't happen again, I am going to change all my tests to use a mock provider. I am going to change all instances of:

```
var ac = new AccountController();
```

to

```
var mockProvider = new Mock<MembershipProvider>();
var ac = new AccountController(mockProvider.Object);
```

Let's run all the tests one more time and make sure our refactoring didn't break anything.

Forms Authentication

We are pretty much done with our Register action except for one thing — we need to log the user in after a successful registration and before we redirect to /home/index. This works just like Web Forms, and all we need to do is call `FormsAuthentication.SetAuthCookie(username, false);`. But before we write the code, let's write a test and see how easy it will be to add this one line of code. I start to write a test and quickly realize that I can't mock the `FormsAuthentication` class because it is sealed and contains static methods. So the following won't even compile:

```
var mockAuthentication = new Mock<FormsAuthentication>();
mockAuthentication
    .Expect(a => a.SetAuthCookie(username, false));
```

To simplify testing, we will create an interface and wrapper class that we can easily mock in our testing.

The interface and wrapper class are already created for you when you create a new ASP.NET MVC web application, but I want to demonstrate the concepts so you can see how they make testing easier.

Let's create the interface first to contain the `SetAuthCookie` method:

```
public interface IFormsAuthentication
{
    void SetAuthCookie(string userName, bool createPersistentCookie);
}
```

Then we create a property in our `AccountController` class and modify the constructor to take an `IFormsAuthentication` as a parameter:

```
public AccountController()
    : this(null, null)
{
}

public AccountController(IFormsAuthentication formsAuth,
                         MembershipProvider provider)
{
    FormsAuth = formsAuth ?? new FormsAuthenticationWrapper();
    Provider = provider ?? Membership.Provider;
}

public IFormsAuthentication FormsAuth
{
    get;
    private set;
}
```

Now we have to create the `FormsAuthenticationWrapper` class, which will just wrap calls to the `FormsAuthentication` class and implement the `IFormsAuthenticaton` interface:

```
public class FormsAuthenticationWrapper : IFormsAuthentication
{
```

```csharp
        public void SetAuthCookie(string userName, bool createPersistentCookie)
        {
            FormsAuthentication.SetAuthCookie(userName, createPersistentCookie);
        }
    }
```

Now we can easily mock the call to `SetAuthCookie` and we can write our test like this:

```csharp
[Test]
public void Register_Should_Call_SetAuthCookie_On_Success()
{
    //create mocks and set expectations
    var mockProvider = new Mock<MembershipProvider>();
    mockProvider
        .Expect(p => p.CreateUser(username, password,
                                    email, question, answer, true,
                                    null, out createstatus))
        .Returns(new Mock<MembershipUser>().Object);

    var mockAuthentication = new Mock<IFormsAuthentication>();
    mockAuthentication
        .Expect(a => a.SetAuthCookie(username, false));


    //run tests
    var ac = new AccountController(mockAuthentication.Object,
        mockProvider.Object);
    var results = ac.Register(username, email,
                                question, answer, password);
    //assert results
    Assert.IsNotNull(results);
    Assert.IsInstanceOfType(typeof(RedirectToRouteResult), results);
    //verify mocks expectations have been met
    mockProvider.VerifyAll();
    mockAuthentication.VerifyAll();
}
```

We can't compile the test project because we have changed our constructor's signature and we need to go back and change all our `AccountController` instantiation code to look something like this:

```csharp
var ac = new AccountController(instanceOfIFormsAuthentication,
                                instanceOfMembershipProvider);
```

Let's run the test now and make sure that it fails because the expectation on the mock forms authentication is not met. Then add this line before we redirect to home/index:

```csharp
FormsAuth.SetAuthCookie(username, false);
```

Run all the tests and make sure they all pass.

The View

Creating the view is really not necessary to proceed with the site, but since we are human and want to actually see something tangible (and so do our customers), we will go ahead and create the Registration page. Here is an overview of the steps we will take:

1. Create a master page (MVC View Master Page) in the Views\Shared folder.

2. Create a Register MVC View Page in the Views\Account folder.

Convention

All views should go under the Views folder, and all shared views should go under the Views\Shared folder. Specific views should be in a subfolder that has the same name as the controller sans the controller part. For example, views for the AccountController should go in a folder named *Account* (under the Views folder). The view name should match the action name. So a view for the Register action would be *Register.aspx*. This greatly simplifies routing and configuration. Of course, we could name the view *Signup.aspx*, but then we will have to remember to change the action to return the proper view. So instead of calling

```
return View();
```

we would call

```
return View("signup");
```

Now we construct the view. This is what we know about the view:

1. We need fields for username, email, password, secret question, and secret answer.

2. We need a button to submit to the Register action, that is, perform a POST request.

3. We need to display validation error messages.

There are a couple of ways to create the input fields for the form. We can use the helper methods and generate a text field like this:

```
<%= Html.TextBox("username") %>
```

The above line will generate the following HTML in the browser:

```
<input id="username" name="username" type="text" value="" />
```

Or we can simply write the HTML ourselves. I prefer to write straight HTML wherever possible, but in this case, I will use the helper methods. One of the benefits is that it makes validation easier — I will explain later.

> **Convention**
>
> Make the field name and ID match the name of the parameter expected by your action (case is not important). So if your action looks like this:
>
> ```
> public ActionResult MyAction(string username, int age)
> ```
>
> your fields should be named *username* and *age*. This allows the framework to properly map each form field to the correct parameter.

Let's see how our view might look:

```
<h2>Account Creation</h2>
<p>
    Use the form below to create a new account.
</p>
<%= Html.ValidationSummary()%>
<form method="post" action="<%=Html.AttributeEncode(Url.Action("Register"))%>">
    <div>
        <label for="username">Username</label>
        <br />
        <%=Html.TextBox("username") %>
        <br />
        <label for="email">Email</label>
        <br />
        <%=Html.TextBox("email") %>
        <br />
        <label for="password">Password</label>
        <br />
        <%=Html.Password("password") %>
        <br />
        <label for="question">Secret Question</label>
        <br />
        <%=Html.TextBox("question") %>
        <br />
        <label for="answer">Secret Answer</label>
        <br />
        <%=Html.TextBox("answer") %>
        <br />
        <input type="submit" value="Register" />
    </div>
</form>
```

Note that the form's action attribute is created with the `Url.Action("Register")` helper method. This will generate the appropriate URL for the Register action according to the defined routing rules. We also use the `Html.AttributeEncode` helper method to ensure that the string is properly encoded as an HTML attribute.

Here is the generated HTML for our view:

```html
<h2>Account Creation</h2>
<p>
    Use the form below to create a new account.
</p>

<form method="post" action="/Account/Register">
    <div>
        <label for="username">Username</label>
        <br />
        <input id="username" name="username" type="text" value="" />
        <br />
        <label for="email">Email</label>
        <br />
        <input id="email" name="email" type="text" value="" />
        <br />
        <label for="password">Password</label>
        <br />
        <input id="password" name="password" type="password" value="" />
        <br />
        <label for="question">Secret Question</label>
        <br />
        <input id="question" name="question" type="text" value="" />
        <br />
        <label for="answer">Secret Answer</label>
        <br />
        <input id="answer" name="answer" type="text" value="" />
        <br />
        <input type="submit" value="Register" />
    </div>
</form>
```

Isn't that beautiful? It's exactly as we designed it — no hidden fields, no view state, no mysterious JavaScripts. The rendered view is shown in Figure 3-1.

Figure 3-1

And if we try to submit the form, we should get to see a summary of our validation errors, as shown in Figure 3-2.

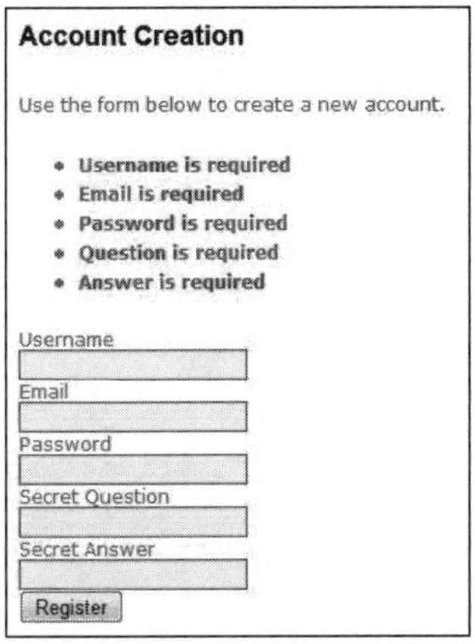

Account Creation

Use the form below to create a new account.

• Username is required
• Email is required
• Password is required
• Question is required
• Answer is required

Username

Email

Password

Secret Question

Secret Answer

Register

Figure 3-2

A quick note about validation: You can display single error messages next to each field by using the helper method `ValidationMessage`. All you do is insert the line below where you want your message to appear. This will display the error message set up in the `ModelState` with the key `username`.

```
<%=Html.ValidationMessage("username") %>
```

I like this approach better than the error summary because it tells the user exactly where the error is. I didn't do it above for the sake of brevity and because I have a feeling that we will be visiting validation again. Plus, my purpose here was to verify that the action is working accordingly and that everything is wired up correctly.

Notice that the fields with errors associated with them are highlighted; actually, if we examine the HTML, you will see that it now looks like this:

```
<h2>Account Creation</h2>
<p>
    Use the form below to create a new account.
</p>
<ul class="validation-summary-errors"><li>Username is required</li>
<li>Email is required</li>
<li>Password is required</li>
<li>Question is required</li>
<li>Answer is required</li>
</ul>
<form method="post" action="/Account/Register">
    <div>
        <label for="username">Username</label>
        <br />
        <input class="input-validation-error" id="username" name="username"
                type="text" value="" />
```

```
        <br />
        <label for="email">Email</label>
        <br />
        <input class="input-validation-error" id="email" name="email"
            type="text" value="" />
        <br />
        <label for="password">Password</label>
        <br />
        <input class="input-validation-error" id="password" name="password"
            type="password" value="" />
        <br />
        <label for="question">Secret Question</label>
        <br />
        <input class="input-validation-error" id="question" name="question"
            type="text" value="" />
        <br />
        <label for="answer">Secret Answer</label>
        <br />
        <input class="input-validation-error" id="answer" name="answer"
            type="text" value="" />
        <br />
        <input type="submit" value="Register" />
    </div>
</form>
```

Can you spot the differences? The fields with errors have the class `input-validation-error` associated with them. This class is defined in the default style sheet, which results in the highlighting. I can hear you in the back ask, "How did this class get added?" The answer is the helper method `Html.TextBox`; it is smart enough to know that there was an error for a field and adds the appropriate style to it. That is a pretty good reason to use the helper methods in this situation.

View State

Houston, we have a problem. I tried to register a new user and ran into two problems. First, I entered a password of **1234**, which resulted in an error, shown in Figure 3-3:

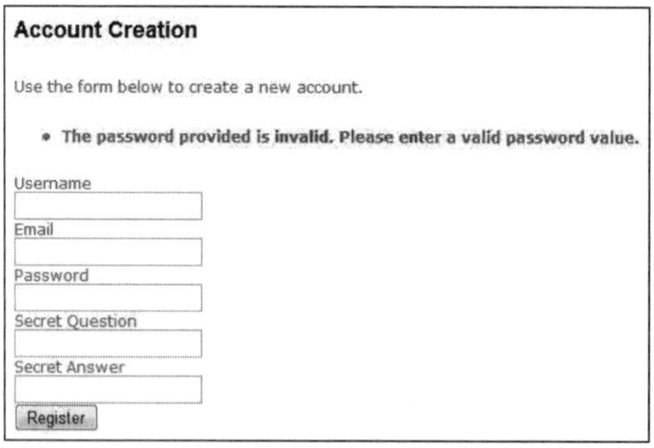

Figure 3-3

This is because I didn't configure the membership provider with the correct values in the web.config file. The second and bigger problem is that, as you can see in Figure 3-3, the form is now blank and all my values are gone. This, of course, is not acceptable from a usability standpoint. This happens because MVC applications do not persist the View state as in Web Forms applications. Don't panic, though; there is an easy fix for it.

Remember that our action returns the view if there are any validation errors?

```
if (!ViewData.ModelState.IsValid)
{
    return View();
}
```

We need to somehow pass to the view the values that were previously entered. There are several ways to do this. One way is to pass a dictionary of all the values using string keys that match field names; for example, we can do the following:

```
return View(new Dictionary<string, object>
                {
                    { "username", username },
                    {"email",email},
                    {"password",password},
                    {"question",question},
                    {"answer",answer}
                });
```

The other way is to pass a model object back to the view. For example, we could create a class to hold the view model:

```
public class RegisterModel
{
    public string Username { get; set; }
    public string Email { get; set; }
    public string Password { get; set; }
    public string Question { get; set; }
    public string Answer { get; set; }
}
```

and return the view with an instance of the class as such:

```
return View(new RegisterModel
                {
                    Username = username,
                    Email = email,
                    Password = password,
                    Question = question,
                    Answer = answer
                });
```

Either way you choose, the view is smart enough to set the values for the fields. Now if we try to submit an invalid form, the values are maintained between requests, and we get what's shown in Figure 3-4.

Account Creation

Use the form below to create a new account.

- Email is invalid
- Password is required

Username
test
Email
e@e.com##
Password

Secret Question
test
Secret Answer
test
Register

Figure 3-4

Let's run all the tests to make sure that we haven't broken anything. All the tests pass, but we still need to make some changes. We need to make sure that the correct model is returned to the view and its values are correct. Since this code will be used in several tests, I decided to create it as an extension method to be called on the model. This extension method along with other extension methods will be in a static class called `ModelAssertions`. The assertion method is as follows:

```
public static void AssertRegisterModel(this RegisterModel model,
                                       string username, string email,
                                       string question, string answer,
                                       string password)
{
    Assert.AreEqual(username, model.Username);
    Assert.AreEqual(email, model.Email);
    Assert.AreEqual(password, model.Password);
    Assert.AreEqual(question, model.Question);
    Assert.AreEqual(answer, model.Answer);
}
```

Now we can easily assert the model by calling:

```
(((ViewResult) results).ViewData.Model as RegisterModel)
    .AssertRegisterModel(string.Empty, email, question, answer, password);
```

It's time to refactor. Many of the unit tests testing the Register method perform the same tasks to assert the results, so I am going to refactor these tasks into one method:

```
private static void AssertRegisterViewResultOnError(AccountController ac,
                                       ActionResult results,
                                       string errorKey,
                                       string errorMessage,
                                       string username,
                                       string email,
                                       string question,
                                       string answer,
                                       string password)
{
```

```
        Assert.IsNotNull(results);
        Assert.IsInstanceOfType(typeof (ViewResult), results);
        ac.ViewData.ModelState.AssertErrorMessage(errorKey, errorMessage);
        Assert.IsInstanceOfType(typeof (RegisterModel),
                                ((ViewResult) results).ViewData.Model);
        var model = (((ViewResult) results).ViewData.Model as RegisterModel);
        model.AssertRegisterModel(username, email, question, answer, password);
    }
```

Now I can simply assert the results in my unit tests by calling one method. For example, the following unit test:

```
[Test]
public void Register_Should_Return_Error_If_Password_Is_Missing()
{
    var mockProvider = new Mock<MembershipProvider>();
    var mockAuthentication = new Mock<IFormsAuthentication>();
    var ac = new AccountController(mockAuthentication.Object, mockProvider.Object);
    var results = ac.Register(username, email,
                              question, answer, string.Empty);
    Assert.IsNotNull(results);
    Assert.IsInstanceOfType(typeof (ViewResult), results);
    ac.ViewData.ModelState.AssertErrorMessage("password", "Password is required");
}
```

can be refactored into:

```
[Test]
public void Register_Should_Return_Error_If_Password_Is_Missing()
{
    var mockProvider = new Mock<MembershipProvider>();
    var mockAuthentication = new Mock<IFormsAuthentication>();
    var ac = new AccountController(mockAuthentication.Object, mockProvider.Object);
    var results = ac.Register(username, email,
                              question, answer, string.Empty);
    AssertRegisterViewResultOnError(ac, results, "password",
                                    "Password is required",
                                    username, email, question,
                                    answer, string.Empty);
}
```

Run all the tests and make sure everything still works.

Summary

We covered a lot of concepts in this chapter and, I hope, by now you are comfortable with the TDD process and the ASP.NET MVC framework. We only covered the registration process, but the rest of the membership follows the same pattern. We create a test, write some code, make sure the tests pass, and repeat. You can now try to create the rest of the membership functionality and then compare it with the accompanying code. You will need to implement login and password resets as well.

Refactor: Model Binders, Mocks, and Asserts

In the previous chapter, I walked you through creating the registration process for new users. I then went ahead and followed the same procedure to create the remaining features of membership:

- ❑ Log in.
- ❑ Reset password.
- ❑ Log out.

As I was going through this process, I refactored the code and the tests and changed some things we previously did. In this chapter, I will discuss these changes.

Problem

There were many similarities in my tests that were being copied and pasted throughout — an egregious violation of the DRY principle. Here are some things that I started to notice as I wrote more tests:

- ❑ My assert statements were very similar and repeated in many tests.
- ❑ My controller instantiation was similar and repeated many times.
- ❑ My mocks were also looking very similar and need to be centralized.

I also did a lot of unnecessary coding for controller actions that needed to be refactored and cleaned up. Most actions were taking several parameters instead of accepting a typed object. It's a lot cleaner to write:

```
public ActionResult Create(User user)
```

than

```
public ActionResult Create(string username, string email, string password,
                           string phone)
```

Design

Let's start with the test code. The assert statements can be grouped into several extension methods that extend the appropriate object. For example, asserting the result of actions that redirect to a different URL can be grouped together into an extension method on the `ActionResult` class.

Several of the tests started off with the same set of statements that created the mocks and initialized the controller with the mocked objects. These lines can also be refactored into a central location for reuse by all tests. All mocked objects can be moved to a static class that can then be accessed by all tests.

Now, on the code side, I wanted to use a strongly typed class as the parameter to my actions instead of using multiple parameters that just resulted in unnecessary typing. This can be achieved by using Model Binders to tell the framework how to convert the form's values posted into a strongly typed object. For example, take a look at the `LoginModel` class in Figure 4-1, which can replace the `Username`, `Password`, and `RememberMe` parameters.

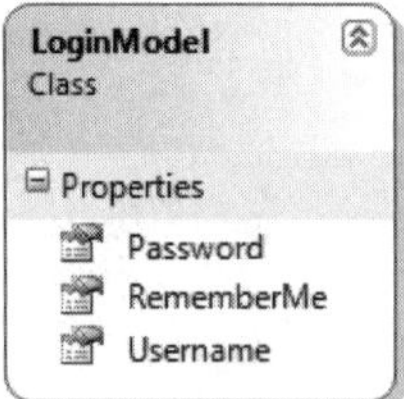

Figure 4-1

Solution

Let's take a look at the implementations of the above design that will address the problems at hand. My objective was to simplify the code and make it elegant. Here is one of my tests before any changes:

```
[Test]
public void Login_Should_Return_Error_If_Username_Is_Missing()
{
    var mockProvider = new Mock<MembershipProvider>();
    var mockAuthentication = new Mock<IFormsAuthentication>();
    var ac = new AccountController(mockAuthentication.Object,
                                   mockProvider.Object);
    var results = ac.Login(string.Empty, password, true);

    var errormessage = "Username is required";
```

```
    var errorKey = "username";

    Assert.IsNotNull(results);
    Assert.IsInstanceOfType(typeof(ViewResult), results);
    ac.ViewData.ModelState.AssertErrorMessage(errorKey, errormessage);
    Assert.IsInstanceOfType(typeof(LoginModel),
                            ((ViewResult)results).ViewData.Model);

    var model = (((ViewResult)results).ViewData.Model as LoginModel);

    Assert.AreEqual(string.Empty, model.Username);
    Assert.AreEqual(password, model.Password);
    Assert.AreEqual(true, model.RememberMe);

    Assert.AreEqual("Login", ac.ViewData["Title"], "Page title is wrong");
}
```

On its own, the above test looks good and doesn't need much refactoring. But the fact that many of the above lines were repeated in other tests gave rise to the need to refactor. To start with, my assertions are very generic and will be called by other methods. These lines can be moved into a method:

```
Assert.IsNotNull(results);
Assert.IsInstanceOfType(typeof(ViewResult), results);
ac.ViewData.ModelState.AssertErrorMessage(errorKey, errormessage);
Assert.IsInstanceOfType(typeof(LoginModel),
                        ((ViewResult)results).ViewData.Model);
var model = (((ViewResult)results).ViewData.Model as LoginModel);
Assert.AreEqual(string.Empty, model.Username);
Assert.AreEqual(password, model.Password);
Assert.AreEqual(true, model.RememberMe);
Assert.AreEqual("Login", ac.ViewData["Title"], "Page title is wrong");
```

The first three lines can also be moved out of here, and since they are part of the setup and get called at the start of every test, we can move them to the setup method. A *setup method* is just a method that is decorated with the `SetUp` attribute that is run before every test. This allows us to add instantiation and initialization code in one place and have it execute before every test. Here is how the setup method might look:

```
[SetUp]
public void SetUp()
{
    var mockProvider = new Mock<MembershipProvider>();
    var mockAuthentication = new Mock<IFormsAuthentication>();
    ac = new AccountController(mockAuthentication.Object,
                               mockProvider.Object);
}
```

The controller variable `ac` is now defined as a field in the class that can be accessed by all tests.

To further improve this, we will move the mocks into a class that we will call `Mocks`. This class will contain all the mocked objects, and we can pass it around easily between methods. We will use a lazy initialization pattern (refer to Chapter 1) for the class properties to make sure that only the mocks we need are initialized; otherwise, it could considerably slow down other tests. Here is the class:

```
internal class Mocks
{
    private static Mock<IFormsAuthentication> formsAuthentication;
    private static Mock<MembershipProvider> membershipProvider;

    public Mock<IFormsAuthentication> FormsAuthentication
    {
        get
        {
            formsAuthentication = formsAuthentication ??
                            new Mock<IFormsAuthentication>();
            return formsAuthentication;
        }
    }

    public Mock<MembershipProvider> MembershipProvider
    {
        get
        {
            membershipProvider = membershipProvider ??
                            new Mock<MembershipProvider>();
            return membershipProvider;
        }
    }
}
```

Now we can change our setup method above to:

```
[SetUp]
public void SetUp()
{
    mocks = new Mocks();
    ac = new AccountController(mocks.FormsAuthentication.Object,
                        mocks.MembershipProvider.Object);
}
```

Since I was going to refactor the controller action, I decided to wait on refactoring the assert statements in the test above. My Login action looked like this:

```
public ActionResult Login(string username, string password, bool rememberMe)
```

I wanted it to look like this:

```
public ActionResult Login(LoginModel model)
```

So, I created the LoginModel class as follows:

```
public class LoginModel
{
    public string Username { get; set; }
```

```
        public string Password { get; set; }
        public bool RememberMe { get; set; }
}
```

Then, all I needed to do is make sure that framework knows how to map my form values to my model object. This is done using model binders, and the framework comes with a model binder called ComplexModelBinder that does exactly that. The only problem with the ComplexModelBinder is that the fields in the views need to be named in the format *classname.fieldname* and thus the line below

```
<%= Html.TextBox("Username")%>
```

would have to be changed to

```
<%= Html.TextBox("LoginModel.Username")%>
```

This is something I didn't want to do because it would make my HTML element names very long and make any JavaScripts that I write down the road too verbose. Luckily, the framework gives us the flexibility to create our own model binders. All I had to do was implement the interface IModelBinder. I went ahead and created a generic model binder that uses reflection to get the values of properties from the forms using the same name. (I also created another binder that gets the values from the query string.)

```
class FormBinder : IModelBinder
{
    public object GetValue(ControllerContext controllerContext,
                           string modelName, Type modelType,
                           ModelStateDictionary modelState)
    {
        var instance = Activator.CreateInstance(modelType);
        PropertyInfo[] propertyInfos;
            propertyInfos = modelType.GetProperties();

        foreach (var prop in propertyInfos)
        {
            prop.SetValue(instance,
                    controllerContext.HttpContext.Request
                                    .Form[prop.Name.ToLower()],
                    null);
        }
        return instance;
    }
}
```

Using the above binder means that we have to abide by a naming convention wherein the field name in the view needs to match the property name in the model. That is not an unreasonable convention.

The only thing left is to wire up the binder to the model so that the framework knows what to do. There are several ways to do that:

❑   We can use a parameter attribute on the action:

```
public ActionResult Login([ModelBinder(typeof(FormBinder))]LoginModel model)
```

❑   We can decorate the model class with an attribute:

```
[ModelBinder(typeof(FormBinder))]
public class LoginModel
{
    public string Username { get; set; }
    public string Password { get; set; }
    public bool RememberMe { get; set; }
}
```

❑   We can register the binder at application startup:

```
protected void Application_Start()
{
    ModelBinders.Binders[typeof(LoginModel)] = new FormBinder();
    RegisterRoutes(RouteTable.Routes);
}
```

❑   We can register a default binder at application start:

```
protected void Application_Start()
{
    ModelBinders.Binders.DefaultBinder = new FormBinder();
    RegisterRoutes(RouteTable.Routes);
}
```

Although the preceding code will work, it was initially written for the RC version of the MVC frame-work. It is not necessary to write all this for the release version, and the solution is a lot simpler. Version 1 of the MVC framework contains a `Bind` *attribute that replaces most of this code. The action would simply look as follows:*

```
public ActionResult Login(
                    [Bind(Prefix = "")] LoginModel model)
```

The `Prefix` *can be set to anything to match the prefix used in your HTML naming. This allows you to use any naming convention you like. For example, if your HTML text field is defined as follows:*

```
<%= Html.TextBox("Login.Username")%>
```

Then you can change your action to the following

```
public ActionResult Login(
                [Bind(Prefix = "Login")] LoginModel model)
```

Then I went back to the test and created an extension method to assert the model:

```
public static void AssertModel(this LoginModel model,
                        LoginModel source)
{
    Assert.AreEqual(source.Username, model.Username);
    Assert.AreEqual(source.Password, model.Password);
    Assert.AreEqual(source.RememberMe, model.RememberMe);
}
```

I also created a helper method to assert the results:

```
private void AssertLoginViewResultOnError(ActionResult results,
                                          string errorKey,
                                          string errorMessage,
                                          LoginModel model)
{
    Assert.IsNotNull(results);
    Assert.IsInstanceOfType(typeof(ViewResult), results);
    ac.ViewData.ModelState.AssertErrorMessage(errorKey, errorMessage);
    Assert.IsInstanceOfType(typeof(LoginModel),
                            ((ViewResult)results).ViewData.Model);
    var outModel = (((ViewResult)results).ViewData.Model as LoginModel);
    outModel.AssertModel(model);
    Assert.AreEqual("Login", ac.ViewData["Title"], "Page title is wrong");
}
```

Now my test is lean, mean, and clean:

```
[Test]
public void Login_Should_Return_Error_If_Username_Is_Missing()
{
    var inModel = new LoginModel
                    {
                        Password = password,
                        RememberMe = true,
                        Username = string.Empty
                    };
    var results = ac.Login(inModel);
    AssertLoginViewResultOnError(results, "username,
        "Username is required", inModel);
}
```

More Refactoring

The code to assert an action result that redirects to another URL is:

```
Assert.IsNotNull(results);
Assert.IsInstanceOfType(typeof(RedirectToRouteResult), results);
var typedResults = results as RedirectToRouteResult;
Assert.AreEqual("Index",
                typedResults.Values["action"],
                "Wrong action");
Assert.AreEqual("Home",
                typedResults.Values["controller"],
                "Wrong controller");
```

I took this code and moved it to an extension method:

```
internal static class ResultsAssertions
{
    public static void AssertRedirectToRouteResult(this ActionResult result,
                                          string actionName,
```

```
                                                   string controllerName)
    {
        Assert.IsNotNull(result);
        Assert.IsInstanceOfType(typeof (RedirectToRouteResult), result);
        var routeResult = (RedirectToRouteResult) result;
        Assert.AreEqual(2, routeResult.Values.Count);
        Assert.AreEqual(actionName.ToLower(),
                    routeResult.Values["action"].ToString().ToLower());
        Assert.AreEqual(controllerName.ToLower(),
                    routeResult.Values["controller"].ToString().ToLower());
    }
}
```

Now I can simply assert the result of an action by writing:

```
results.AssertRedirectToRouteResult("Index", "home");
```

Summary

So far, we have created some extension methods to simplify our testing and implemented a generic model binder that can be used by all our model objects to retrieve items from data. We have also cleaned up our tests and consolidated our mocks, which should dramatically increase our productivity when writing tests.

As much as I love writing code, I love refactoring it even more. That's when you go back to your code and try to find a better and more elegant solution. The power of TDD is in full display when you are refactoring your code. You have the comfort of knowing that there are tests to validate your changes, which is incredibly empowering. We have all been in situations in which we refactor a few lines of code and then something breaks a few days later; but with TDD, the odds of this happening are greatly diminished.

5

Client and Server Validation

Regardless of how trusting you are, you should not trust anyone on the Internet, and you should validate all the data you receive. With that said, there are two places where you can perform form validation — on the client and on the server. Why do both? Client validation improves usability by not performing a round-trip to the server; it also makes the application more scalable because of fewer hits on the server. Server validation is critical because client validation can be disabled or circumvented. In this chapter, we will lay out a framework for validating on the server and on the client in order to automate and reduce the amount of code that we would have to write for each page requiring validation.

Problem

Now that we have our membership working, users can sign up, log in, log out, and reset their passwords. Before we start delving into the rest of the application, we need to determine our validation strategy and make sure it works with the rest of the application before we go too far and create a bunch of views.

So far, we have implemented server validation using `if` statements and the model state to indicate errors. Functionally this works well, but we need to do better. Ideally, we want to validate on both the client and the server. Client validation allows us to give users instant feedback without the overhead of a server round-trip. Server validation ensures that the data is valid even if client validation fails or the client doesn't support JavaScript or has it disabled. We also need an easy way to define validation rules, preferably on the model itself. Lastly, we need to get the validation out of the controller and into the service (business logic) layer, so that our validation logic is not tightly coupled to the controller.

To summarize, we need to:

- ❑ Validate on the client.
- ❑ Validate on the server.

❑ Define validation rules on the model.

❑ Perform validation in the service (business logic) layer.

Design

Instead of talking about the membership code we just wrote, let's add some new functionality and use the new validation design. One of the requirements is the ability for the users to create a new message, so let's start with that.

First, we should understand what a message is made up of:

❑ A descriptive name, for example, *October Newsletter*

❑ An email subject, for example, "October's exclusive offers to our valued members"

❑ Message content in HTML

❑ Message content in plaintext

The name, subject, and text body are required, whereas the HTML body is optional. Figure 5-1 shows the class diagram for the model.

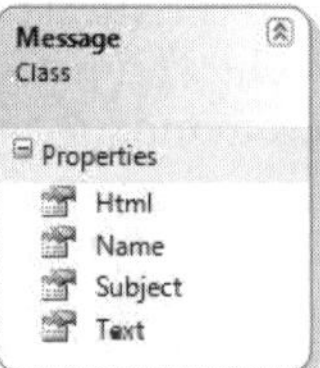

Figure 5-1

For the sake of this chapter, we are only concerned with the message creation operation and not the process itself. This will make it clearer to talk about validation without getting bogged down in the process details.

Solution

We start off by creating a new test class — `MessageControllerTest` — and adding our first test:

```
[TestFixture]
public class MessageControllerTest
{
    private MessageController controller;
    [SetUp]
    public void SetUp()
    {
        controller = new MessageController();
```

```
    }

    [Test]
    public void Create_Returns_View()
    {
        ActionResult result = controller.Create();
        result.AssertViewResult(controller, "New Message");
    }
}
```

In order for the above code to compile, we have to create the `MessageController` class and add a `Create` method to it:

```
public class MessageController : Controller
{
    [AcceptVerbs("get")]
    [Authorize]
    public ActionResult Create()
    {
        ViewData["Title"] = "New Message";
        return View();
    }
}
```

The next test is as follows:

```
[Test]
public void Create_Returns_Error_If_Name_Is_Missing()
{
    var model = new Message()
                    {
                        Subject = _subject,
                        Name = string.Empty,
                        Text = _text
                    };
    var result = controller.Create(model);

    var errorKey = "name";
    var errorMessage = "Name is required";

    //assert results
    Assert.IsNotNull(result);
    Assert.IsInstanceOfType(typeof(ViewResult), result);
    controller.ViewData.ModelState.AssertErrorMessage(errorKey, errorMessage);
    Assert.IsInstanceOfType(typeof(Message),
                            ((ViewResult)result).ViewData.Model);
    //asser that the ViewData.Model
    var outModel = (((ViewResult)result).ViewData.Model as Message);
    Assert.AreEqual(model.Subject, outModel.Subject);
    Assert.AreEqual(model.Name, outModel.Name);
    Assert.AreEqual(model.Text, outModel.Text);

    Assert.AreEqual("Login", controller.ViewData["Title"], "Page title is wrong");
}
```

The _subject and _text variables are defined at the class level because they will be used by other tests.

Nothing new so far; this is just the same stuff we have been doing. The next step is to create the `Create` method that will receive the POST request:

```
[AcceptVerbs("post")]
[Authorize]
public ActionResult Create(Message model)
{
    ViewData["Title"] = "New Message";

    //validate input
    if (string.IsNullOrEmpty(model.Name) )
    {
        ViewData.ModelState.AddModelError("name",
                                          model.Name,
                                          "Name is required");
    }

    if (!ViewData.ModelState.IsValid)
    {
        return View(model);
    }
    return View();
}
```

There is enough code written here to pass the previous test, which is good enough for now. Now let's quickly create a view to make sure that the validation works:

```
<h2>
    Create New Message</h2>
<%= Html.ValidationSummary()%>
<form action="/message/create" method="post">
<div>
    <label for="name">
        Name</label>
    <br />
    <%=Html.TextBox("name") %>
    <br />
    <label for="subject">
        Subject</label>
    <br />
    <%=Html.TextBox("subject") %>
    <br />
    <label for="html">
        Html Body (optional)</label>
    <br />
    <%=Html.TextArea("html") %>
    <br />
    <label for="text">
        Text Body</label>
    <br />
    <%=Html.TextArea("text") %>
    <br />
```

```
    <input type="submit" value="Create Message" />
</div>
</form>
```

And if we try to submit without filling in a name, we get an error as shown in Figure 5-2.

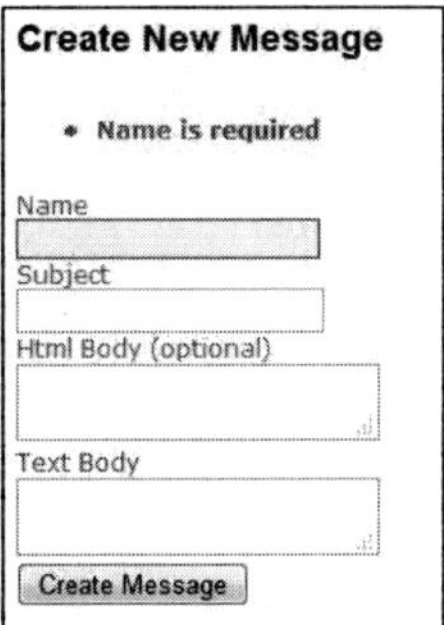

Figure 5-2

Now, we have just enough to start creating a better validation component. As we have already agreed, we need to move the validation out of the controller. We need to create a business logic object to handle the creation of the message and perform validation. Being good designers and because we want to make this easy to test and mock, we will use interfaces. At the moment, we only need an `Add` method, so here is our interface:

```
public interface IMessageService
{
    long Add(Message message);
}
```

Let's create a simple implementation of this interface. Remember that we are using TDD, so let's create some tests first. Our first test will make sure that the `Add` method throws an exception if the validation fails.

```
[Test]
[ExpectedException(typeof(ValidationException))]
public void Add_Throws_Exception_If_Validation_Returns_Errors()
{
    var invalidMessage = new Message();

    //mock a failed validation
    var mockValidationRunner = new Mock<IValidationRunner>();
    mockValidationRunner.Expect(v => v.Run(invalidMessage))
        .Returns(new List<ValidationError>
                {
                    new ValidationError("prop",
                                        "error")
                });

    IMessageService service = new MessageService(mockValidationRunner.Object);
    service.Add(invalidMessage); //should throw error
    mockValidationRunner.VerifyAll();
}
```

The test above includes the `ExpectedException` attribute, which tells the test framework that for this test to be successful, an exception of type `ValidationException` must be thrown. This is very convenient for testing.

Since none of these classes have been created, our project will not compile and we cannot run our test. Based on the test above, it looks like we need:

- An `IValidationRunner` interface with a `Run` method
- A `ValidationException` exception
- A `ValidationError` class with a constructor that takes two string parameters
- An implementation of `IMessageService` with a constructor that takes an instance, `IValidationRunner`

Here is what we have so far:

```
public interface IValidationRunner
{
    List<ValidationError> Run(object modelToValidate);
}

public class ValidationException : Exception { }

public class ValidationError
{
    public ValidationError(string propertyName, string errorMessage)
    {
    }
}

public class MessageService : IMessageService
{
    public MessageService(IValidationRunner validationRunner)
    {
    }

    public int Add(Message message)
    {
        throw new NotImplementedException();
    }
}
```

The project now compiles, but the test fails. If we change the `Add` method to throw an exception, the test will pass.

```
public int Add(Message message)
{
    throw new ValidationException();
}
```

There is a problem, however: The test should not have passed because the `mockValidationRunner.VerifyAll();` should fail; but the `mockValidationRunner.VerifyAll();` did not run because the `Add` method threw an exception. That is a problem with testing for exceptions using the `ExpectedException` attribute. A much better pattern is to use the `Assert.Throws` with a delegate or lambda expression.

```
[Test]
public void Add_Throws_Exception_If_Validation_Returns_Errors()
{
    var invalidMessage = new Message();

    //mock a failed validation
    var mockValidationRunner = new Mock<IValidationRunner>();
    mockValidationRunner.Expect(v => v.Run(invalidMessage))
        .Returns(new List<ValidationError>
            {
                new ValidationError("prop",
                                    "error")
            });

    IMessageService service = new MessageService(mockValidationRunner.Object);
    Assert.Throws<ValidationException>(() => service.Add(invalidMessage));

    mockValidationRunner.VerifyAll();
}
```

This will test the same condition as well as allow the test to continue after the exception. Now the test is failing for the correct reason: The `Run` method on the `ValidationRunner` has not been called. The following changes will make the test pass:

```
public class MessageService : IMessageService
{
    private IValidationRunner ValidationRunner { get; set; }
    public MessageService(IValidationRunner validationRunner)
    {
        ValidationRunner = validationRunner;
    }

    public int Add(Message message)
    {
        var errors = ValidationRunner.Run(message);
        if (errors != null && errors.Count > 0)
        {
            throw new ValidationException();
        }
        return -1;
    }
}
```

Moving on, we need to test the validation for every field. Let's start with Name:

```
[Test]
public void Add_Throws_Exception_If_Name_Is_Missing()
{
    message.Name = string.Empty;
```

```
IValidationRunner vrunner = new ValidationRunner();
IMessageService service = new MessageService(vrunner);
var ex = Assert.Throws<ValidationException>(() => service.Add(message));
Assert.IsNotNull(ex.ValidationErrors);
Assert.GreaterThan(ex.ValidationErrors.Count, 0);
//asser the correct error
Assert.AreEqual(ex.ValidationErrors
                    .Count(e => e.PropertyName == "Name" &&
                        e.ErrorMessage == "Name is required"), 1);
}
```

In the above test, we test that the `Add` method throws the correct exception and that the exception contains the validation error to indicate that the name is required. To make the above code run, we need to create the `ValidationRunner` and implement the `IValidationRunner` interface:

```
public class ValidationRunner : IValidationRunner
{
    public List<ValidationError> Run(object modelToValidate)
    {
        return null;
    }
}
```

And we need to add a `ValidationErrors` property to the `ValidationException`:

```
public class ValidationException : Exception
{
    public List<ValidationError> ValidationErrors { get; set; }
}
```

Now let's write code to make the test pass. First, we need to change the exception-throwing code to include the validation errors:

```
public int Add(Message message)
{
    var errors = ValidationRunner.Run(message);
    if (errors != null && errors.Count > 0)
    {
        throw new ValidationException(errors);
    }
    return -1;
}
```

Then change the `ValidationException`'s constructor:

```
public class ValidationException : Exception
{
    public ValidationException(List<ValidationError> errors)
    {
        ValidationErrors = errors;
    }
    public List<ValidationError> ValidationErrors { get; private set; }
}
```

Next, we change the `Run` method to return the appropriate errors. We are going to use reflection to iterate through the object's properties and look for validation attributes. We can easily create our own attributes, but, even easier, we can use the attributes defined in the `System.ComponentModel.DataAnnotations` namespace. Our `ValidationRunner` now looks like this:

```csharp
public class ValidationRunner : IValidationRunner
{
    public List<ValidationError> ValidationErrors { get; private set; }

    public List<ValidationError> Run(object modelToValidate)
    {
        ValidationErrors = new List<ValidationError>();
        var props = TypeDescriptor.GetProperties(
                                    modelToValidate.GetType());
        foreach (PropertyDescriptor prop in props)
        {
            var value = prop.GetValue(modelToValidate);
            foreach (var attrib in prop.Attributes
                .OfType<ValidationAttribute>())
            {
                if (!attrib.IsValid(value))
                {
                    ValidationErrors.Add(
                        new ValidationError(prop.Name,
                                            attrib.ErrorMessage));
                }
            }
        }
        return ValidationErrors;
    }
}
```

In the above code, we are looking for the `ValidationAttribute`. If we find it, we will check if the property value is valid, and if not, we will add a validation error to our collection of validation errors.

The test still fails because we haven't decorated our Message with the proper attributes. We simply add the appropriate attribute to each property:

```csharp
public class Message
{
    [Required(ErrorMessage = "Name is required")]
    public string Name { get; set; }
    [Required(ErrorMessage = "Subject is required")]
    public string Subject { get; set; }
    public string Html { get; set; }
    [Required(ErrorMessage = "A plain text body is required")]
    public string Text { get; set; }
}
```

The test passes. Now we can just add more tests to test the other validation conditions.

It's important to note that the above code tests the `MessageService` class and not the validation class. We could have easily mocked all the validation calls and got the same results. We need to test the validation component separately. Let's create a new test fixture to test all validation scenarios and then create a model to use for our testing:

```
internal class ModelToValidate
{
    [Required(ErrorMessage = "Name is required")]
    public string Name { get; set; }

    [Range(18, 35, ErrorMessage = "Age should be 18 to 35")]
    public int? Age { get; set; }

    [RegularExpression(@"\w+([-+.']\w+)*@\w+([-.]\w+)*\.\w+([-.]\w+)*",
        ErrorMessage = "Email is invalid")]
    public string Email { get; set; }
}
```

Instead of walking through each test, let's look at the tests for the model we just created:

```
[TestFixture]
public class ValidationRunnerTests
{
    private ModelToValidate model;
    private ValidationRunner runner;

    [SetUp]
    public void SetUp()
    {
        runner = new ValidationRunner();
        model = new ModelToValidate()
                    {
                        Age = 24,
                        Email = "test@test.com",
                        Name = "Jessica Alba"
                    };
    }

    [Test]
    public void Validate_Required_Erros_If_Value_Is_Missing()
    {
        model.Name = string.Empty;
        var errors = runner.Run(model);
        AssertValidationError(errors, "Name", "Name is required");
    }

    [Test]
    public void Validate_Required_No_Erros_If_Value_Is_Set()
    {
        var errors = runner.Run(model);
        if (errors != null)
            Assert.AreEqual(errors.Count, 0);
    }

    [Test]
    public void Validate_Range_Errors_If_Value_Less_Than_Min()
    {
```

```
    model.Age = 2;
    var errors = runner.Run(model);
    AssertValidationError(errors, "Age", "Age should be 18 to 35");
}

[Test]
public void Validate_Range_Errors_If_Value_More_Than_Max()
{
    model.Age = 36;
    var errors = runner.Run(model);
    AssertValidationError(errors, "Age", "Age should be 18 to 35");
}

[Test, Row(18), Row(25), Row(35)]
public void Validate_Range_No_Errors_If_Within_Range(int? value)
{
    model.Age = value;
    var errors = runner.Run(model);
    if (errors != null)
        Assert.AreEqual(errors.Count, 0);
}

[Test]
public void Validate_RegEx_Errors_If_Value_Is_Invalid()
{
    model.Email = "bad email#@#";
    var errors = runner.Run(model);
    AssertValidationError(errors, "Email", "Email is invalid");
}

[Test]
public void Validate_RegEx_No_Errors_If_Value_Is_Valid()
{
    var errors = runner.Run(model);
    if (errors != null)
        Assert.AreEqual(errors.Count, 0);
}

[Test]
public void Validate_Only_If_Required_And_Set()
{
    model.Age = null;
    model.Email = null;
    var errors = runner.Run(model);
    if (errors != null)
        Assert.AreEqual(errors.Count, 0);
}

private static void AssertValidationError(List<ValidationError> errors,
                                          string propertyName,
                                          string errorMessage)
{
    Assert.IsNotNull(errors);
    Assert.GreaterThan(errors.Count, 0);
    Assert.AreEqual(errors.Count(e =>
                            e.PropertyName == propertyName &&
```

```csharp
                                         e.ErrorMessage == errorMessage),
                    1);
        }

        internal class ModelToValidate
        {
            [Required(ErrorMessage = "Name is required")]
            public string Name { get; set; }

            [Range(18, 35, ErrorMessage = "Age should be 18 to 35")]
            public int? Age { get; set; }

            [RegularExpression(@"\w+([-+.']\w+)*@\w+([-.]\w+)*\.\w+([-.]\w+)*",
                ErrorMessage = "Email is invalid")]
            public string Email { get; set; }
        }
    }
```

Using required, range, and regular expression attributes, we should be able to cover pretty much all
our validation needs. If not, we can always create our own validation attributes. For example, we could
encapsulate the email validation into its own class like so:

```csharp
class EmailValidationAttribute : RegularExpressionAttribute
{
    public EmailAttribute()
        : base(@"\w+([-+.']\w+)*@\w+([-.]\w+)*\.\w+([-.]\w+)*")
    {
    }
}
```

Or, we can inherit from the virtual class `ValidationAttribute` and write our own custom validation logic:

```csharp
class UsernameValidationAttribute : ValidationAttribute
{
    public override bool IsValid(object value)
    {
        if (value.GetType() != typeof(string))
            return false;
        var str = value.ToString();
        if (str.Length < 4)
            return false;
        //test other conditions
        return true;
    }
}
```

Now that we have a validation framework up and running, let's see if we can apply it to the controller.
The controller is going to need an instance of IMessageService, so we will add the following code to the
`MessageController`:

```csharp
public MessageController()
    : this(null) { }
```

```csharp
public MessageController(IMessageService service)
{
    Service = service ?? new MessageService();
}

public IMessageService Service { get; set; }
```

Now we change our `Create` method to use the service:

```csharp
[AcceptVerbs("post")]
[Authorize]
public ActionResult Create(Message model)
{
    ViewData["Title"] = "New Message";

    try
    {
        var id = Service.Add(model);
    }
    catch (ValidationException ex)
    {
        foreach (var error in ex.ValidationErrors)
        {
            ViewData.ModelState.AddModelError(
                error.PropertyName,
                null,
                error.ErrorMessage);
        }
    }

    if (!ViewData.ModelState.IsValid)
    {
        return View(model);
    }
    return View();
}
```

The `Create_Returns_Error_If_Name_Is_Missing` test should still pass, but now we are using the model-based validation and there's no need to write more `if` statements.

I was happy to see it work right away, but I wanted to make sure, so I changed the error message on the `Required` *attribute on the* `Name` *property just to make sure the test would fail, and it did.*

Validation is now finished for the `Create` method, but we still need tests to make sure all the validation works. After some refactoring, our message controller test fixture looks as follows:

```csharp
[TestFixture]
public class MessageControllerTest
{
    private MessageController controller;
    private Message model;

    [SetUp]
```

```csharp
public void SetUp()
{
    controller = new MessageController();
    model = new Message()
                {
                    Subject = "My newsletter subject",
                    Name = "October newsletter",
                    Text = "Hello subscriber",
                    Html = "Hello <b>subscriber</b>"
                };
}


[Test]
public void Create_Returns_View()
{
    var result = controller.Create();
    result.AssertViewResult(controller, "New Message");
}


[Test]
public void Create_Returns_Error_If_Name_Is_Missing()
{
    model.Name = string.Empty;
    var result = controller.Create(model);
    var errorKey = "Name";
    var errorMessage = "Name is required";
    AssertValidationError(result, errorKey, errorMessage);
}


[Test]
public void Create_Returns_Error_If_Text_Is_Missing()
{
    model.Text = string.Empty;
    var result = controller.Create(model);
    var errorKey = "Text";
    var errorMessage = "A plain text body is required";
    AssertValidationError(result, errorKey, errorMessage);
}


[Test]
public void Create_Returns_Error_If_Subject_Is_Missing()
{
    model.Subject = string.Empty;
    var result = controller.Create(model);
    var errorKey = "Subject";
    var errorMessage = "Subject is required";
    AssertValidationError(result, errorKey, errorMessage);
}


private void AssertValidationError(ActionResult result,
                                  string errorKey,
                                  string errorMessage)
{
    //assert results
```

```
            Assert.IsNotNull(result);
            Assert.IsInstanceOfType(typeof (ViewResult), result);
            controller.ViewData.ModelState.AssertErrorMessage(errorKey, errorMessage);
            Assert.IsInstanceOfType(typeof (Message),
                                ((ViewResult) result).ViewData.Model);
            //asser that the ViewData.Model
            var outModel = (((ViewResult) result).ViewData.Model as Message);
            Assert.AreEqual(model.Subject, outModel.Subject);
            Assert.AreEqual(model.Name, outModel.Name);
            Assert.AreEqual(model.Text, outModel.Text);

            Assert.AreEqual("New Message", controller.ViewData["Title"],
                        "Page title is wrong");
        }
    }
```

Let's confirm that everything is working as it should. If we run the project and try to submit, we see the validation in action, and the page looks like Figure 5-3:

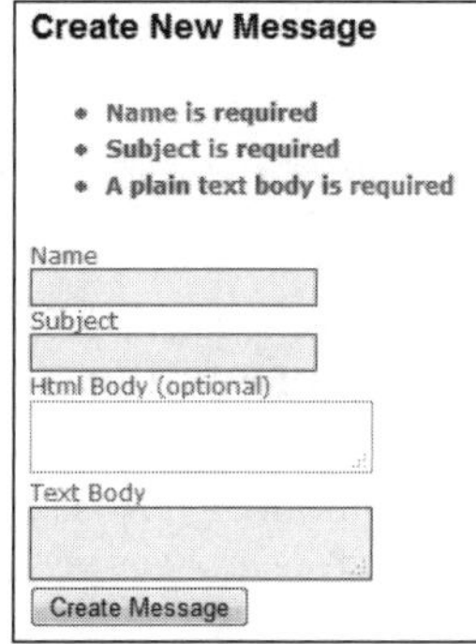

Figure 5-3

Client-Side Validation

So far, server-side validation is working pretty well. Now, let's get client-side validation in place. There are two options to consider:

❑   Write our JavaScript.

❑   Use a third-party JavaScript validation library.

Again, why reinvent the wheel? Let's use a third-party library. There are several options out there, but here we'll use the jQuery Validation plug-in. It is a very flexible validation library that allows us to validate forms in two different ways. We can use classes on the input fields. For example, the following line of code is telling the validation library to validate the input field txtemail as a required field and as an email field:

```
<input id="txtemail" name="txtemail" size="25"  class="required email" />
```

The second method uses rules that are defined in JavaScript. We can achieve the same results as the above example using the following JavaScript:

```html
<script type="text/javascript">
$("#createForm").validate({
    rules: {
        txtemail: {
            required: true,
            email: true
        }
    },
    messages: {
        txtemail: "Please enter a valid email address"
    }
});
</script>
```

Since we are going to generate the client-side validation code dynamically based on the model's definition, it will be easier to generate the JavaScript code than to generate the classes on each field. It is also a better design since it encapsulates the validation logic in one location versus having it spread out through the HTML.

We need to create a method that generates the JavaScript based on the model's definition. Let's start with a test.

> ### Convention
> We will use the convention that the HTML element has the same name as the property/field name being validated and is all lowercased. This simplifies our script generation code and minimizes script errors.

Here is our test class:

```csharp
[TestFixture]
public class JQueryValidationGeneratorTests
{
    private ModelToValidate model;
    private JQueryValidationGenerator generator;
    [SetUp]
    public void SetUp()
    {
        generator = new JQueryValidationGenerator();
        model = new ModelToValidate()
        {
            Age = 24,
            Email = "test@test.com",
            Name = "Jessica Alba"
        };
    }
    [Test]
    public void Generates_Rule_For_Required_Field()
    {
```

```
        string script = generator.Generate("createForm", model);
        Assert.IsTrue(script.Contains("name:{required:true}"));
    }


    internal class ModelToValidate
    {
        [Required(ErrorMessage = "Name is required")]
        public string Name { get; set; }

        [Range(18, 35, ErrorMessage = "Age should be 18 to 35")]
        public int? Age { get; set; }

        [RegularExpression(@"\w+([-+.']\w+)*@\w+([-.]\w+)*\.\w+([-.]\w+)*",
            ErrorMessage = "Email is invalid")]
        public string Email { get; set; }
    }
}
```

The project will not compile until we create the missing classes and methods. The design should be flexible, so we can easily replace the jQuery validation library if need be. We start by creating the following interface:

```
interface IValidationGenerator
{
    string Generate(string formToValidate, object modelToValidate);
}
```

Then we implement it for the jQuery library and write enough code to pass our first test:

```
public class JQueryValidationGenerator : IValidationGenerator
{
    public string Generate(string formToValidate, object modelToValidate)
    {
        var props = TypeDescriptor.GetProperties(modelToValidate.GetType());
        var rules = string.Empty;
        var script = string.Empty;
        foreach (PropertyDescriptor prop in props)
        {
            var rule = string.Empty;
            foreach (var attrib in prop.Attributes
                .OfType<ValidationAttribute>())
            {
                var subrule = string.Empty;
                if (attrib.GetType() == typeof(RequiredAttribute))
                    subrule = "required:true";

                rule += string.Format("{0}{1}",
                                string.IsNullOrEmpty(rule) ? "" : ",",
                                subrule);
            }

            if (!string.IsNullOrEmpty(rule))
            {
                rule = string.Format("{0}:{{{1}}}",
```

```
                                    prop.Name.ToLower(),
                                    rule);
                rules += string.Format("{0}{1}",
                                    string.IsNullOrEmpty(rules) ? "" : ",",
                                    rule);
            }


        }

        if (!string.IsNullOrEmpty(rules))
        {
            script = string.Format("<script type=\"text/javascript\">\r\n" +
                            "$().ready(function() {{\r\n" +
                            "$('#{0}')." +
                            "validate({{rules:{{{1}}},\r\n" +
                            "messages:{{{2}}}}});}});" +
                            "\r\n</script>",
                            formToValidate, rules, messages);
        }
        return script;
    }
}
```

Let's test email validation:

```
[Test]
public void Generates_Rule_For_Email_Field()
{
    string script = generator.Generate("createForm", model);
    Assert.IsTrue(script.Contains("email:{email:true}"));
}
```

This code will not work because our model validates for email using a regular expression:

```
[RegularExpression(@"\w+([-+.']\w+)*@\w+([-.]\w+)*\.\w+([-.]\w+)*",
    ErrorMessage = "Email is invalid")]
public string Email { get; set; }
```

It would be much better if we could validate email using an email attribute, such as:

```
[Email(ErrorMessage = "Email is invalid")]
public string Email { get; set; }
```

Unfortunately, there are two problems. First, there is no regular expression rule in the jQuery Validation framework. Second, there is no `Email` attribute in the `DataAnnotations` namespace. So, we can either create an `Email` attribute or extend jQuery's Validation framework with a regular expression rule. Luckily, both are easy to implement.

We can create a new validation rule type by calling this JavaScript:

```
$(document).ready(function() {
    jQuery.validator.addMethod("regex", function(value, element, param) {
        return this.optional(element) || new RegExp(param).test(value);
```

```
    }, "Invalid data");
});
```

Or, we can create an `Email` attribute like this:

```
public class EmailAttribute : ValidationAttribute
{
    public override bool IsValid(object value)
    {
        var regex = new Regex(@"\w+([-+.']\w+)*@\w+([-.]\w+)*\.\w+([-.]\w+)*");
        return regex.IsMatch((string)value);
    }
}
```

Since we don't have a need for a regular expression rule at the moment, we will go ahead and create the `EmailAttribute` instead. Now we can generate our rule by simply adding another `if` statement to the generator shown in the preceding code.

```
if (attrib.GetType() == typeof(EmailAttribute))
    subrule = "email:true";
```

The preceding generator code doesn't include the messages part of the validation script for clarity. We will create tests for the messages and add more tests as we progress through our project and require more validation types.

Let's test this in the View. We will create a helper method that generates the script. Then all we need to do to get the script into the View is add this one line of code:

```
<%= Html.JQueryGenerator("createmessage", ViewData.Model) %>
```

The helper method looks like this:

```
public static string JQueryGenerator(this HtmlHelper htmlHelper,
                                     string formName, object model)
{
    return (new JQueryValidationGenerator()).Generate(formName, model);
}
```

If we try to navigate to /message/create, we get an error:

```
Object reference not set to an instance of an object.
```

The reason is the model is not set, so the `ViewData.Model` is null. This is a simple fix. All we have to do is change the Create action to:

```
[AcceptVerbs("get")]
[Authorize]
public ActionResult Create()
{
    ViewData["Title"] = "New Message";
    return View(new Message());
}
```

All we are doing is passing an empty model of type `Message` that allows our generator code to probe the model and examine its attributes to generate the appropriate JavaScript. The generated JavaScript is:

```
<script type="text/javascript">
$().ready(function() {
$('#createmessage').validate({
rules:{name:{required:true},subject:{required:true},text:{required:true}},
messages:{name:{required:'Name is required'},subject:{required:'Subject is
required'},text:{required:'A plain text body is required'}}});});
</script>
```

If we try to submit the form, the script will validate it on the client without ever reaching the server, as shown in Figure 5-4.

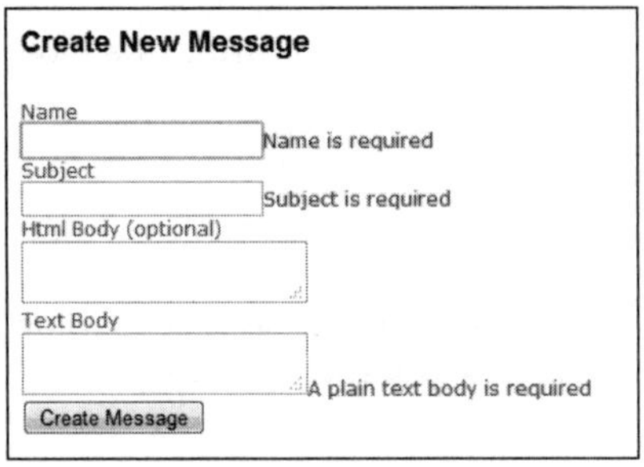

Create New Message

Name

Name is required

Subject

Subject is required

Html Body (optional)

Text Body

A plain text body is required

Create Message

Figure 5-4

Summary

In this chapter, we have discussed client and server validation. Validation is a very common problem and will pretty much be needed in every project you work on. If you can only implement one type of validation, then it should be on the server. Client-side validation alone is not secure enough because, as previously mentioned, it is not secure and can be circumvented.

We discussed how to simplify validation by simply adding attributes to the model. In my opinion, this is a very clean and loosely coupled solution to the validation problem. Using the attributes defined on the model, we can then have a validation framework that reads these attributes and validates the model accordingly.

We also used the attribute to generate the appropriate JavaScript to perform client validation. Again, this is very clean and repeatable throughout the project and even throughout other projects. We will not have to write JavaScript code for every form and every field; we simply generate the scripts based on the model attributes.

6

Data Layer and IRepository Pattern

Our application is heavily data-driven, and a good amount of attention needs to be given to the data layer. At the same time, we don't want to bother with database design and modeling right now and just want to keep moving along with our application. We need to keep creating our application without being bogged down by the database and slowing down our tests. In this chapter, we will do exactly that. We will lay the groundwork for a data layer that will enable us to keep working on our application without creating and configuring a database, creating a single database table, or worrying about maintaining the database schema during the development phase.

Problem

Other than standard ASP.NET tables, we have not touched the database or created any tables. I deliberately wanted to delay doing anything with the database until we needed to, and so far we haven't. Dealing with databases can complicate testing. We have to worry about managing data and maintaining the state of the database during testing. We also have to restore the database to a neutral state after each test. You can see how this could complicate our testing and also considerably slow it down. If your tests are too slow, you will run them less often, you will be less likely to write them, and you will very quickly lose interest in Test Driven Development.

We need to abstract the data layer so that we can run our tests without ever touching the database. We also want to be able to run our website and have it function without needing to create or populate the database with anything. We basically want to be able to use an in-memory database but at the same be able to easily switch to using the real database without re-writing any code.

Design

A good design for our problem is to use the IRepository pattern. This is a simple but yet very powerful pattern that allows us to abstract the data layer from our code. Abstracting the data layer gives us a lot of flexibility in our design and simplifies our testing. Don't worry if all this sounds too theoretical right now — the next few pages will help clarify all the concepts.

In the previous chapter, we created an `IMessageService` interface that, so far, has only one method that adds a message to the database. The beauty of using the service layer is that the application code doesn't need to know anything about the underlying details of the what, how, and where of dealing with the database. It just knows that it needs to call the `Add` method and handle any validation exceptions. Using an interface at this layer makes our testing easier by giving us the ability to mock the interface and/or implement a test-specific implementation. We now take this same concept and abstract it one more layer. We will pass an `IMessageRepository` interface into the `MessageService` class; the `IMessageRepository` interface will deal strictly with working with the repository/database/data store. That's its single responsibility.

Let's think about what we need to do here. We want to basically perform CRUD (create, read, update, and delete) operations on the data, so our `IRepository` interface, at the least, needs to include these operations. Our class diagrams so far are shown in Figure 6-1.

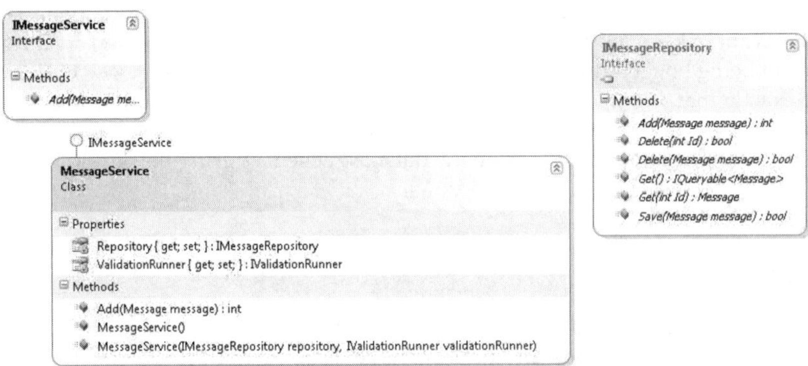

Figure 6-1

Solution

Let's implement the above design and refactor our tests and make sure that they work. We start by creating the interface:

```
public interface IMessageRepository
{
    int Add(Message message);
    bool Delete(int Id);
    bool Save(Message message);
```

```
    IQueryable<Message> Get();
}
```

> **To improve the code's readability, I am going to rename the** `MessageService` **class to** `InMemoryMessageService`. **Later we will create a** `SqlMessageService` **class that will use a** `SqlMessageRepository`.

Then we change the `InMemoryMessageService` to use the new repository:

```
public class InMemoryMessageService : IMessageService
{
    private IValidationRunner ValidationRunner { get; set; }
    private IMessageRepository Repository { get; set; }

    public InMemoryMessageService()
        : this(null, null)
    {
    }

    public InMemoryMessageService(IMessageRepository repository,
                    IValidationRunner validationRunner)
    {
        ValidationRunner = validationRunner ?? new ValidationRunner();
        Repository = repository ?? new InMemoryMessageRepository();
    }
}
```

Now we make sure we can build the projects and run all the tests. Once everything is fine, we write a new test to make sure that we are using the repository:

```
[Test]
public void Create_Adds_Message_To_Repository()
{
    //mock the repo
    var mockRepo = new Mock<IMessageRepository>();
    //set expectations
    mockRepo.Expect(r => r.Add(model)).Returns(1);
    var mockValidationRunner = new Mock<IValidationRunner>();
    var service = new InMemoryMessageService(mockRepo.Object,
                                        mockValidationRunner.Object);
    controller = new MessageController(service);
    var result = controller.Create(model);
    mockRepo.VerifyAll();
}
```

By mocking the `IMessageRepository` interface, we limit our test to the fact that the `Add` method is getting called. This narrows down our test and isolates us from the actual implementation of the `IMessageRepository` implementation. The implementation should be tested separately, as you will soon see.

To make the previous test work, we change our `Add` method in the `InMemoryMessageService` class to use the repository:

```csharp
public int Add(Message message)
{
    var errors = ValidationRunner.Run(message);
    if (errors != null && errors.Count > 0)
    {
        throw new ValidationException(errors);
    }
    return Repository.Add(message);
}
```

As you can see from the preceding code, the service layer knows nothing about the persistence mechanism or destination. Instead, it delegates that task to the `IRepository`. We can now implement the `IMessageRepository` interface any way we want. We can have an implementation that writes to memory for testing purposes, another that writes to XML for integration testing, and a production implementation that talks to SQL Server.

Let's implement the `IMessageRepository` interface without having to deal with the database. We will create an in-memory implementation, but, as we have always done, we will start by writing tests. Let's create the test fixture:

```csharp
[TestFixture]
public class InMemoryRepositoryTests
{
    private Message message;

    [SetUp]
    public void SetUp()
    {
        message = new Message()
        {
            Subject = "My newsletter subject",
            Name = "October newsletter",
            Text = "Hello subscriber",
            Html = "Hello <b>subscriber</b>"
        };
    }
}
```

Then we create a test for adding a message:

```csharp
[Test]
public void Add_Message_To_Repository()
{
    var repo = new InMemoryMessageRepository();
    repo.Add(message);
    //verify message is added correctly
    var msg = repo.Get().Where(m => m.Id == 1).Single();
    Assert.IsNotNull(msg);
    Assert.AreEqual(message.Html, msg.Html);
    Assert.AreEqual(message.Text, msg.Text);
    Assert.AreEqual(message.Subject, msg.Subject);
```

```
        Assert.AreEqual(message.Name, msg.Name);
    }
```

We can then make the previous test pass by writing the following code:

```
public class InMemoryMessageRepository : IMessageRepository
{
    private List<Message> Messages { get; set; }

    public InMemoryMessageRepository()
    {
        Messages = new List<Message>();
    }

    public int Add(Message message)
    {
        message.Id = 1;
        Messages.Add(message);
        return message.Id;
    }

    public bool Delete(int Id)
    {
        throw new System.NotImplementedException();
    }

    public bool Save(Message message)
    {
        throw new System.NotImplementedException();
    }

    public IQueryable<Message> Get()
    {
        var q = from m in Messages select m;
        return q.AsQueryable();
    }
}
```

Now we need to make sure that the repository is properly assigning a unique ID to each message:

```
[Test]
public void Add_Assigns_Unique_Ids()
{
    var repo = new InMemoryMessageRepository();
    repo.Add(new Message()); //1
    repo.Add(new Message()); //2
    repo.Add(new Message()); //3
    var msgs = repo.Get();
    Assert.IsNotNull(msgs);
    Assert.AreEqual(3, msgs.Count());
    Assert.AreEqual(1, msgs.Count(m => m.Id == 1));
    Assert.AreEqual(1, msgs.Count(m => m.Id == 2));
    Assert.AreEqual(1, msgs.Count(m => m.Id == 3));
}
```

We can modify the `Add` method to assign a unique ID like so:

```csharp
private int _autoId;
private int AutoId
{
    get
    {
        _autoId += 1;
        return _autoId;
    }
}
public int Add(Message message)
{
    message.Id = AutoId;
    Messages.Add(message);
    return message.Id;
}
```

Moving on, let's test the delete functionality:

```csharp
[Test]
public void Delete_Message_From_Repository()
{
    var repo = new InMemoryMessageRepository();
    repo.Add(message);
    //make sure message is added
    var msgs = repo.Get();
    Assert.IsNotNull(msgs);
    Assert.AreEqual(1, msgs.Count());
    var result = repo.Delete(1);
    Assert.IsTrue(result);
    msgs = repo.Get();
    Assert.IsNotNull(msgs);
    Assert.AreEqual(0, msgs.Count());
}
```

We are simply adding a message, verifying that it was added, removing it, and then verifying that it was removed. The `Delete` method is implemented as follows:

```csharp
public bool Delete(int Id)
{
    try
    {
        Messages.Remove(Messages.Single(m => m.Id == Id));
        return true;
    }
    catch (Exception ex)
    {
        return false;
    }
}
```

We should also make sure that the `Delete` method doesn't throw any exceptions but instead returns `False` on any error. We can ensure that with the following test:

```
[Test]
public void Delete_Message_Returns_False_On_Exception()
{
    var repo = new InMemoryMessageRepository();
    repo.Add(message);
    //make sure message is added
    var msgs = repo.Get();
    Assert.IsNotNull(msgs);
    Assert.AreEqual(1, msgs.Count());
    var result = repo.Delete(12); //Id doesn't exist
    Assert.IsFalse(result);
    msgs = repo.Get();
    Assert.IsNotNull(msgs);
    Assert.AreEqual(1, msgs.Count());
}
```

Finally, let's make sure that we can save changes to an existing message. We will add a message, get it, make changes to it, and then save it. Here is the test:

```
[Test]
public void Save_Message_To_Repository()
{
    var repo = new InMemoryMessageRepository();
    repo.Add(message);
    //get message
    var msg = repo.Get().Where(m => m.Id == 1).Single();
    Assert.IsNotNull(msg);
    //make changes
    var text = "new text";
    var name = "new name";
    var html = "new html";
    var subject = "new subject";
    msg.Name = name;
    msg.Html = html;
    msg.Subject = subject;
    msg.Text = text;
    //save message
    repo.Save(msg);
    //get message again
    var msgAfterSave = repo.Get().Where(m => m.Id == 1).Single();
    //verify changes were saved
    Assert.AreEqual(html, msgAfterSave.Html);
    Assert.AreEqual(text, msgAfterSave.Text);
    Assert.AreEqual(subject, msgAfterSave.Subject);
    Assert.AreEqual(name, msgAfterSave.Name);
}
```

and here is the implementation:

```
public bool Save(Message message)
{
```

```
        try
        {
            var original = Messages.Single(m => m.Id == message.Id);
            var index = Messages.IndexOf(original);
            Messages[index] = message;
            return true;
        }
        catch (Exception)
        {
            return false;
        }
    }
```

The full implementation of the `InMemoryMessageRepository` class is as follows:

```
    public class InMemoryMessageRepository : IMessageRepository
    {
        private List<Message> Messages { get; set; }

        public InMemoryMessageRepository()
        {
            Messages = new List<Message>();
        }

        private int _autoId;
        private int AutoId
        {
            get
            {
                _autoId += 1;
                return _autoId;
            }
        }

        public int Add(Message message)
        {
            message.Id = AutoId;
            Messages.Add(message);
            return message.Id;
        }


        public bool Delete(int Id)
        {
            try
            {
                Messages.Remove(Messages.Single(m => m.Id == Id));
                return true;
            }
            catch (Exception ex)
            {
                return false;
            }
```

```csharp
    }

    public bool Save(Message message)
    {
        try
        {
            var original = Messages.Single(m => m.Id == message.Id);
            var index = Messages.IndexOf(original);
            Messages[index] = message;
            return true;
        }
        catch (Exception)
        {
            return false;
        }
    }

    public IQueryable<Message> Get()
    {
        var q = from m in Messages select m;
        return q.AsQueryable();
    }
}
```

This implementation will now allow us to run tests much more quickly than if we had to touch the database. We also don't need to worry about cleanup code, since the data is stored in memory and it automatically goes away after test execution. We can also add some more code to this implementation to create some test data that we can experiment with.

There are a few things I want to clarify, however. Notice that the `Get` method returns an IQueryable list of messages. This was specifically chosen over a `List<Message>` because it allows us to use the power of LINQ's lazy loading. Using this design, we can write several methods in the service class to apply different or even multiple filtering on the returned results. For example, we can have a method get a specific message by ID, get all messages for a user, search messages for a specific text, and even apply paging. To clarify further, take a look at this method in the `MessageService` class (and `IMessageService` interface):

```csharp
public Message GetById(int Id)
{
    return Repository.Get().Single(m => m.Id == Id);
}
```

In this method, we call the `Get` method on the repository, which returns an `IQueryable<Message>` but doesn't execute the SQL until `Single` executes with the appropriate filter. So we are not executing a `select * from messages` and then filtering it in code, we are actually executing something like `select * from messages where Id = @id`.

And for the sake of clarification, here is another example:

```csharp
public List<Message> Search(string searchTerm)
{
    return Repository.Get().Where(m => m.Text.Contains(searchTerm)).ToList();
}
```

In the previous method, we search the text of the message for a specific search term. If the repository implementation is using LINQ to SQL, the SQL generated might look something like `select * from messages where text like searchTerm`.

Something important to note is that we haven't used any data context in the preceding implementation because we are working with an in-memory repository. When we switch to the production repository using LINQ to SQL, we have to consider the data context and release any resources. We cannot release the data context in the data layer because we are using LINQ's lazy load and the returned `IQueryable` will throw an exception if you try to access it after disposing of the data context. So the data context has to be managed in the service layer. Some argue that this is a bad design because it creates a tight coupling between the two layers and the `IQueryable` crosses layer boundaries. These are valid concerns and must be considered in your design. I personally think that they are an acceptable trade-off.

Summary

We have done such a good job abstracting each layer that we won't have to make any changes to the controller. The following `MessageController` constructors will work as is:

```
public MessageController()
    : this(null)
{
}

public MessageController(IMessageService service)
{
    Service = service ?? new InMemoryMessageService();
}
```

We were also able to use the IRepository pattern and abstract the persistence mechanism from the business logic. That allowed us to create an in-memory database implementation that is used relatively easily during testing but can easily be replaced with a SQL-backed implementation. In the coming chapters, you will see the benefits of this design and how much it simplifies our testing and maintenance.

7

Declare Your Independence with Dependency Injection

It is always a good idea to reduce dependencies in your code and abstract as much as possible; but that is not always realistic. It is inevitable that you will introduce dependencies between your classes and even assemblies. Fortunately, there is a way to mitigate the effects of dependencies and reduce the coupling in the code.

Using the Inversion of Control (IoC) and Dependency Injection (DI) principles, we are able to create loosely coupled systems and mitigate the effects of dependencies. Inversion of Control is the indirection of object instantiation so that objects do not directly create other objects. Instead, an IoC Container will inject the dependencies into an object through constructor parameters or public properties.

Combined with mocking, Dependency Injection can greatly simplify testing. Imagine if we have a class that calls a web service. Using DI, we can inject a mocked version of that class which is used for our testing.

Problem

Our controllers so far have parameterized constructors that expect some interfaces. For example, our `AccountController` expects an `IFormsAuthentication` and a `MembershipProvider`, and our `MessageController` expects an `IMessageService`. Currently our `MessageController` class has two constructors:

```
public MessageController()
    : this(null)
{
}
```

```
public MessageController(IMessageService service)
{
    Service = service ?? new InMemoryMessageService();
}
```

The default constructor is called by the MVC framework, which, in turn, calls the parameterized constructor with `null` values. The parameterized constructor instantiates an implementation of the interface if the passed value is null. This works well and allows us to use the parameterized constructor without changing the framework's instantiation process. The problem with this pattern is that our code is tightly coupled to a specific implementation of the interface — specifically, the `InMemoryMessageService` implementation. Remember that we used interfaces because they simplify testing and mocking, as well as enable us to plug in different implementations throughout the life of the application. If we wanted to use a different implementation — say, SqlMessageService — we would have to recompile and redeploy the application. That is not an acceptable price to pay and defeats the plugability enabled by the use of interfaces.

Design

We can solve these problems by using an IoC Container that will be able to decide at run time which implementation of the interfaces to instantiate — this is where we invert the control and redirect the instantiation away from the dependent object. The container would then pass the correct instance into the dependent object's constructor; that is, it will inject the dependency.

Without an IoC Container, our class diagram would look like Figure 7-1.

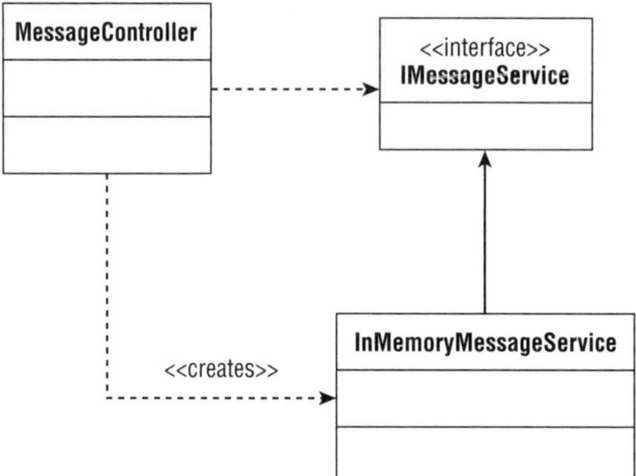

Figure 7-1

If we use an IoC container, we will eliminate the dependency on the concrete implementation and remove the instantiation logic from the dependent class. Our class diagram would look like Figure 7-2.

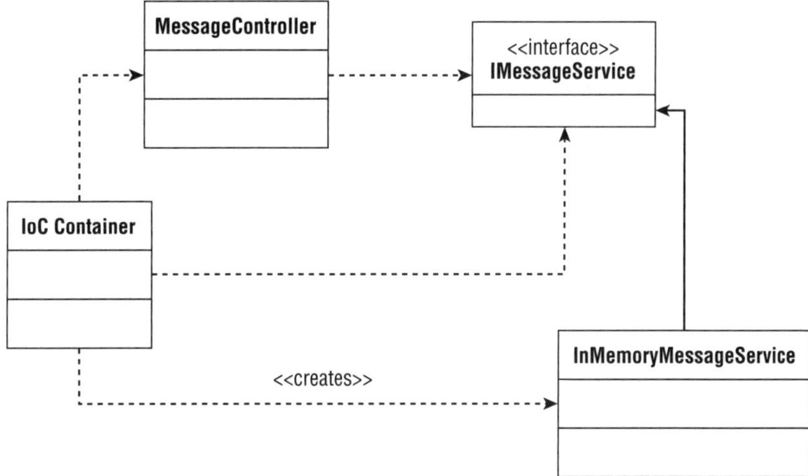

Figure 7-2

Solution

There are several IoC Containers out there that we can choose from. There are also several online articles and resources comparing the pros and cons of each container. Most of the popular containers are very comparable in features, and your decision might come down to style. I personally like Ninject (`www.ninject.org`) for its ease of use, fluent interface, light weight, and good online and community support.

The first thing to do is download Ninject and reference the `Ninject.core.dll` and `Ninject.Framework.Mvc.dll` assemblies in the web project. Next, we change the Global.asax file so that the `MvcApplication` class inherits from `NinjectHttpApplication` instead of `System.Web.HttpApplication`. `NinjectHttpApplication` is an abstract class that will replace the default controller factory with a Ninject-aware factory that will handle the injection of controllers. There are two virtual methods that we have to override, `RegisterRoutes` and `CreateKernel`. The final class looks like this:

```
public class MvcApplication : NinjectHttpApplication
{
    protected override void RegisterRoutes(RouteCollection routes)
    {
        routes.IgnoreRoute("{resource}.axd/{*pathInfo}");

        routes.MapRoute(
            "Default",                              // Route name
            "{controller}/{action}/{id}", // URL with parameters
            new
            {
                controller = "Home",
                action = "Index",
                id = ""
            }                                       // Parameter defaults
        );
```

```
        }

        private StandardKernel _kernel;

        protected override IKernel CreateKernel()
        {
            IModule[] modules = new IModule[]
                    {
                            new AutoControllerModule(
                                Assembly.GetExecutingAssembly()),
                            new InMemoryModule()
                    };
            _kernel = new StandardKernel(modules);
            return _kernel;

        }

    }
```

In the `CreateKernel` method, we instruct the Ninject kernel to manage all the controllers in the executing assembly. This is done using the `AutoControllerModule`, which is part of the `Ninject.Framework.Mvc` assembly and automatically goes through the assembly and configures all controllers for injection. We can configure Ninject in the `InMemorModule` and tell it what to inject, as shown in the following:

```
public class InMemoryModule : StandardModule
{
    public override void Load()
    {
        //authentication & memebership
        Bind<IFormsAuthentication>().To<FormsAuthenticationWrapper>();
        Bind<MembershipProvider>().ToConstant(Membership.Provider);

        //services
        Bind<IMessageService>().To<InMemoryMessageService>();

        //repositories
        Bind<IMessageRepository>().To<InMemoryMessageRepository>();

        //misc
        Bind<IValidationRunner>().To<ValidationRunner>();
    }
}
```

In the previous code, we tell the Ninject kernel how to inject the interfaces. In our case, we are using simple bindings and are just telling the kernel which implementation of each interface to use. Now, all we have to do to inject the appropriate interface into a constructor is to decorate the constructor with the `Inject` attribute. For example, here is the `AccountController` constructor:

```
[Inject]
public AccountController(IFormsAuthentication formsAuth,
    MembershipProvider provider)
{
    FormsAuth = formsAuth ?? new FormsAuthenticationWrapper();
    Provider = provider ?? Membership.Provider;
}
```

To clarify what the injection does, let's add a breakpoint on the first line and debug the project once without injection and again with injection. Without injection, you will notice that the `formsAuth` parameter is null, as shown in Figure 7-3. This is because the default constructor is executed, which calls the parameterized constructor with null values.

```
public AccountController()
    : this(null, null)
{
}
```

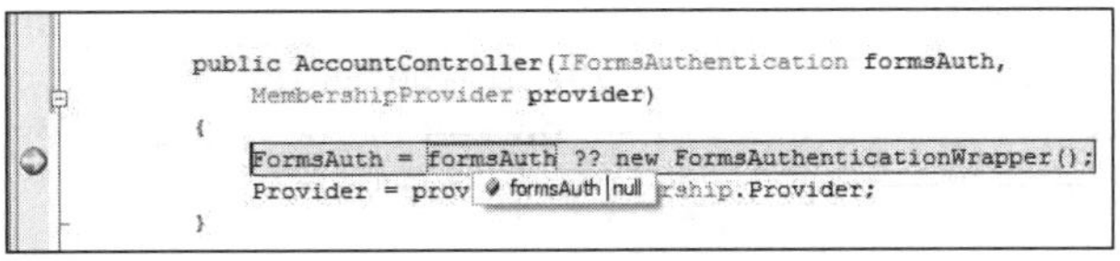

Figure 7-3

If we enable injection and debug the project again, the Ninject kernel will look for the constructor with the `Inject` attribute and inject the appropriate instance. (If more than one constructor has the `Inject` attribute, Ninject will apply some logic to choose the appropriate construct. Refer to Ninject's documentation for more details.) Now, you will see that the `formsAuth` parameter is instantiated with the appropriate implementation, as shown in Figure 7-4.

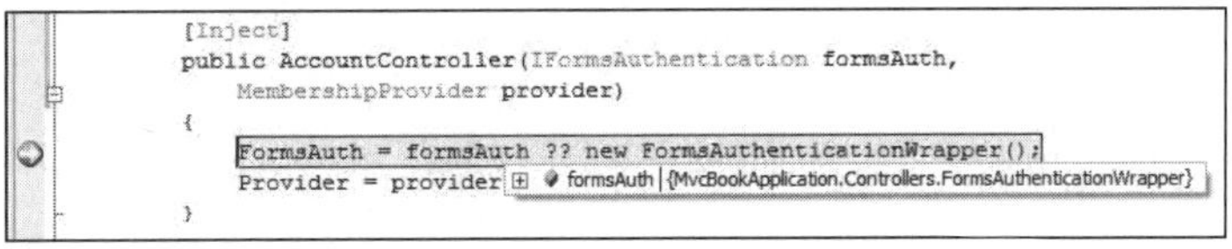

Figure 7-4

Ninject is also clever enough to inject dependencies through the object tree. For example, the `MessageController` depends on the `IMessageService` and our `InMemoryMessageService` implementation of the `IMessageService` interface depends on the `IMessageRepository` interface. We need Ninject to inject the appropriate instance of `IMessageService` and `IMessageRepository`. We have already told the Ninject kernel which implementations to use for these interfaces in the `InMemoryModule` class shown previously. Now, all we have to do is apply the `Inject` property to the `InMemoryMessageService` constructor:

```
[Inject]
public InMemoryMessageService(IMessageRepository repository,
    IValidationRunner validationRunner)
{
    ValidationRunner = validationRunner ?? new ValidationRunner();
    Repository = repository ?? new InMemoryMessageRepository();
}
```

If you place a breakpoint and debug the code, you will see that an instance of `InMemoryMessageRepository` is injected into the `InMemoryMessageService` constructor, as shown in Figure 7-5. This indicates that the Ninject kernel injected dependencies recursively throughout the object dependency hierarchy.

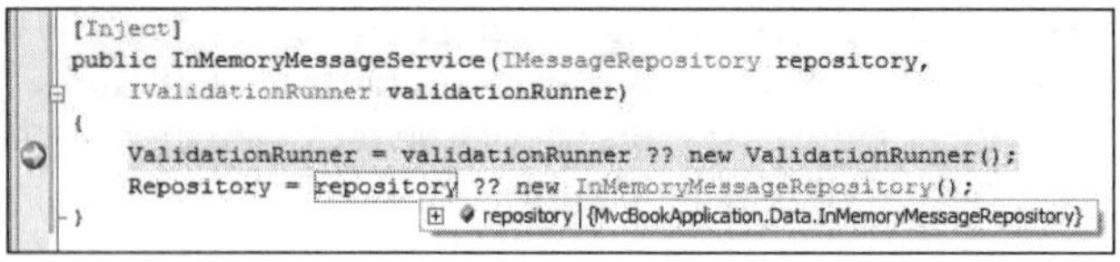

```
[Inject]
public InMemoryMessageService(IMessageRepository repository,
    IValidationRunner validationRunner)
{

    ValidationRunner = validationRunner ?? new ValidationRunner();
    Repository = repository ?? new InMemoryMessageRepository();
                            repository  {MvcBookApplication.Data.InMemoryMessageRepository}
}
```

Figure 7-5

We can now easily replace our `InMemoryModule` class to bind interfaces to different implementations. I used Ninject's fluent interface to configure its kernel for the sake of clarity and type-safety. I could have easily done the same thing using a configuration file. The benefit of using a configuration file is that I can replace the injected implementations by simply editing the configuration file and without having to recompile the application.

Summary

Using an IoC Container and Dependency Injection, we have reduced coupling between components and created a very agile solution. We are able to easily replace implementations with very minimal changes. We can focus our efforts on creating a great application without having to worry about all the details right away and can easily plug in new and better components in the future.

8

Contact Management

We have established a good foundation so far and are now familiar with the TDD process. It is time to build on top of this foundation and create our application. Since a fundamental piece of this application is to send messages to users, I think a good place to start is with contact management.

Problem

Contacts are a centerpiece of this application, and the ability to manage these contacts is fundamental to the application. The user needs to create, modify, and delete contacts as well as group them in lists and target them in mailing campaigns.

For contacts, we need the following actions:

- Create a contact manually.
- Import contacts from a file.
- Edit an existing contact.
- View an existing contact.
- Browse/list existing contacts.
- Delete an existing contact.
- Search contacts.

For Contact Lists, we need the following actions:

- ❑ Create a Contact List.
- ❑ Edit an existing Contact List.
    - ❑ Edit Contact List details.
    - ❑ Add a contact to a list.
    - ❑ Remove a contact from a list.
- ❑ View an existing Contact List.
- ❑ Browse/list existing Contact Lists.
- ❑ Delete an existing Contact List.

We also need to implement basic web application functions such as paging and sorting.

Design

It is important to note that a contact is associated with the logged-in user and the user cannot access contacts that do not belong to her. The user cannot have multiple contacts with the same email address; an email address is unique in relation to a user. However, the user can have multiple Contact Lists, and a contact can appear in multiple lists. The diagram in Figure 8-1 clarifies the relationships between user, contact, and CONTACT LIST.

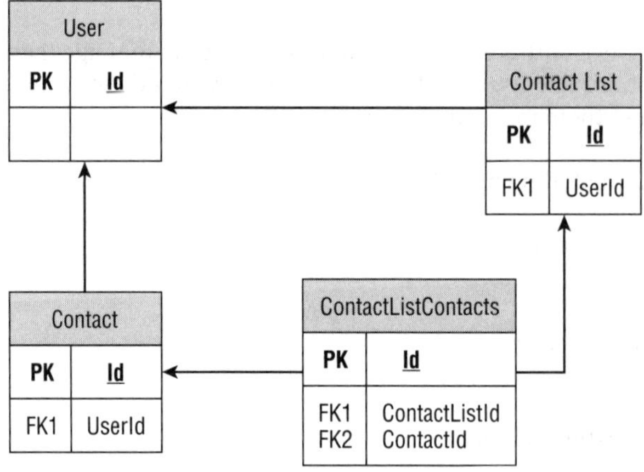

Figure 8-1

Figure 8-1 illustrates that:

- ❑ A user can have multiple Contact Lists.
- ❑ A user can have multiple contacts with unique emails.
- ❑ A Contact List can have multiple contacts with unique emails.

So, what exactly is a contact? At the most basic level, a *contact* is simply an email address, but most likely we want to gather more information about a contact than just an email address. For now, we will say that the contact entity has these properties:

❑ Email address

❑ Name

❑ Date of birth

❑ Sex

The email address is the only *required* value.

Create a Contact

A contact can be created manually by filling out a form or can be imported from a file. We focus on manual creation for now. When adding a contact, we want to ensure that it doesn't already exist, and if it does, we should display an error to the user. We will also notify the user upon a successful creation. To improve usability, we will also give the user the option to add the new contact to an existing Contact List or to a newly created Contact List.

Browse Contacts

The user needs to be able to browse all his or her contacts in order to edit, view, and delete them. Browsing contacts will display contacts in a grid format that can be paged and sorted. We want to make sure that we retrieve only the records that we want to view from the database so we will retrieve one page at a time. The same is true for sorting which will be performed by clicking on the grid header. Contacts can be sorted by email, name, sex, and date of birth. Each row in the grid will have hyperlinks for editing and deleting the related contact.

Edit a Contact

A user can edit a contact and change all its properties. We need to make sure that only the owner of a contact can edit it. Saving changes will fail with an error if the contact's email is changed to an email address that already belongs to another contact owned by the user.

Delete a Contact

A user will see a confirmation page when requesting to delete a contact. If the user confirms, the contact is deleted. We need to check that the user has permission to delete a contact before performing the delete operation.

Solution

We will implement the functionality to manage contacts by creating tests followed by implementation code to pass the tests. This will ensure that we cover all the cases and that future additions don't break existing tests. It makes sense to start with creating contacts so that we have a foundation to build on to browse, edit, and delete.

Create a Contact

First, we need a View to create a contact, so let's create a new test class called
`ContactControllerTests`:

```
[TestFixture]
public class ContactControllerTests
{
    private ContactController controller;
    private Contact model;

    [SetUp]
    public void SetUp()
    {
        controller = new ContactController();
        model = new Contact()
                {
                        Email = "test@test.com",
                        Name = "Julia Roberts",
                        Dob = new DateTime(1967, 10, 28),
                        Sex = Sex.Female
                };
    }
    [Test]
    public void create_returns_view ()
    {
        var result = controller.Create();
        Assert.IsInstanceOfType(typeof(Contact), controller.ViewData.Model);
        result.AssertViewResult(controller, "New Contact", "create");
    }
}
```

In the code, we are testing that there is a Create action that returns a View. To make the test pass, we
first create our Model:

```
public class Contact
{
    public int Id { get; set; }
    public string Email { get; set; }
    public string Name { get; set; }
    public Sex Sex { get; set; }
    public DateTime? Dob { get; set; }
}
```

We then need an enumeration for sex:

```
public enum Sex
{
    Undefined = 0,
    Male = 1,
    Female = 2
}
```

Next, we create our `ContactController` and add a Create action to it:

```
public class ContactController : Controller
{
    [AcceptVerbs(HttpVerbs.Get)]
    [Authorize]
    public ActionResult Create()
    {
        ViewData["Title"] = "New Contact";
        return View("create");
    }
}
```

Let's create the View to make sure that everything is working as it should:

```
<h2>
    Create New Contact</h2>
<form id="createcontact" action="/contact/create" method="post">
<div>
    <label for="email">
        Email</label>
    <br />
    <%=Html.TextBox("email")%>
    <br />
    <label for="name">
        Name</label>
    <br />
    <%=Html.TextBox("name")%>
    <br />
    <label for="sex">
        Sex</label>
    <br />
    <%=Html.DropDownList("sex" )%>
    <br />
    <label for="dob">
        Date of Birth</label>
    <br />
    <%=Html.TextBox("dob")%>
    <br />
    <input type="submit" value="Create Contact" />
</div>
</form>
```

For the dropdown to work correctly, we need to add an item to the `ViewData` with the key `"sex"` and of type `SelectList`. Let's create a test for that:

```
[Test]
public void create_should_define_sex_in_viewdata()
{
    var result = controller.Create();
    var sexlist = controller.ViewData["sex"];
    Assert.IsNotNull(sexlist);
    Assert.IsInstanceOfType(typeof(SelectList), sexlist);
}
```

The modified Create action now looks like this:

```
[AcceptVerbs(HttpVerbs.Get)]
[Authorize]
public ActionResult Create()
{
    ViewData["Title"] = "New Contact";
    ViewData["sex"] = new SelectList(new Dictionary<string, object>
                        {
                            {"-1"," "},
                            {"1", "Male"},
                            {"2", "Female"}
                        }, "key", "value");
    return View("create" , new Contact());
}
```

The resulting View is shown in Figure 8-2.

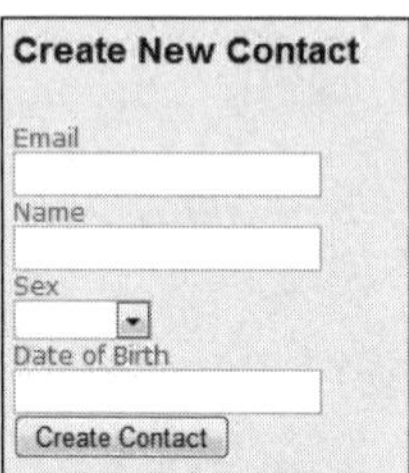

Figure 8-2

Now that we can render our View, let's make sure that we add validation. We start by defining the validation on the model class. We want to make sure that a valid email is provided and that if a date of birth is provided, it should be a valid date.

```
public class Contact
{
    public int Id { get; set; }
    [Required(ErrorMessage = "Email is required")]
    [Email(ErrorMessage = "Invalid email")]
    public string Email { get; set; }
    public string Name { get; set; }
    public Sex Sex { get; set; }
    [Date(ErrorMessage = "Invalid date")]
    public DateTime? Dob { get; set; }
}
```

In the previous code, we define the validation rules using the attributes we previously created. The Date attribute doesn't exist and needs to be created. First, we create a test for the validation runner:

```
[Test]
public void validate_date_errors_if_value_is_not_date()
{
```

```
    model.Dob = "bad date";
    var errors = runner.Run(model);
    AssertValidationError(errors, "Dob", "Invalid date");
}

[Test]
public void validate_date_no_errors_if_value_is_a_date()
{
    model.Dob = "10/01/2009";
    var errors = runner.Run(model);
    if (errors != null)
        Assert.AreEqual(errors.Count, 0);
}
```

Then create the date validation attribute and make sure that the tests work:

```
public class DateAttribute : ValidationAttribute
{
    public override bool IsValid(object value)
    {
        if (value.GetType() == typeof(DateTime))
        {
            return true;
        }
        if (value.GetType() == typeof(string))
        {
            DateTime result;
            var svalue = value as string;
            return svalue == null || DateTime.TryParse(svalue, out result);
        }
        return false;
    }
}
```

We also have to modify our jQuery generator to validate for dates, but first, let's create the test:

```
[Test]
public void generates_rule_for_date_field()
{
    string script = generator.Generate("createForm", model);
    Assert.IsTrue(script.Contains("date:{date:true}"));
}
```

To make the previous test pass, we simply add the following `if` statement to the `Generate` method in the `JQueryValidationGenerator`:

```
if (attrib.GetType() == typeof(DateAttribute))
{
    subrule = "date:true";
    ruletype = "date";
}
```

Let's make sure that client validation is working as it should in the view. Add the following statement to the View:

```
<%=Html.JQueryGenerator("createcontact", ViewData.Model)%>
```

If we try to submit an invalid view, we will get client validation errors as shown in Figure 8-3.

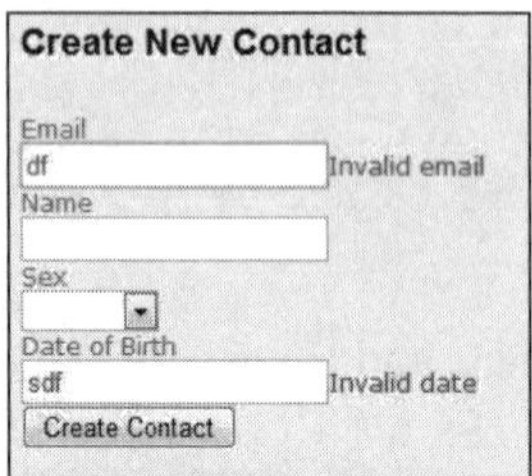

Figure 8-3

Let's now write tests for creating the contact. We will start with a test to validate that an email address has been provided:

```
[Test]
public void create_returns_error_if_email_is_missing()
{
    model.Email = null;
    var result = controller.Create(model);
    AssertValidationError(result, "Email", "Email is required");
}
```

The AssertValidationError is a helper method that will assert a validation error; this code was refactored into a method so that it can be reused by other tests.

```
private void AssertValidationError(ActionResult result,
                                   string errorKey,
                                   string errorMessage)
{
    //assert results
    Assert.IsNotNull(result);
    Assert.IsInstanceOfType(typeof(ViewResult), result);
    controller.ViewData.ModelState.AssertErrorMessage(errorKey, errorMessage);
    Assert.IsInstanceOfType(typeof(Contact),
                            ((ViewResult)result).ViewData.Model);
    //asser that the ViewData.Model
    var outModel = (((ViewResult)result).ViewData.Model as Contact);
    Assert.AreEqual(model.Email, outModel.Email);
    Assert.AreEqual(model.Name, outModel.Name);
    Assert.AreEqual(model.Sex, outModel.Sex);
    Assert.AreEqual(model.Dob, outModel.Dob);

    Assert.AreEqual("New Contact", controller.ViewData["Title"],
                    "Page title is wrong");
}
```

We have to make several changes to make the projects compile and the test pass. First, we need to add the Create action:

```
[AcceptVerbs(HttpVerbs.Post)]
[Authorize]
public ActionResult Create([Bind(Prefix = "", Exclude = "Id")] Contact model)
{
    ViewData["Title"] = "New Contact";
    ViewData["sex"] = new SelectList(new Dictionary<string, object>
                                {
                                    {"-1"," "},
                                    {"1", "Male"},
                                    {"2", "Female"}
                                }, "key", "value");
    try
    {
        var id = Service.Add(model);
    }
    catch (ValidationException ex)
    {
        foreach (var error in ex.ValidationErrors)
        {
            ViewData.ModelState.AddModelError(
                error.PropertyName,
                error.ErrorMessage);
        }
    }

    if (!ViewData.ModelState.IsValid)
    {
        return View("create", model);
    }
    return RedirectToAction("create");
}
```

We are using the same pattern we previously used to create a message, and now we have to change our controller constructors:

```
public IContactService Service { get; set; }

public ContactController()
    : this(null)
{
}

[Inject]
public ContactController(IContactService service)
{
    Service = service ?? new InMemoryContactService();
}
```

Next, we create the `IContactService` and an in-memory implementation:

```
public interface IContactService
{
```

```csharp
    int Add(Contact contact);
}

public class InMemoryContactService : IContactService
{
    private IValidationRunner ValidationRunner { get; set; }

    public InMemoryContactService()
        : this(null)
    {

    }
    [Inject]
    public InMemoryContactService(IValidationRunner validationRunner)
    {
        ValidationRunner = validationRunner ?? new ValidationRunner();
    }

    public int Add(Contact contact)
    {
        var errors = ValidationRunner.Run(contact);
        if (errors != null && errors.Count > 0)
        {
            throw new ValidationException(errors);
        }
        return -1;
    }
}
```

We also have to add code to our application bootstrapper to tell the Ninject kernel how to handle the new interfaces. We only created one interface, so we just need to add this one line of code:

```csharp
Bind<IContactService>().To<InMemoryContactService>();
```

The previous line tells Ninject to inject an instance of `InMemoryContactService` whenever it encounters an `IContactService` interface.

It's important to note that the preceding code is not a full implementation but is just enough code to pass the test. As we add more tests, the code will become complete.

Next up, we test that validation fails for invalid emails:

```csharp
[Test]
public void create_returns_error_if_email_is_invalid()
{
    model.Email = "bad email";
    var result = controller.Create(model);
    AssertValidationError(result, "Email", "Invalid email");
}
```

The previous test should pass without any changes, since all the validation code is already in place.

After a contact is successfully created, we want to re-display the view but with a blank form. This can be done by simply redirecting to the Create action:

```
[Test]
public void create_redirects_to_create_action_if_successful ()
{
    var result = controller.Create(model);
    result.AssertRedirectToRouteResult("create");
}
```

We also want to notify the user that the contact was successfully created. We will use a notification message at the top of the page to notify the user. This notification message needs to display only once, and we will probably use it throughout the application, so we should probably display it on the master page. Ruby on Rails calls this a *flash message*, so for the sake of simplicity, I will call this the *flash message pattern*. Luckily, it is easy to create flash messages in MVC using the TempData dictionary.

> ### TempData
>
> `TempData` is a property on the controller of type `TempDataDictionary`. It is a special dictionary of values that can be passed to the View just like the ViewData dictionary. The only difference is that TempData is only available for the life of one request — that is, it is temporary.

This will all make sense shortly, but let's start with a test:

```
[Test]
public void create_adds_flash_message_if_contact_creation_is_successful()
{
    var result = controller.Create(model);
    Assert.IsTrue(controller.ModelState.IsValid, "model state is invalid");
    Assert.Contains(controller.TempData,
                  new KeyValuePair<string, object>
                      ("flash",
                       "Contact successfully created"),
                  "Flash message is missing");
}
```

All we are doing in the previous test is making sure that a flash message is added to the TempData dictionary upon a successful creation. To make the test work, we simply add this line to the `Create` method right before we return from a successful creation:

```
TempData["flash"] = "Contact successfully created";
```

Before we get too far ahead of ourselves, let's make sure that our notification works. We will create a user control called `FlashMessage` in the Views\Shared folder, and it will simply display a flash message if one exists.

```
<%
    if (ViewContext.TempData.ContainsKey("flash"))
    {
%>
```

```
<div class="flash">
    <%= Html.Encode(ViewContext.TempData["flash"])%>
</div>
<%
    }
%>
```

We can then style the flash message to fit our site design by adding this to our style sheet:

```
.flash
{
 color:Green;
 padding:5px;
 border:solid 2px black;
 background: yellow;
}
```

Lastly, we add the `FlashMessage` user control to the master page, so that it will be accessible from the entire application by simply adding this line:

```
<% Html.RenderPartial("flashmessage");%>
```

Now, if we add a new contact, we should see the flash message as shown in Figure 8-4.

Figure 8-4

Our next task is to make sure that before we add a contact, the email is unique. We can't just add a validation attribute to the Model because we have to actually check the data store. There are two ways to do this. We can make a call to the Repository to check if the contact exists right before we add it; or we can call the `Add` and rely on the Repository to enforce the constraints. I think it is a good design to actually perform the check before we add *and* enforce the constraints in the repository. This way, we are applying the business rules at the application level, and the repository constraint works as a safeguard in case of faulty logic. We are also not solely relying on the Repository to enforce business rules because in the case of an in-memory or XML repository, there might not be an easy way to define constraints. Since we are performing the validation at the service level, it makes sense to perform the uniqueness check in the same place. Here is the test:

```
[Test]
public void create_returns_error_if_contact_already_exists()
{
    //add it once
```

```
    var result = controller.Create(model);
    //make sure it gets added
    result.AssertRedirectToRouteResult("create");
    //add it again
    result = controller.Create(model);
    AssertValidationError(result, "Email", "Contact already exists");
}
```

To make the preceding test work, we will add an `IContactRepository` interface, implement it in `InMemoryContactRepository`, and configure Ninject to inject the new dependencies. I am not going to detail all the steps, since they are similar to what we previously did with the `IMessageRepository` interface and `InMemoryMessageRepository` class. We can then change the `Add` method in the `InMemoryContactService` to apply the appropriate logic.

```
public int Add(Contact contact)
{
    var errors = ValidationRunner.Run(contact);
    if (errors != null && errors.Count > 0)
    {
        throw new ValidationException(errors);
    }
    //check if email is unique
    if (Repository.Get()
        .Count(c => c.Email.ToLower() == contact.Email.ToLower()) > 0)
    {
        throw new ValidationException(
            new List<ValidationError>
                {
                    new ValidationError("Email", "Contact already exists")
                });
    }
    return Repository.Add(contact);
}
```

If you have been paying attention, you will notice that we have a logical bug. The problem is that this code will prevent duplicate email addresses globally, so if user `John` adds a contact with the email `customer@gmail.com`, other users will not be able to add the same customer. We need to check uniqueness for the logged-in user only. This requires multiple changes across the application, so let's get started.

We need to establish a relationship between contact and user, so let's add a `User` property to the `Contact` class:

```
public class Contact
{
    public User User { get; set; }
    public int Id { get; set; }
    [Required(ErrorMessage = "Email is required")]
    [Email(ErrorMessage = "Invalid email")]
    public string Email { get; set; }
    public string Name { get; set; }
    public Sex Sex { get; set; }
    public DateTime? Dob { get; set; }
}
```

I don't want to define all the details of what a user class is. All I am interested in right now is just a couple of properties, so let's keep it simple for now, and when the time comes, we will add to it.

```csharp
public class User
{
    public Guid UserId { get; set; }
    public string Username { get; set; }
}
```

Now, the `Add` method can check the email uniqueness in the context of the logged-in user:

```csharp
public int Add(Contact contact)
{
    var errors = ValidationRunner.Run(contact);
    if (errors != null && errors.Count > 0)
    {
        throw new ValidationException(errors);
    }

    //check if email is unique
    if (Repository.Get()
        .Count(c => c.Email.ToLower() == contact.Email.ToLower() &&
            c.User.UserId == contact.User.UserId) > 0)
    {
        throw new ValidationException(
            new List<ValidationError>
        {
            new ValidationError("Email", "Contact already exists")
        });
    }
    return Repository.Add(contact);
}
```

For the preceding code to work, we have to set the `User` property before we call the `Add` method from the Create action, as shown in the following code:

```csharp
model.User =  new User
            {
                Username = User.Identity.Name,
                UserId = (Guid)Provider.
                        GetUser(User.Identity.Name, false)
                        .ProviderUserKey
            };
var id = Service.Add(model);
```

The code snippet creates a dependency on the `MembershipProvider` class. In this scenario, we are using property injection instead of constructor injection since the `MembershipProvider` is not really conceptually related to the `ContactController`. It also makes it easier to change the code, since we do not have to change the constructor. The fact that we are using an IoC Container makes this task easy. All we have to do is add a property and add the `Inject` attribute to it, and the IoC Container will take care of initializing it with the right implementation.

```csharp
[Inject]
public MembershipProvider Provider { get; set; }
```

We didn't start with a test this time because there were a lot of changes that needed to take place, but that doesn't mean that we shouldn't write the tests. We need to test that multiple users can add the same contact.

Before we can write the test, we need to change the setup to mock some classes and define the dependency injection.

First, we define some mock objects as fields at the class level in the `ContactControllerTests` class:

```
private static Mock<MembershipProvider> MockMembership =
    new Mock<MembershipProvider>();
private static Mock<MembershipUser> MockMembershipUser =
    new Mock<MembershipUser>();
private static Mock<IPrincipal> user =
    new Mock<IPrincipal>();
private static Mock<IIdentity> identity =
    new Mock<IIdentity>();
private static Mock<HttpContextBase> httpContext =
    new Mock<HttpContextBase>();
private static Mock<ControllerBase> controllerbase =
    new Mock<ControllerBase>();
```

Then we have to set up the mock objects for the membership provider to work:

```
private static void SetupMocks(string username, Guid userid)
{
    identity.Expect(i => i.Name).Returns(username);
    user.Expect(u => u.Identity).Returns(identity.Object);
    httpContext.Expect(h => h.User).Returns(user.Object);
    MockMembership.Expect(m => m.GetUser(username, false))
        .Returns(MockMembershipUser.Object);
    MockMembershipUser.Expect(u => u.ProviderUserKey)
        .Returns(userid);
}
```

Next, we have to instantiate the controller using Dependency Injection (DI), but first, let's configure the IoC Container:

```
private static StandardKernel GetIoCKernel()
{
    var modules = new IModule[]
                    {
                        new InlineModule(
                            new Action<InlineModule>[]
                                {
                                    m => m.Bind<MembershipProvider>()
                                            .ToConstant(MockMembership.Object),
                                    m => m.Bind<IContactService>()
                                            .To<InMemoryContactService>(),
                                    m => m.Bind<IContactRepository>()
                                            .To<InMemoryContactRepository>()
                                            .Using<SingletonBehavior>(),
                                    m => m.Bind<IValidationRunner>()
                                            .To<ValidationRunner>()
```

```
                                            })
                    };
        return new StandardKernel(modules);
    }
```

The important thing to note here is the `Using<SingletonBehavior>` call on the `IContactRepository` binding. This tells the IoC to only create a single instance of the `InMemoryContactRepository`. If we don't do that, then multiple instances will be created and our test will fail because each contact will be added to its own instance of the Repository. Then we create the controller using the IoC Container's kernel with the above configuration:

```
private static ContactController GetController()
{
    kernel = GetIoCKernel();
    var contactController = (ContactController)kernel
        .Get(typeof(ContactController));
    contactController.ControllerContext = new ControllerContext(
        httpContext.Object,
        new RouteData(),
        controllerbase.Object);
    return contactController;
}
```

Now our test setup method looks like this:

```
[SetUp]
public void SetUp()
{
    SetupMocks(Username, UserId);
    controller = GetController();
    model = new Contact()
                {
                    Email = "test@test.com",
                    Name = "Julia Roberts",
                    Dob = new DateTime(1967, 10, 28),
                    Sex = Sex.Female
                };
}
```

Now we can write the test:

```
[Test]
public void create_succeeds_for_duplicate_contacts_by_different_users()
{
    //add a contact to the repository
    var anotherUsername = Username + 2;
    var anotherUserId = Guid.NewGuid();
    var repo = (IContactRepository)kernel.Get(typeof(IContactRepository));
    repo.Add(new Contact()
                {
                    Email = "test@test.com",
```

```
                    Name = "Julia Roberts",
                    Dob = new DateTime(1967, 10, 28),
                    Sex = Sex.Female,
                    User = new User
                        {
                            UserId = anotherUserId,
                            Username = anotherUsername
                        }

            });

    //add the same contact for a different user
    var result = controller.Create(model);
    //make sure it gets added
    result.AssertRedirectToRouteResult("create");
    Assert.AreEqual(2,repo.Get().Count());

    //verify mocks
    MockMembership.VerifyAll();
    MockMembershipUser.VerifyAll();
}
```

We first added a contact for a user — say, `UserA` — to the Repository, then we added the same contact for a different user — say, `UserB`. We then made sure that both contacts made it into the Repository. Since the `IContactRepository` is defined as a singleton and we instantiated it using the IoC Container in our test, we will be able to access the same instance of the Repository as the controller.

Bug

I had to change the `InMemoryModule` class to use the singleton behavior for the application to work as expected. If I don't do that, then a new repository instance is created every time the controller is instantiated, that is, at every request.

If every request creates a new instance of the *fake* data, then changes will not be persisted. This means that if we try to edit a contact and save it, the next request will regenerate the fake in-memory data, and the changes we made will be overwritten.

By using a singleton for the in-memory data class, we persist the in-memory data throughout the session lifetime. This is good enough for testing and development. In production, this will not be necessary since the data will be persisted to a persistent data store.

Browse Contacts

The user needs to be able to browse all of his or her contacts in order to edit, view, and delete them. Browsing contacts will display contacts in a grid format that can be paged and sorted. We want to make sure that we retrieve only the records that we want to view from the database so we will retrieve one page at a time.

We need to write a test to make sure that we can retrieve only one page of contacts. The grid is paged every 20 contacts.

```
[Test]
public void browse_contacts_should_retrieve_20_or_less_contacts_at_once()
{
    PopulateRepository();
    var result = controller.Browse(null);
    Assert.IsInstanceOfType(typeof(PagedList<Contact>),
                            controller.ViewData.Model,
                            "View data is the wrong type");
    Assert.LessThanOrEqualTo(((PagedList<Contact>)controller.ViewData.Model).Count,
                             20, "Page size is wrong");
    result.AssertViewResult(controller, "Browse Contacts", "browse");
}
```

The `PopulateRepository` method, as the name suggests, will populate our Repository with some test data. The test data will have 50 contacts with 25 assigned to one user and 25 assigned to a different user.

```
private void PopulateRepository()
{
    var anotherUsername = Username + 2;
    var anotherUserId = Guid.NewGuid();
    var repo = (IContactRepository)kernel.Get(typeof(IContactRepository));
    for (var i = 0; i < 50; i++)
    {
        repo.Add(
            new Contact
                {
                    Id = i,
                    Email = ("user" + i + "@test.com"),
                    Name = string.Format("First{0} Last{1}", i, i),
                    Dob - (new DateTime(1967, 10, 28)).AddDays(i),
                    Sex = (i % 3 == 0
                            ?
                                Sex.Undefined
                            :
                                (i % 2 == 0
                                    ?
                                        Sex.Female
                                    :
                                        Sex.Male)),
                    User = i % 2 == 0
                            ? new User
                                {
                                    UserId = UserId,
                                    Username = Username
                                }
                            :
                                new User
                                    {
                                        UserId = anotherUserId,
                                        Username = anotherUsername
```

```
                }
        });

    }
}
```

The Browse controller action is pretty straightforward:

```
[AcceptVerbs(HttpVerbs.Get), Authorize]
public ActionResult Browse(int? page)
{
    ViewData["Title"] = "Browse Contacts";
    page = page ?? 1;
    ViewData.Model = Service.GetPage(page);
    return View("browse");
}
```

For the above code to work, we need to add a `Browse` method to the `IContactService` interface:

```
public interface IContactService
{
    int Add(Contact contact);
    PagedList<Contact> GetPage(int? page);
}
```

and implement it to retrieve the requested page. To prevent any errors, we will get the first page if the page variable is null or is less than 1.

```
public PagedList<Contact> GetPage(int? page)
{
    page = page ?? 1;
    page = page < 1 ? 1 : page;
    return Repository.Get().ToPagedList((int)(page - 1), 20);
}
```

You are probably wondering about the `PagedList` class. The `PagedList` is a collection class that facilitates paging through an `IQueryable` or `IEnumerable` collection. It implements the `IPagedList<T>` interface.

```
public interface IPagedList<T> : IList<T>
{
    int PageCount { get; }
    int TotalItemCount { get; }
    int PageIndex { get; }
    int PageNumber { get; }
    int PageSize { get; }
    bool HasPreviousPage { get; }
    bool HasNextPage { get; }
    bool IsFirstPage { get; }
    bool IsLastPage { get; }
}
```

Here is the `PagedList` class itself:

```csharp
public class PagedList<T> : List<T>, IPagedList<T>
{
    public PagedList(IEnumerable<T> source, int index, int pageSize)
    {
        if (source is IQueryable<T>)
            Initialize(source as IQueryable<T>, index, pageSize);
        else
            Initialize(source.AsQueryable(), index, pageSize);
    }

    public PagedList(IQueryable<T> source, int index, int pageSize)
    {
        Initialize(source, index, pageSize);
    }

    public int PageCount { get; private set; }
    public int TotalItemCount { get; private set; }
    public int PageIndex { get; private set; }
    public int PageNumber { get { return PageIndex + 1; } }
    public int PageSize { get; private set; }
    public bool HasPreviousPage { get; private set; }
    public bool HasNextPage { get; private set; }
    public bool IsFirstPage { get; private set; }
    public bool IsLastPage { get; private set; }

    protected void Initialize(IQueryable<T> source, int index, int pageSize)
    {
        if (source == null)
            source = new List<T>().AsQueryable();

        TotalItemCount = source.Count();
        PageSize = pageSize;
        PageIndex = index;
        if (TotalItemCount > 0)
            PageCount = (int)Math.Ceiling(TotalItemCount / (double)PageSize);
        else
            PageCount = 0;
        HasPreviousPage = (PageIndex > 0);
        HasNextPage = (PageIndex < (PageCount - 1));
        IsFirstPage = (PageIndex <= 0);
        IsLastPage = (PageIndex >= (PageCount - 1));

        if (index < 0)
            throw new
                ArgumentOutOfRangeException("PageIndex cannot be below 0.");
        if (pageSize < 1)
            throw new
                ArgumentOutOfRangeException("PageSize cannot be less than 1.");

        if (TotalItemCount > 0)
            AddRange(source.Skip((index) * pageSize).Take(pageSize).ToList());
    }
}
```

There is also a static `Pagination` class that contains a couple of extension methods **to convert** `IQueryable` and `IEnumerable` collections to a `PagedList` collection.

```
public static class Pagination
{
    public static PagedList<T> ToPagedList<T>(this IQueryable<T> source,
                                              int index, int pageSize)
    {
        return new PagedList<T>(source, index, pageSize);
    }

    public static PagedList<T> ToPagedList<T>(this IEnumerable<T> source,
                                              int index, int pageSize)
    {
        return new PagedList<T>(source, index, pageSize);
    }
}
```

The previous paging code was modified from the original source, which can be found on Troy Goode's blog SquaredRoot at `www.squaredroot.com`.

Another important thing to note is that the page parameter on the action is a nullable integer, which allows us to handle the case when the page is not defined and assume the first page. We have to define a new route in the Global.asax.cs file to be able to use the URL `http://localhost/contact/browse/{page}` to point to the Browse action and pass the `{page}` parameter to the action method.

```
routes.MapRoute(
    "BrowseContacts",
    "contact/browse/{page}",
    new
        {
            controller = "Contact",
            action = "browse",
            page = 1
        }
    );
```

We are basically telling our route handler to map any `contact/browse/{page}` URL to the Contact controller and Browse action, and if the page parameter is not defined, then default to the **first page**.

The test should now pass, so let's move on to the next one. We need to make sure that we are only retrieving contacts for the logged-in user. So our total item count should be 25.

```
[Test]
public void browse_contacts_should_retrieve_contacts_for_loggedin_user_only()
{
    PopulateRepository();
    var result = controller.Browse(null);
    Assert.AreEqual(25,
        ((PagedList<Contact>)controller.ViewData.Model).TotalItemCount,
        "Item count is wrong");
}
```

The previous test will fail because the total item count will be 50 since we are not filtering the results based on the logged-in user. We need to change our `Browse` service method to:

```
PagedList<Contact> GetPage(Guid userid, int? page);
```

Then we change the implementation to:

```
public PagedList<Contact> GetPage(Guid userid, int? page)
{
    page = page ?? 1;
    page = page < 1 ? 1 : page;
    return Repository.Get()
        .Where(c => c.User.UserId == userid)
        .ToPagedList((int)(page - 1), 20);
}
```

Then change the controller to pass the user ID to the service call:

```
[AcceptVerbs(HttpVerbs.Get), Authorize]
public ActionResult Browse(int? page)
{
    ViewData["Title"] = "Browse Contacts";
    page = page ?? 1;
    ViewData.Model = Service.GetPage((Guid) Provider.
                                        GetUser(User.Identity.Name, false)
                                        .ProviderUserKey,
                                page);
    return View("browse");
}
```

The test should now pass. It's time to create a View and make sure things look right. We will create a strongly typed View:

```
public partial class Browse : ViewPage<PagedList<Data.Models.Contact>>
{
}
```

The View itself will be a simple table that iterates through the list of contacts. For now, we will just create non-functioning links to get a good idea of the look. We will add functionality later.

```
<h2>
    Browse Contacts</h2>
<table class="grid">
    <thead>
        <tr>
            <th>
                Email
            </th>
            <th>
                Name
            </th>
```

```
            <th>
                Actions
            </th>
        </tr>
    </thead>
    <tbody>
        <%foreach (var contact in ViewData.Model)
          {%>
        <tr>
            <td>
                <%=contact.Email %>
            </td>
            <td>
                <%=contact.Name %>
            </td>
            <td>
                <a href=''>edit</a> <a href=''>delete</a>
            </td>
        </tr>
        <%} %>
    </tbody>
</table>
```

If we navigate to `http://localhost/contact/browse`, we should get the first page, as shown in Figure 8-5.

Browse Contacts

Email	Name	Actions
user0@test.com	First0 Last0	edit delete
user2@test.com	First2 Last2	edit delete
user4@test.com	First4 Last4	edit delete
user6@test.com	First6 Last6	edit delete
user8@test.com	First8 Last8	edit delete
user10@test.com	First10 Last10	edit delete
user12@test.com	First12 Last12	edit delete
user14@test.com	First14 Last14	edit delete
user16@test.com	First16 Last16	edit delete
user18@test.com	First18 Last18	edit delete
user20@test.com	First20 Last20	edit delete
user22@test.com	First22 Last22	edit delete
user24@test.com	First24 Last24	edit delete
user26@test.com	First26 Last26	edit delete
user28@test.com	First28 Last28	edit delete
user30@test.com	First30 Last30	edit delete
user32@test.com	First32 Last32	edit delete
user34@test.com	First34 Last34	edit delete
user36@test.com	First36 Last36	edit delete
user38@test.com	First38 Last38	edit delete

Figure 8-5

And if we try `http://localhost/contact/browse/2`, we should get the second page, as shown in Figure 8-6.

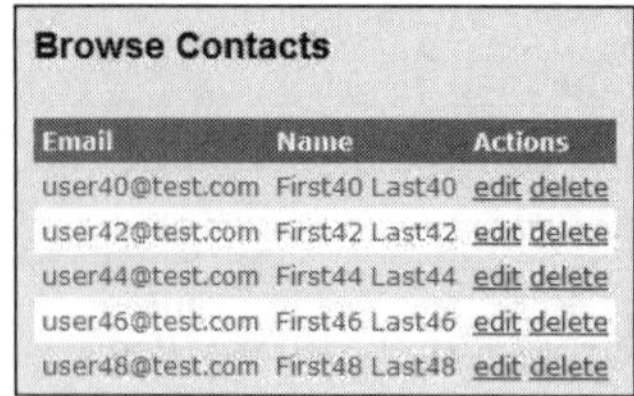

Figure 8-6

The dummy data shown in Figures 8-5 and 8-6 was populated in the `InMemoryModule` *class, where we configure the IoC to ensure that the entire application has access to some data.*

Obviously, we don't expect the user to page through our grid by typing the page number into the URL. We need to add a pager to the grid, and since we know that we will have more than one grid and that they will also need paging, we will go ahead and create the pager as a user control.

The pagination user control code was modified from the original source, which can be found on Robert Muehsig's blog at `http://code-inside.de`.

The pager style was modified from the original source, which can be found on Antonio Lupetti's blog at `http://woork.blogspot.com`.

The Pagination.ascx user control is as follows:

```
<div class="pagination">
    <ul>
        <% if (ViewData.Model.HasPreviousPage)
           { %>
        <li class="previous">
           <a href="<%=ViewData.Model.PageActionLink.Replace("{page}",
                             (ViewData.Model.PageIndex - 1).ToString())%>">
            « Previous</a></li>
        <% }
           else
           { %>
        <li class="previous-off">« Previous</li>
        <% } %>
        <%for (int page = 1; page <= ViewData.Model.TotalPages; page++)
          {
             if (page == ViewData.Model.PageIndex)
             { %>
        <li class="active">
           <%=page.ToString()%></li>
        <% }
             else
             { %>
        <li>
           <a href="<%=ViewData.Model.PageActionLink.Replace("{page}",
                                          page.ToString())%>">
           <%=page.ToString()%></a></li>
        <% }
```

```
            }

        if (ViewData.Model.HasNextPage)
        { %>
      <li class="next">
        <a href="<%=ViewData.Model.PageActionLink.Replace("{page}",
                          (ViewData.Model.PageIndex + 1).ToString())%>">
          Next »</a></li>
      <% }
        else
        { %>
      <li class="next-off">Next »</li>
      <% } %>
    </ul>
</div>
```

The `Pagination` control is strongly typed and expects a `PaginationViewData` object as the model. The `PaginationViewData` is a simple wrapper to wrap the data needed to render the pager.

```
public class PaginationViewData
{
    public int PageIndex { get; set; }
    public int TotalPages { get; set; }
    public int PageSize { get; set; }
    public int TotalCount { get; set; }
    public string PageActionLink { get; set; }
    public bool HasPreviousPage
    {
        get
        {
            return (PageIndex > 1);
        }
    }
    public bool HasNextPage
    {
        get
        {
            return (PageIndex * PageSize) <= TotalCount;
        }
    }
}
```

Now, we can use the pager in our View by rendering the `Pagination` control:

```
<%Html.RenderPartial("pagination", new PaginationViewData
                        {
                            PageActionLink = "/contact/browse/{page}",
                            PageIndex = ViewData.Model.PageNumber,
                            PageSize = ViewData.Model.PageSize,
                            TotalCount = ViewData.Model.TotalItemCount,
                            TotalPages = ViewData.Model.PageCount
                        }); %>
```

Our View will now have a pager as shown in Figure 8-7.

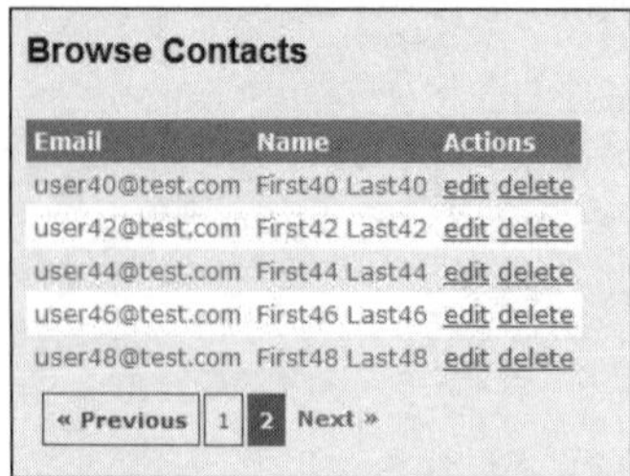

Figure 8-7

The next order of business is sorting the table. Before we write any tests, let's lay the foundation to handle sorting. Sorting requires two arguments:

❑ The field being sorted

❑ The direction of the sort

The first thing we need to do is change the Browse action to handle sorting:

```
[AcceptVerbs(HttpVerbs.Get), Authorize]
public ActionResult Browse(int? page, string sortBy, string sortDir)
{
    ViewData["Title"] = "Browse Contacts";
    ViewData["sortdir"] = sortDir;
    ViewData["sortby"] = sortBy;

    page = page ?? 1;
    ViewData.Model = Service.GetPage((Guid)Provider.
                                            GetUser(User.Identity.Name, false)
                                            .ProviderUserKey,
                                page, sortBy, sortDir);
    return View("browse");
}
```

We then need to pass the sort parameters to the service layer, so let's overload the `GetPage` method in the `IContactService` interface:

```
PagedList<Contact> GetPage(Guid userid, int? page,
                    string sortBy, string sortDirection);
```

Before we implement the new `GetPage` method, it is important to note that we cannot use a sort string in a LINQ query. We cannot do the following:

```
return Repository.Get()
    .Where(c => c.User.UserId == userid)
    .OrderBy(sortBy + " " + sortDirection)
    .ToPagedList((int) (page - 1), 20);
```

LINQ queries are strongly typed and expect a sort expression like this:

```
return Repository.Get()
    .Where(c => c.User.UserId == userid)
    .OrderBy(o => o.Email)
    .ToPagedList((int) (page - 1), 20);
```

Luckily, there is a way to execute dynamic LINQ using the LINQ Dynamic Query Library, which can be downloaded from MSDN (www.msdn.com). This library adds some extension methods that allow us to execute dynamic LINQ.

Now that we have downloaded the LINQ Dynamic Query Library and included it in our code, we can now change both implementations for GetPage:

```
public PagedList<Contact> GetPage(Guid userid, int? page)
{
    return GetPage(userid, page, "email", "asc");
}

public PagedList<Contact> GetPage(Guid userid, int? page,
                                  string sortBy, string sortDirection)
{
    sortBy = sortBy ?? "email";
    sortDirection = sortDirection ?? "asc";
    page = page ?? 1;
    page = page < 1 ? 1 : page;
    return Repository.Get()
        .Where(c => c.User.UserId == userid)
        .OrderBy(sortBy + " " + sortDirection)
        .ToPagedList((int)(page - 1), 20);
}
```

Note the OrderBy, *which uses dynamic LINQ to sort the query.*

Let's update the View to see if sorting will work. We first hyperlink the grid headers:

```
<thead>
    <tr>
        <th>
            <%=Html.ActionLink<ContactController>(
                            c => c.Browse(ViewData.Model.PageNumber,
                                    "email",
                                    ViewData.GetSortDirection("email")),
                            "Email")%>
        </th>
        <th>
            <%=Html.ActionLink<ContactController>(
                            c => c.Browse(ViewData.Model.PageNumber,
                                    "name",
                                    ViewData.GetSortDirection("name")),
                            "Name")%>
        </th>
        <th>
```

```
            Actions
        </th>
    </tr>
</thead>
```

The preceding code uses a `ViewData` extension method, `GetSortDirection`, that reverses the sort direction when the grid header is clicked.

```
public static string GetSortDirection(this ViewDataDictionary ViewData,
                                      string field)
{
    return (string)ViewData["sortby"] != field
                ? "asc"
                : ((string)ViewData["sortdir"] == "asc"
                      ? "desc"
                      : "asc");
}
```

Finally, we need to make sure that the pager control understands sorting. We first add two new properties to the `PaginationViewData` class:

```
public string SortBy { get; set; }
public string SortDirection { get; set; }
```

Then we change the user control to add the sort parameters to the pager links. For example, here is the previous hyperlink:

```
<a href='<%=ViewData.Model.PageActionLink
                .Replace("{page}",
                        (ViewData.Model.PageNumber - 1).ToString()) +
                (string.IsNullOrEmpty(ViewData.Model.SortBy)
                ? ""
                : "?sortby=" + ViewData.Model.SortBy
                + "&sortdir=" + ViewData.Model.SortDirection)%>'>« Previous</a>
```

Before we move on, let's add one test to ensure that the sort options are saved to the View data:

```
[Test]
public void browse_contacts_should_save_sort_options_to_viewdata()
{
    var result = controller.Browse(null, "email", "asc");
    controller.ViewData.AssertItem("sortby", "email");
    controller.ViewData.AssertItem("sortdir", "asc");
    result.AssertViewResult(controller, "Browse Contacts", "browse");
}
```

Edit Contact

A user can edit a contact and change all of its properties. We need to make sure that only the owner of a contact can edit it. Saving changes will fail with an error if the contact's email is changed to an email address that already belongs to another contact owned by the user.

First, we need to make sure that we can get a View:

```
[Test]
public void edit_contact_should_return_view()
{
    PopulateRepository();
    var result = controller.Edit(1);
    result.AssertViewResult(controller, "Edit Contact", "edit");
}
```

Then we create the action method in the controller:

```
[AcceptVerbs(HttpVerbs.Get), Authorize]
public ActionResult Edit(int id)
{
    ViewData["Title"]="Edit Contact";
    return View("edit");
}
```

Now that we have a View, let's make sure that it will retrieve the correct contact item:

```
[Test]
public void edit_contact_should_get_requested_contact()
{
    PopulateRepository();
    var result = controller.Edit(1);
    Assert.IsInstanceOfType(typeof(Contact), controller.ViewData.Model);
    Assert.AreEqual(1, ((Contact)controller.ViewData.Model).Id);
    result.AssertViewResult(controller, "Edit Contact", "edit");
}
```

Then we modify the Edit action to retrieve the contact using the service class:

```
[AcceptVerbs(HttpVerbs.Get), Authorize]
public ActionResult Edit(int id)
{
    ViewData["Title"]="Edit Contact";
    ViewData.Model = Service.Get(id);
    return View("edit");
}
```

The `Get` method is added to the `IContactService` interface and implemented in the `InMemoryContactService`:

```
public Contact Get(int id)
{
    return Repository.Get().Where(c => c.Id == id).SingleOrDefault();
}
```

We also want to make sure that a proper error message is displayed if the contact ID provided doesn't exist:

```
[Test]
public void edit_should_return_error_page_if_requested_contact_is_not_found()
{
    try
    {
        PopulateRepository();
        var result = controller.Edit(45789); //non-existing contact
        Assert.Fail("Failed to throw exception");
    }
    catch (ArgumentException)
    {
        controller.TempData.AssertItem("error",
                            "The contact you requested could not be found");
    }
}
```

In this test, we try to edit a contact that doesn't exist, and we expect an exception to be thrown as well as an error message be added to the TempData dictionary. Here is the modified action:

```
[AcceptVerbs(HttpVerbs.Get), Authorize]
public ActionResult Edit(int id)
{
    ViewData["Title"] = "Edit Contact";
    ViewData.Model = Service.Get(id);
    if (ViewData.Model == null)
    {
        TempData["error"] = "The contact you requested could not be found";
        throw new ArgumentException ();
    }
    return View("edit");
}
```

Let's create an empty view for now to test the error condition. If we navigate to `http://localhost/contact/edit/23424`, where 23424 is a non-existing contact, we should see the error page shown in Figure 8-8.

Server Error in '/' Application.

Specified argument was out of the range of valid values.

Description: An unhandled exception occurred during the execution of the current web request. Please review th

Exception Details: System.ArgumentOutOfRangeException: Specified argument was out of the range of valid va

Source Error:

```
Line 111:    {
Line 112:        TempData["error"] = "The contact you requested could n
Line 113:        throw new ArgumentOutOfRangeException();
Line 114:    }
Line 115:    return View("edit");
```

Source File: t:\projects\MvcBookApplication\MvcBookApplication\Controllers\ContactController.cs   Line: 113

Stack Trace:

Figure 8-8

Obviously, this is not a good error to show to the end-user. We need to create a custom and more friendly error page. First, we need to turn on custom errors in the web.config file by adding the following line under the `<system.web>` node:

```
<customErrors mode="On"></customErrors>
```

The next thing is to instruct the MVC framework to handle the error by adding the `HandleError` attribute to the action:

```
[AcceptVerbs(HttpVerbs.Get), Authorize]
[HandleError]
public ActionResult Edit(int id)
{
    ViewData["Title"] = "Edit Contact";
    ViewData.Model = Service.Get(id);
    if (ViewData.Model == null)
    {
        TempData["error"] = "The contact you requested could not be found";
        throw new ArgumentException ();
    }
    return View("edit");
}
```

The `HandleError` will handle any unhandled exception thrown during action execution and will render an error view. It does that by looking for a view named *error* in the controller's folder; if one is not found, then it looks in the shared folder. So, let's create an error page in the shared folder so that we can use it throughout the application:

```
<h2>
    Sorry, an error occurred while processing your request.
</h2>
<%if (TempData.ContainsKey("error"))
  {%>
<div>
    <%= TempData["error"] %></div>
<%} %>
```

The error view will display a generic error message followed by a customized message from the TempData dictionary — if one exists.

Now, if we try to navigate to the same page again, we should see a more informative error message, as shown in Figure 8-9.

Sorry, an error occurred while processing your request.

The contact you requested could not be found

Figure 8-9

We now need to make sure that the logged-in user can only edit contacts that belong to him or her. There are many ways to enforce this. We can enforce it in the controller, or we can enforce it in the service class. I prefer enforcing the security check in the service layer in case we need to use the service layer for another project — for example, a mobile website, a web service, or a Windows client. We don't want to rewrite the security enforcement code for each of these applications. The test looks very similar to the previous one:

```
[Test]
public void edit_should_return_error_page_if_user_is_not_owner()
{
    var id = 2;
    try
    {
        PopulateRepository();
        var result = controller.Edit(id); //owned by another user
        Assert.Fail("Failed to throw exception");
    }
    catch (ArgumentException)
    {
        var repo = (IContactRepository)kernel.Get(typeof(IContactRepository));
        Assert.AreEqual(1, repo.Get().Count(c => c.Id == id));
        controller.TempData.AssertItem("error",
                            "The contact you requested could not be found");
    }
}
```

The difference is that the contact we are looking for exists but belongs to a different user. To make this work, we have to change the Get method signature to:

```
Contact Get(Guid userd, int id);
```

The implementation looks like this:

```
public Contact Get(Guid userid, int id)
{
    return Repository.Get().Where(c =>
                            c.Id == id &&
                            c.User.UserId == userid)
                    .SingleOrDefault();
}
```

The next step is to create the Edit action that will handle the form submission. Since the steps here are very similar to the way we created the Create action, I will skip the details and show you the final results. Here is the action method that handles the saving (post), which is very similar to the Create action we wrote previously:

```
[AcceptVerbs(HttpVerbs.Post), Authorize]
[HandleError]
public ActionResult Edit(int id, [Bind(Prefix = "")] Contact model)
{
    ViewData["Title"] = "Edit Contact";
    try
    {
```

```
            model.Id = id;
            if (!Service.Save(UserId, model))
            {
                ViewData.ModelState.AddModelError("save",
                    "Error saving the contact");
            }
        }
        catch (ValidationException ex)
        {
            foreach (var error in ex.ValidationErrors)
            {
                ViewData.ModelState.AddModelError(
                    error.PropertyName,
                    error.ErrorMessage);
            }
        }
        if (!ViewData.ModelState.IsValid)
        {
            return View("edit", model);
        }
        TempData["flash"] = "Contact successfully saved";
        return RedirectToAction("browse");
    }
```

Just as we did previously, we validate the input, then call the save method on the service class.

```
public bool Save(Guid userid, Contact contact)
{
    var errors = ValidationRunner.Run(contact);
    if (errors != null && errors.Count > 0)
    {
        throw new ValidationException(errors);
    }
    //check if email is unique
    if (Repository.Get()
        .Count(c => c.Email.ToLower() == contact.Email.ToLower() &&
            c.User.UserId == userid && c.Id != contact.Id) > 0)
    {
        throw new ValidationException(
            new List<ValidationError>
                {
                    new ValidationError("Email", "Email already exists")
                });
    }
    //make sure user has permission to save
    if(Repository.Get().Count(c =>
                        c.Id == contact.Id &&
                        c.User.UserId == userid) == 0)
        return false;
    return Repository.Save(contact);
}
```

The view is also similar to the create view:

```
<script type="text/javascript">
    $(document).ready(function() {
        $("#sex option[value=<%= (int) ViewData.Model.Sex %>]")
                                    .attr("selected", "selected");
    });
</script>

<h2>
    Edit Contact</h2>
<%=Html.ValidationSummary()%>
<%=Html.JQueryGenerator("editcontact", ViewData.Model)%>
<form id="editcontact"
    action="/contact/edit/<%=ViewData.Model.Id %>" method="post">
<div>
    <label for="email">
        Email</label>
    <br />
    <%=Html.TextBox("email")%>
    <br />
    <label for="name">
        Name</label>
    <br />
    <%=Html.TextBox("name")%>
    <br />
    <label for="sex">
        Sex</label>
    <br />
    <select id="sex" name="sex">
        <option value="0"></option>
        <option value="1">Male</option>
        <option value="2">Female</option>
    </select>
    <br />
    <label for="dob">
        Date of Birth</label>
    <br />
    <input id="dob" name="dob" type="text"
value='<%=ViewData.Model.Dob.ToShortDateString()  %>' />
    <br />
    <input type="submit" value="Save Contact" />
</div>
</form>
```

There are some important differences to note in the previous view as compared to the create view. We need to select the correct value from the dropdown, so I used a JavaScript call to do that. I simply get the value of the sex and use it to set the selected attribute on the corresponding option in the dropdown.

```
$("#sex option[value=<%= (int) ViewData.Model.Sex %>]")
                    .attr("selected", "selected");
```

The `$("#sex option[value=<%= (int) ViewData.Model.Sex %>]")` part simply selects an element of type `option` that has a parent with ID `sex` and that has a `value` attribute equal to the sex of the contact being edited. The `attr("selected", "selected")` part adds a `selected` attribute to the element and sets its value to `selected`. The resulting HTML would look like this:

```
<select id="Select1" name="sex">
    <option value="0"></option>
    <option value="1">Male</option>
    <option value="2" selected="selected">Female</option>
</select>
```

> ### $(document).ready()
>
> `$(document).read()` is a jQuery function that is executed as soon as the page document object model (DOM) is loaded and before the page contents load.

The other thing to note is that I didn't use the TextBox Html helper to generate the date field because I wanted to format the date into a short date string, that is, `01/01/2008` instead of `01/01/2008 12:00`. And since Dob is of type `DateTime?`, I had to write an extension method to get the short date string.

```
public static string ToShortDateString(this DateTime? date)
{
    return date == null ? "" : ((DateTime) date).ToShortDateString();
}
```

> ### Refactor
>
> The Create and Edit views are almost identical and are good candidates for refactoring. We can refactor the form's HTML into a user control that we can reuse in both pages.

Delete Contact

When the user clicks on the Delete link in the grid, he or she will be directed to a confirmation page like the one shown in Figure 8-10.

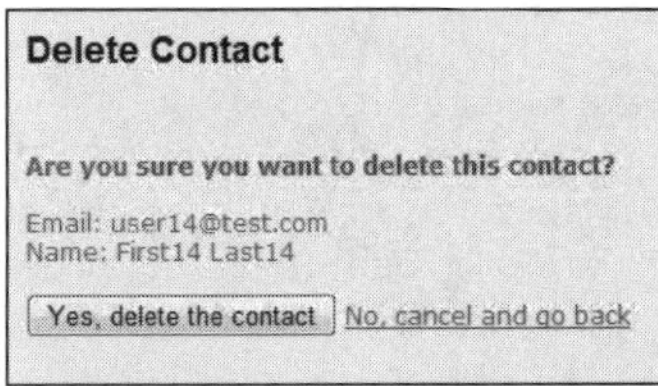

Figure 8-10

I followed the same process as previously noted — created tests, wrote code, and created some views to confirm proper functionality. Here are the action methods:

```
[AcceptVerbs(HttpVerbs.Get), Authorize]
[HandleError]
public ActionResult Delete(int id)
{
    ViewData["title"] = "Delete Contact";
    ViewData.Model = Service.Get(UserId, id);
    if (ViewData.Model == null)
    {
        TempData["error"] = "The contact you are trying to delete does not exist";
        throw new ArgumentException();
    }
    return View("delete");
}


[AcceptVerbs(HttpVerbs.Post), Authorize, ActionName("Delete")]
[HandleError]
public ActionResult DeleteSubmit(int id)
{
    if (!Service.Delete(UserId, id))
    {
        TempData["error"] = "Error deleting the contact";
        throw new ArgumentException();
    }
    TempData["flash"] = "Contact successfully deleted";
    return RedirectToAction("browse");
}
```

The one thing to note in the previous actions is the use of the `ActionName` attribute on the `DeleteSubmit` method. The `ActionName` attribute allows us to define an action name that is different from the method name, which is necessary in this situation since both methods have the same signature and cannot be both called `Delete`. This allows us to post the Delete form to the URL `/contact/delete/{id}` instead of `/contact/deletesubmit/{id}`.

Here is the implementation of the `Delete` method in the `InMemoryContactService` class:

```
public bool Delete(Guid userid, int id)
{
    //make sure user has permission to delete
    if (Repository.Get().Count(c =>
                        c.Id == id &&
                        c.User.UserId == userid) == 0)
        return false;
    return Repository.Delete(id);
}
```

Summary

We have covered many topics in this chapter. We discussed paging and sorting of data grids. We registered a custom route. We talked about error handling and redirecting to a friendly error page using the `HandleError` attribute. We saw our validation framework in action on the client and on the server. We used a little bit of jQuery magic to select the item of a dropdown when the page loads. We used the `ActionName` attribute to assign a name to the action that is different from the method name. We did all this using TDD and have unit tests covering all the conditions that we can think of, so we should be feeling pretty comfortable and confident with our code so far.

9

Import Contacts

It's unreasonable to expect users to create one contact at a time. We need a way to allow them to import or enter multiple contacts at once. There are several ways to accomplish this task, and we will talk about them in this chapter. We will enable users to quickly import their existing Contact Lists easily so they can start using our application right away.

Problem

There is no doubt that users of this application have hundreds if not thousands of contacts that they want to reach. They need to get these contacts into our application, but so far, we have only enabled them to do that one contact at a time. In a real-life application this will not work. We need to enable the users to enter contacts in bulk either by typing them (copying and pasting) or by uploading a text file with their contacts.

Design

In this book, we focus on the importing of text files only, but we want to design our application with the flexibility to support other file formats such as an Excel spreadsheet or an Outlook Personal File.

For the purpose of this chapter, we will create two implementations of this interface — one to handle an uploaded text file and another to handle a string of multiple contacts.

Multiple contacts will be entered in a multiline textbox as one contact per line with the contact details comma-delimited. For example:

    user1@acme.com,firstname,lastname,male,12/17/1964

    user2@hotmail.com,firstname

    user3@gmail.com,,,female

We will also assume that the uploaded text file will be in the same format. Again, this is what we will support for now, but we have designed it in a way that will enable us to easily support other formats down the road.

Solution

We will start with our usual test to make sure that a View exists for us with the appropriate title setup:

```
[Test]
public void import_should_return_view()
{
    var result = controller.Import();
    result.AssertViewResult(controller, "Import Contacts", "import");
}
```

We then make the test work with this action in the ContactController:

```
[AcceptVerbs(HttpVerbs.Get)]
public ActionResult Import()
{
    ViewData["Title"] = "Import Contacts";
    return View("import");
}
```

In our next test, we will make sure that either a string or an uploaded file is posted to the server. The uploaded file is part of the Request object and is in the Files collection, so we will access the file by calling Request.Files[0]. We need to add a mock for these objects for our test to work:

```
httpContext.Expect(h => h.Request).Returns(request.Object);
request.Expect(r => r.Files).Returns(files.Object);
```

The above objects are declared as follows:

```
private static Mock<HttpRequestBase> request;
private static Mock<HttpFileCollectionBase> files;
```

Here is the test:

```
[Test]
public void import_should_return_error_if_contacts_and_file_are_missing()
{
    var result = controller.Import(null);
    Assert.IsNotNull(result);
    Assert.IsInstanceOfType(typeof(ViewResult), result);
    controller.ViewData.ModelState
        .AssertErrorMessage("Import",
                            "You must enter some contacts or upload a file");
    result.AssertViewResult(controller,"Import Contacts", "import");
}
```

To make the test pass, we create the import action that handles the post and validates the input and uploaded files as follows:

```
[AcceptVerbs(HttpVerbs.Post)]
public ActionResult Import(string contacts)
{
    ViewData["Title"] = "Import Contacts";
    if (string.IsNullOrEmpty(contacts) && Request.Files.Count == 0)
    {
        ViewData.ModelState.AddModelError("Import",
                                "You must enter some contacts or upload a file");
    }
    if (!ViewData.ModelState.IsValid)
    {
        return View("import");
    }
    throw new NotImplementedException();
}
```

The exception being thrown at the end is deliberate until we implement the rest of the action.

Now, let's make sure that the Import action adds a flash message when it succeeds:

```
[Test]
public void import_should_add_flash_message_if_import_is_successful()
{
    var result = controller.Import("user1@test.com");
    Assert.IsTrue(controller.ModelState.IsValid, "model state is invalid");
    Assert.Contains(controller.TempData,
                new KeyValuePair<string, object>
                    ("flash",
                     "Contacts successfully imported"),
                "Flash message is missing");

}
```

We pass the test by simply adding the following line to the above action:

```
TempData["flash"] = "Contacts successfully imported";
```

Next, we want to ensure that we are redirected to the Browse action if the import is successful:

```
[Test]
public void import_should_redirect_to_browse_action_if_successful()
{
    var result = controller.Import("user1@test.com");
    Assert.IsTrue(controller.ModelState.IsValid, "model state is invalid");
    result.AssertRedirectToRouteResult("browse");
}
```

Our Import action so far looks as follows:

```
[AcceptVerbs(HttpVerbs.Post)]
public ActionResult Import(string contacts)
```

```
    {
        ViewData["Title"] = "Import Contacts";
        if (string.IsNullOrEmpty(contacts) &&
            (Request.Files.Count == 0 || Request.Files[0].ContentLength == 0))
        {
            ViewData.ModelState.AddModelError("Import",
                                    "You must enter some contacts or upload a file");
        }
        if (!ViewData.ModelState.IsValid)
        {
            return View("import");
        }
        TempData["flash"] = "Contacts successfully imported";
        return RedirectToAction("browse");
    }
}
```

So far, it's not really doing any importing, so we need to make sure that it actually imports the entered contacts. But before we get too far, let's quickly create a View to make sure that everything is working correctly. The View contains a text area and a button and looks as follows:

```
<h2>
    Import Contacts</h2>
<%=Html.ValidationSummary()%>
<form id="importcontacts" action="/contact/import" method="post"
enctype="multipart/form-data">
<div>
    Enter email address below. One address per line.
    <label for="contacts">
        Email Addresses</label>
    <br />
    <textarea id="contacts" name="contacts" rows="10" cols="55"></textarea>
</div>
<div>
    <input type="file" id='file' name='file' /></div>
<div>
    <input type="submit" id="import" name="import" value="Import Email" /></div>
</form>
```

If we click on the Submit button, we should get a validation error as shown in Figure 9-1.

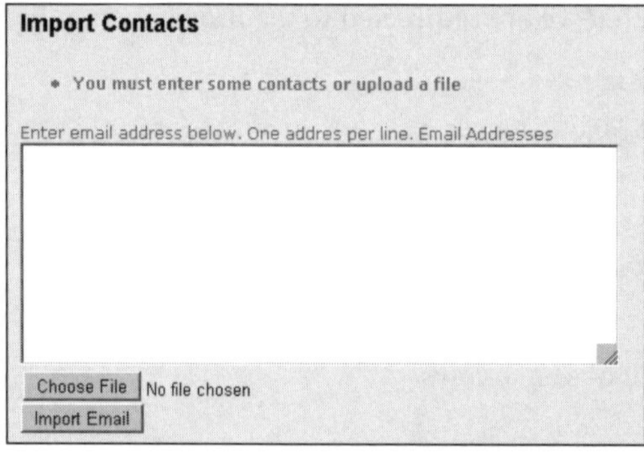

Figure 9-1

Now, we need to instantiate an importer instance. One way to do this is to write an `if` statement that will determine which implementation of the `IContactsImporter` interface to instantiate and then call the appropriate `Parse` method. The problem is that testing this logic will be difficult, and we will not be able to mock the `IContactsImporter` interface easily. To clarify, let's examine this further. We could write the following code in our action:

```
if(!string.IsNullOrEmpty(contacts))
{
    //use text importer
    ContactsImporter = new TextImporter();
    ContactsImporter.Parse(contacts);
}else
{
    //use file importer
    ContactsImporter = new FileImporter();
    ContactsImporter.Parse(Request.Files[0]);
}
```

Look at the previous code and ask yourself, how can I pass a mock instance of `IContactsImporter` to the controller? How can I verify that the correct instance is created? The answer to both questions is that you cannot. It seems like this is an ideal situation for a factory method pattern. We can create a factory class that will know how to create an instance of `IContactsImporter`, and by using an interface, we will be able to mock.

We need to create a parser factory that will return a parser that has a `Parse` method that will return a list of contacts. We then send the list of contacts into an `Import` method that will populate the database. This might sound confusing, but it will all make sense as we move along. The parser factory interface looks like this:

```
public interface IParserFactory
{
    IParser Create(string contacts, HttpPostedFileBase file);
}
```

The parser interface is as follows:

```
public interface IParser
{
    IList<Contact> Parse();
}
```

We now need to implement the `IParserFactory` interface so that it returns the appropriate instance of `IParser`. We will first create a new test class to test the parser factory as follows and add our first test:

```
[TestFixture]
public class ParserFactoryTests
{
    [Test]
    public void factory_should_return_string_parser_if_contacts_are_passed_in()
    {
        ParserFactory factory = new ParserFactory();
        string contacts = "bob@email.com";
```

```
        IParser parser = factory.Create(contacts, null);
        Assert.IsInstanceOfType(typeof (StringParser), parser,
                                "Wrong parser type returned");
    }
}
```

This test needs an implementation of `IParser` called `StringParser` in order to compile. The `StringParser` class is as follows:

```
public class StringParser : IParser
{
    public string Contacts { get; set; }

    public StringParser(string contacts)
    {
        Contacts = contacts;
    }

    public IList<Contact> Parse()
    {
        throw new System.NotImplementedException();
    }
}
```

We are not going to implement the `Parse` method right now; we will get to that shortly. Next, we need to create the `ParserFactory` class. We don't need to implement the entire logic for now; instead, we implement just enough to pass the test:

```
public class ParserFactory : IParserFactory
{
    public IParser Create(string contacts, HttpPostedFileBase file)
    {
        if (!string.IsNullOrEmpty(contacts))
            return new StringParser(contacts);

        throw new NotImplementedException();
    }
}
```

Our test should now pass. Our second test will check to make sure that we get a text file parser if the user uploads a text file. In this test, we will mock the uploaded file as follows:

```
[Test]
public void factory_should_return_text_file_parser_for_uploaded_text_files()
{
    var factory = new ParserFactory();
    var contacts = string.Empty;
    var mockUploadedTextFile = new Mock<HttpPostedFileBase>();
    mockUploadedTextFile.Expect(f => f.FileName).Returns("textfile.txt");
    var parser = factory.Create(contacts, mockUploadedTextFile.Object);
    Assert.IsInstanceOfType(typeof(TextFileParser), parser,
                            "Wrong parser type returned");
}
```

This test will fail. We need to create the `TextFileParser`:

```csharp
public class TextFileParser:IParser
{
    public HttpPostedFileBase PostedFile { get; set; }

    public TextFileParser(HttpPostedFileBase postedFile)
    {
        PostedFile = postedFile;
    }

    public IList<Contact> Parse()
    {
        throw new System.NotImplementedException();
    }
}
```

Now, we modify the `Create` factory method as follows to make the test pass:

```csharp
public class ParserFactory : IParserFactory
{
    public IParser Create(string contacts, HttpPostedFileBase file)
    {
        if (!string.IsNullOrEmpty(contacts))
            return new StringParser(contacts);

        if(file !=null)
        {
            if (Path.GetExtension(file.FileName).ToLower() == ".txt")
                return new TextFileParser(file);
        }
        throw new NotImplementedException();
    }
}
```

We need to add a couple more tests to ensure that the `Create` factory method throws an exception when it cannot create an appropriate parser. We want to throw an `ArgumentNullException` if neither a string nor an uploaded file is provided and throw a `NotImplementedException` if a non-supported file format is provided.

```csharp
[Test]
public void factory_should_throw_exception_if_file_format_is_not_supported()
{
    var factory = new ParserFactory();
    var contacts = string.Empty;
    var mockUploadedTextFile = new Mock<HttpPostedFileBase>();
    mockUploadedTextFile.Expect(f => f.FileName).Returns("textfile.xls");
    Assert.Throws(typeof(NotImplementedException),
                () => factory.Create(contacts, mockUploadedTextFile.Object));
}

[Test]
public void factory_should_throw_exception_if_arguments_are_invalid()
{
```

```
            var factory = new ParserFactory();
            var contacts = string.Empty;
            Assert.Throws(typeof(ArgumentNullException),
                         () => factory.Create(contacts, null));
        }
```

Finally, we make one last change to the `Create` factory method to pass the previous tests:

```
public IParser Create(string contacts, HttpPostedFileBase file)
{
    if (!string.IsNullOrEmpty(contacts))
        return new StringParser(contacts);

    if (file != null)
    {
        if (Path.GetExtension(file.FileName).ToLower() == ".txt")
            return new TextFileParser(file);
        else
            throw new NotImplementedException();
    }
    throw new ArgumentNullException();
}
```

Before can go back to our controller action and use the new factory we just created, let's implement the missing pieces in our parsers. We will start with the `StringParser` class and create a new test fixture for it with one method.

```
[TestFixture]
public class StringParserTests
{
    [Test]
    public void parser_should_return_collection_of_valid_emails()
    {
        var emails = "user1@test.com\r\n" +
                     "user2@test.com\r\n" +
                     "bad email @ test. com\r\n" +
                     "user3@test.com";
        var parser = new StringParser(emails);
        var contacts = parser.Parse();
        Assert.AreEqual(3, contacts.Count);
        Assert.AreEqual("user1@test.com", contacts[0].Email);
        Assert.AreEqual("user2@test.com", contacts[1].Email);
        Assert.AreEqual("user3@test.com", contacts[2].Email);
    }
}
```

After writing the `Parse` method to pass the previous test, our `StringParser` class looks as follows:

```
public class StringParser : IParser
{
    public string Contacts { get; set; }

    public StringParser(string contacts)
    {
        Contacts = contacts;
```

```csharp
        }

        public IList<Contact> Parse()
        {
            var parsedContacts = new List<Contact>();
            var emails = Contacts.Split(new char[]
                                            {
                                                Convert.ToChar("\r"),
                                                Convert.ToChar("\n")
                                            });
            foreach (var email in emails)
            {
                if(AppHelper.IsValidEmail(email))
                {
                    parsedContacts.Add(new Contact{Email = email.Trim()});
                }
            }
            return parsedContacts;
        }
    }
```

We need to do the same thing for the text file parser; here is the test:

```csharp
[Test]
public void parser_should_return_collection_of_valid_emails()
{
    var mockFile = new Mock<HttpPostedFileBase>();

    var emails = "user1@test.com\r\n" +
                 "user2@test.com\r\n" +
                 "bad email @ test. com\r\n" +
                 "user3@test.com";
    var encoding = new ASCIIEncoding();
    var buffer = encoding.GetBytes(emails);
    var stream = new MemoryStream(buffer);

    mockFile.Expect(f => f.InputStream)
        .Returns(stream);

    var parser = new TextFileParser(mockFile.Object);
    var contacts = parser.Parse();
    Assert.AreEqual(3, contacts.Count);
    Assert.AreEqual("user1@test.com", contacts[0].Email);
    Assert.AreEqual("user2@test.com", contacts[1].Email);
    Assert.AreEqual("user3@test.com", contacts[2].Email);

}
```

This looks similar to the string parser test we wrote earlier. An important difference to note here is that we are mocking the posted file. The `Parse` method will read the underlying stream and populate the collection with email addresses.

```csharp
public IList<Contact> Parse()
{
    var reader = new StreamReader(PostedFile.InputStream);
```

```
            var filecontent = reader.ReadToEnd();
            var parsedContacts = new List<Contact>();
            var emails = filecontent.Split(new char[]
                                        {
                                                Convert.ToChar("\r"),
                                                Convert.ToChar("\n")
                                        });
            foreach (var email in emails)
            {
                if (AppHelper.IsValidEmail(email))
                {
                    parsedContacts.Add(new Contact { Email = email.Trim() });
                }
            }
            return parsedContacts;
        }
```

Now that we have all our parsers and parser factory working, we can get back to creating the import action in the controller. Our first test will test the fact that the `ParserFactory` create method is called.

```
    [Test]
    public void import_should_call_the_parser_factory()
    {
        var mockFile = new Mock<HttpPostedFileBase>();
        mockFile.Expect(f => f.ContentLength)
            .Returns(5000);

        var mockParser = new Mock<IParser>();
        mockParserFactory.Expect(f => f.Create(string.Empty, mockFile.Object))
            .Returns(mockParser.Object);
        mockParser.Expect(p => p.Parse())
            .Returns(new List<Contact>());

        mockFiles.Expect(f => f.Count).Returns(1);
        mockFiles.Expect(f => f[0]).Returns(mockFile.Object);

        var result = controller.Import(string.Empty);

        mockParserFactory.VerifyAll();
    }
```

We mock quite a few objects in the above test to ensure that we are only testing the specific piece of code under examination. First, we mock the file to return a content length greater than zero. We mock the file collection to indicate that it contains one file, and finally, we mock the parser factory because we are not interested in its functionality but are only interested in the fact that its `Create` method is called with the correct parameters.

We then add a couple of lines to the import action to pass this test:

```
    [Test]
    public void import_should_call_the_parser_factory()
    {
```

```
        var mockFile = new Mock<HttpPostedFileBase>();
        mockFile.Expect(f => f.ContentLength).Returns(5000);

        var mockParser = new Mock<IParser>();
        mockParserFactory.Expect(f => f.Create(string.Empty, mockFile.Object))
            .Returns(mockParser.Object);

        mockFiles = new Mock<HttpFileCollectionBase>();
        mockFiles.Expect(f => f.Count).Returns(1);
        mockFiles.Expect(f => f[0]).Returns(mockFile.Object);
        request.Expect(r => r.Files).Returns(mockFiles.Object);

        controller.Import(string.Empty);
        mockParserFactory.VerifyAll();
    }
```

For the next test, we want to make sure that the `Parse` method is called:

```
    [Test]
    public void import_should_call_the_parse_method()
    {
        var mockFile = new Mock<HttpPostedFileBase>();
        mockFile.Expect(f => f.ContentLength).Returns(5000);
        var mockParser = new Mock<IParser>();
        mockParserFactory.Expect(f => f.Create(string.Empty, mockFile.Object))
            .Returns(mockParser.Object);
        mockParser.Expect(p => p.Parse())
            .Returns(new List<Contact>
                    {
                        new Contact {Email = "user1@test.com"},
                        new Contact {Email = "user2@test.com"},
                        new Contact {Email = "user3@test.com"}
                    });
        mockFiles = new Mock<HttpFileCollectionBase>();
        mockFiles.Expect(f => f.Count).Returns(1);
        mockFiles.Expect(f => f[0]).Returns(mockFile.Object);
        request.Expect(r => r.Files).Returns(mockFiles.Object);
        controller.Import(string.Empty);
        mockParser.VerifyAll();
    }
```

This is similar to the previous test, and to make it work, we just add one line of code to the import action to call the `Parse` method. There is a problem, though; if we run all the tests, we find that the tests `import_should_add_flash_message_if_import_is_successful` and `import_should_redirect_to_browse_action_if_successful` are failing. This is happening because the action is trying to call the `Create` method on a null parser factory and the `Parse` method on a null parser. This is easy to fix by simply mocking these calls.

The last step is to ensure that the `import` method on the contacts service is called:

```
    [Test]
    public void import_should_call_import_on_service()
    {
```

```csharp
    var mockFile = new Mock<HttpPostedFileBase>();
    mockFile.Expect(f => f.ContentLength).Returns(5000);

    var mockParser = new Mock<IParser>();
    mockParserFactory.Expect(f => f.Create(string.Empty, mockFile.Object))
        .Returns(mockParser.Object);
    var contacts = new List<Contact>
                    {
                            new Contact {Email = "user1@test.com"},
                            new Contact {Email = "user2@test.com"},
                            new Contact {Email = "user3@test.com"}
                    };
    mockParser.Expect(p => p.Parse())
        .Returns(contacts);
    mockFiles = new Mock<HttpFileCollectionBase>();
    mockFiles.Expect(f => f.Count).Returns(1);
    mockFiles.Expect(f => f[0]).Returns(mockFile.Object);
    request.Expect(r => r.Files).Returns(mockFiles.Object);

    var mockService = new Mock<IContactService>();
    mockService.Expect(s => s.Import(UserId, contacts));
    controller.Service = mockService.Object;
    controller.Import(string.Empty);

    mockService.VerifyAll();
}
```

This is just like the previous test, except that we are testing that the service's `Import` method is called. This method doesn't exist and needs to be created on the `IContactService` interface. Its signature looks as follows:

```csharp
void Import(IList<Contact> contacts);
```

The final action on the contact controller is shown next:

```csharp
[AcceptVerbs(HttpVerbs.Post)]
public ActionResult Import(string contacts)
{
    ViewData["Title"] = "Import Contacts";
    if (string.IsNullOrEmpty(contacts) &&
        (Request.Files.Count == 0 || Request.Files[0].ContentLength == 0))
    {
        ViewData.ModelState.AddModelError("Import",
                            "You must enter some contacts or upload a file");
    }
    if (!ViewData.ModelState.IsValid)
    {
        return View("import");
    }

    var file = Request.Files.Count == 0 ? null : Request.Files[0];
    var parser = ParserFactory.Create(contacts, file);
    var parsedContacts = parser.Parse();
```

```
        Service.Import(UserId, parsedContacts);

        TempData["flash"] = "Contacts successfully imported";
        return RedirectToAction("browse");
}
```

As you might have expected, this code breaks a few tests since the `Import` method has not been implemented. We can fix these broken tests by mocking the call to `Import` without having to worry about its
implementation details. Here is how we do that:

```
var mockService = new Mock<IContactService>();
mockService.Expect(s => s.Import(UserId,contacts));
controller.Service = mockService.Object;
```

Import Implementation

So far, we have implemented the controller action to import contacts. This included the use of a factory method pattern to handle the instantiation of the appropriate parser. The parser implementation
returned a collection of contacts. We need to add these contacts to our data store (repository).

We will start by adding writing tests in the `ContactServiceTests` class. Our first test will ensure that
an error is returned for contacts that already exist. Here is the test:

```
[Test]
public void import_should_return_errors_for_existing_emails()
{
    var userid = Guid.NewGuid();
    var contact1 = new Contact
                        {
                            Email = "user1@abc.com",
                            User = new User {UserId = userid}
                        };
    var contact2 = new Contact
                        {
                            Email = "existing@abc.com",
                            User = new User {UserId = userid}
                        };
    var contact3 = new Contact
                        {
                            Email = "user2@abc.com",
                            User = new User {UserId = userid}
                        };
    var contacts = new List<Contact>
                        {
                            contact1,
                            contact2,
                            contact3
                        };

    var repository = new InMemoryContactRepository();
    repository.Add(contact2);

    var mockRunner = new Mock<IValidationRunner>();
```

```
mockRunner.Expect(v => v.Run(contact1))
    .Returns(new List<ValidationError>());
mockRunner.Expect(v => v.Run(contact2))
    .Returns(new List<ValidationError>());
mockRunner.Expect(v => v.Run(contact3))
    .Returns(new List<ValidationError>());

var service = new InMemoryContactService(
    repository,
    mockRunner.Object);

var exception = (ValidationException)
                Assert.Throws(typeof(ValidationException),
                              () => service.Import(userid, contacts));
Assert.AreEqual(1, exception.ValidationErrors.Count);
Assert.AreEqual(string.Format("{0} already exists",
                      contact2.Email),
            exception.ValidationErrors[0].ErrorMessage);
Assert.AreEqual(1, repository.Get()
                        .Count(c => c.Email == contact2.Email));
mockRunner.VerifyAll();
}
```

The first thing we do is create three contact objects and add one of them to our repository. We then mock our validation to succeed and then call the `Import` method. The `Import` method should throw a validation exception that includes one validation error with the message `existing@abc.com already exists`. We also verify that the repository contains only one contact with that email. Here is the code to make this test pass:

```
public void Import(Guid userid, IList<Contact> contacts)
{
    var errors = new List<ValidationError>();
    for (int i = 0; i < contacts.Count; i++)
    {
        var contact = contacts[i];
        try
        {
            var contactErrors = ValidationRunner.Run(contact);
            if (contactErrors != null && contactErrors.Count > 0)
            {
                errors.AddRange(contactErrors);
                continue;
            }
            //check if email exists
            if (Repository.Get()
                    .Count(c => c.Email.ToLower() == contact.Email.ToLower() &&
                            c.User.UserId == contact.User.UserId) > 0)
            {
                errors.Add(
                    new ValidationError("Import",
                                    string.Format("{0} already exists",
                                        contact.Email))));
            }
```

```
        }
        catch
        {
            errors.Add(
                new ValidationError("Import",
                                  string.Format("Error importing {0}",
                                       contact.Email)));
        }
    }
    if (errors.Count > 0)
    {
        throw new ValidationException(errors);
    }
}
```

You will notice that in the previous code, I reuse the validation logic to validate each contact. But instead of throwing an exception right away, I add the validation error to a collection and continue on to the next contact. At the end of the method, I throw one exception that contains all the validation errors. These errors can then be parsed by the controller to display an informative message to the user about the status of the import.

Bug Found

I discovered a bug while writing the previous test for the `Import` method. It turns out that we forgot to set the `User` object on each contact being imported, which results in a null exception being thrown. Being good Test Driven Development (TDD) practitioners, we should write a test to exercise this bug and then fix it. Basically, our test should ensure that all contacts have the `User` object set.

```
[Test]
public void import_should_set_user_object_on_each_contact()
{
    var userid = Guid.NewGuid();
    var username = "testuser";
    var contact1 = new Contact
    {
        Email = "user1@abc.com"
    };
    var contact2 = new Contact
    {
        Email = "user2@abc.com"
    };
    var contact3 = new Contact
    {
        Email = "user3@abc.com"
    };
    var contacts = new List<Contact>
        {
            contact1,
            contact2,
            contact3
        };

    var repo = new InMemoryContactRepository();
```

```
var mockRunner = new Mock<IValidationRunner>();
mockRunner.Expect(v => v.Run(contact1))
    .Returns(new List<ValidationError>());
mockRunner.Expect(v => v.Run(contact2))
    .Returns(new List<ValidationError>());
mockRunner.Expect(v => v.Run(contact3))
    .Returns(new List<ValidationError>());

var service = new InMemoryContactService(
    repo,
    mockRunner.Object);

service.Import(new User
{
    UserId = userid,
    Username = username
}, contacts);

Assert.AreEqual(3, repo.Get().Count());
Assert.AreEqual(3, repo.Get().Count(
                        c => c.User.UserId == userid &&
                            c.User.Username == username));
mockRunner.VerifyAll();
}
```

The important things to note in the previous test are the last two `Assert` calls. We first make sure that all three contacts were added to the repository; then we make sure that all of them have the `User` object set with the correct values. To get this test to work, we add one line to the `Import` method:

```
contact.User = user;
```

We continue to create more tests and change our code to make them pass. Here are a couple more tests:

```
[Test]
public void import_should_add_contacts_to_repository()
{
    var userid = Guid.NewGuid();
    var contact1 = new Contact
                    {
                        Email = "user1@abc.com",
                        User = new User { UserId = userid }
                    };
    var contact2 = new Contact
                    {
                        Email = "user2@abc.com",
                        User = new User { UserId = userid }
                    };
    var contact3 = new Contact
                    {
                        Email = "user3@abc.com",
                        User = new User { UserId = userid }
                    };
```

```
        var contacts = new List<Contact>
                {
                    contact1,
                    contact2,
                    contact3
                };

        var mockRepo = new Mock<IContactRepository>();
        mockRepo.Expect(r => r.Add(contact1)).Returns(1);
        mockRepo.Expect(r => r.Add(contact2)).Returns(2);
        mockRepo.Expect(r => r.Add(contact3)).Returns(3);
        mockRepo.Expect(r => r.Get())
            .Returns((new List<Contact>()).AsQueryable());

        var mockRunner = new Mock<IValidationRunner>();
        mockRunner.Expect(v => v.Run(contact1))
            .Returns(new List<ValidationError>());
        mockRunner.Expect(v => v.Run(contact2))
            .Returns(new List<ValidationError>());
        mockRunner.Expect(v => v.Run(contact3))
            .Returns(new List<ValidationError>());

        var service = new InMemoryContactService(
            mockRepo.Object,
            mockRunner.Object);

        service.Import(userid, contacts);

        mockRepo.VerifyAll();
        mockRunner.VerifyAll();
}

[Test]
public void import_should_return_error_for_invalid_emails_and_not_add_them()
{
    var userid = Guid.NewGuid();
    var contact1 = new Contact
    {
        Email = "user1@abc.com",
        User = new User { UserId = userid }
    };
    var contact2 = new Contact
    {
        Email = "user 2 bad email@abc.com",
        User = new User { UserId = userid }
    };
    var contact3 = new Contact
    {
        Email = "user3@abc.com",
        User = new User { UserId = userid }
    };
    var contacts = new List<Contact>
        {
```

```
            contact1,
            contact2,
            contact3
        };

    var mockRepo = new Mock<IContactRepository>();
    mockRepo.Expect(r => r.Add(contact1)).Returns(1);
    mockRepo.Expect(r => r.Add(contact3)).Returns(3);
    mockRepo.Expect(r => r.Get())
        .Returns((new List<Contact>()).AsQueryable());

    var mockRunner = new Mock<IValidationRunner>();
    mockRunner.Expect(v => v.Run(contact1))
        .Returns(new List<ValidationError>());
    mockRunner.Expect(v => v.Run(contact2))
        .Returns(new List<ValidationError>
                    {
                        new ValidationError("Email","Invalid email")
                    });
    mockRunner.Expect(v => v.Run(contact3))
        .Returns(new List<ValidationError>());

    var service = new InMemoryContactService(
        mockRepo.Object,
        mockRunner.Object);


    var exception = (ValidationException)
                Assert.Throws(typeof(ValidationException),
                            () => service.Import(userid, contacts));
    Assert.AreEqual(1, exception.ValidationErrors.Count);
    Assert.AreEqual(string.Format("{0}: Invalid email",
                            contact2.Email),
                    exception.ValidationErrors[0].ErrorMessage);

    mockRunner.VerifyAll();
    mockRepo.VerifyAll();
    mockRunner.VerifyAll();
}
```

The final `Import` method follows:

```
public void Import(User user, IList<Contact> contacts)
{
    var errors = new List<ValidationError>();
    for (int i = 0; i < contacts.Count; i++)
    {
        var contact = contacts[i];
        contact.User = user;
        try
        {
```

```csharp
            var contactErrors = ValidationRunner.Run(contact);
            if (contactErrors != null && contactErrors.Count > 0)
            {
                foreach (var contactError in contactErrors)
                {
                    contactError.ErrorMessage = string.Format("{0}: {1}",
                                                    contact.Email,
                                        contactError.ErrorMessage);
                }
                errors.AddRange(contactErrors);
                continue;
            }
            //check if email exists
            if (Repository.Get()
                    .Count(c => c.Email.ToLower() == contact.Email.ToLower() &&
                            c.User.UserId == contact.User.UserId) > 0)
            {
                errors.Add(
                    new ValidationError("Import",
                                string.Format("{0} already exists",
                                        contact.Email)));
            }
            else
            {
                Repository.Add(contact);
            }
        }
        catch
        {
            errors.Add(
                new ValidationError("Import",
                            string.Format("Error importing {0}",
                                    contact.Email)));
        }
    }
    if (errors.Count > 0)
    {
        throw new ValidationException(errors);
    }
}
```

The project might not compile and some tests will fail because the Import signature was changed. You will have to go back and fix these tests to work with the new signature.

Test Drive

Let's take everything we just built for a test drive. If we type a few contacts as shown in Figure 9-2 and then click on the Import button, we will be directed to the Browse page in Figure 9-3, where we see the contacts correctly imported.

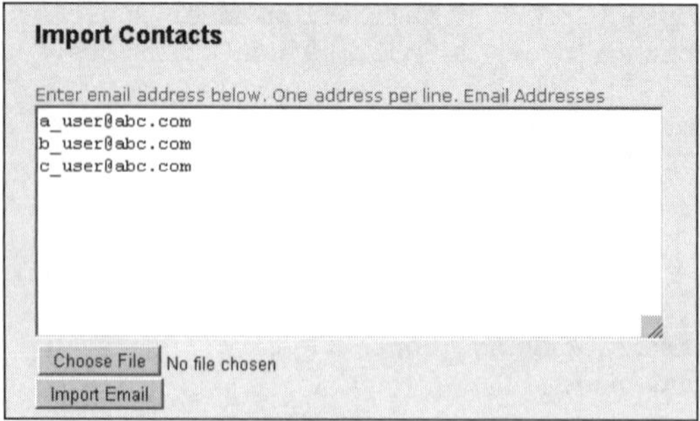

Figure 9-2

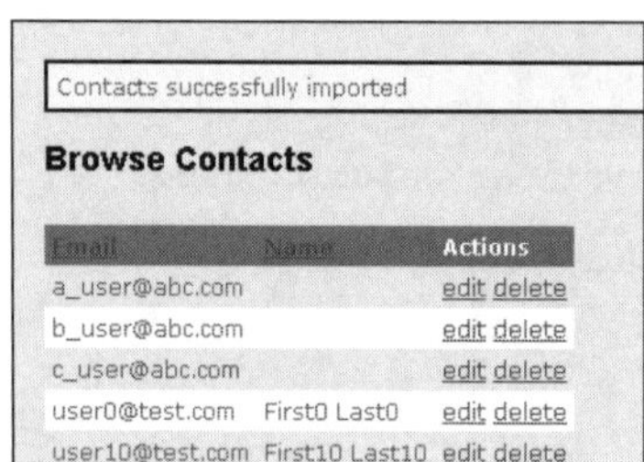

Figure 9-3

Summary

In this chapter, we implemented the critical functionality to deal with contact management. We have created contacts one at a time; imported them in bulk; and browsed, edited, and deleted them as well. We implemented each functionality using a TDD approach, starting with a test and writing the necessary code to pass the test. We also created views to ensure that everything is working together and saw validation working in action.

The concepts discussed in this chapter can be applied to other entities in this project — for example, messages, Contact Lists, and so on. Everything is not identical, but the concepts in general are the same and can be tweaked for every individual entity.

10

Composing Messages

The ultimate purpose of this application is to send out emails to your contacts. In this chapter, we will develop functionality to enable users to create and edit their messages.

Problem

Our users are now able to add and edit their address books, but currently they have nothing they can use it for. We need to allow our users to send a message to one or more of their contacts. The first step in this process is creating a new message.

Design

An email message is made of up of:

- ❑   **Name** — The message's name
- ❑   **Subject** — The subject of the email/message
- ❑   **Text** — The text body of the email/message
- ❑   **HTML** — The HTML body of the email/message

The name field is used to identify your message for your internal use, for example: "Newsletter #4 to subscribers," "Newsletter #4 to non-subscribers," and so on. Name, subject, and text are required fields.

In this chapter, we will only discuss the editing and creating of text-only messages; we will discuss HTML editing in Chapter 11.

Solution

We start by creating a message controller and a test class. The message controller is currently empty, and in the test class, we will create our first test:

```
[TestFixture]
public class MessageControllerTests
{
    private MessageController controller;
    private Message model;

    [SetUp]
    public void SetUp()
    {
        controller = new MessageController();
    }

    [Test]
    public void create_should_return_view()
    {
        var result = controller.Create();
        result.AssertViewResult(controller, "Create New Message");
    }
}
```

The previous code will not compile until we create the `Create` action method in the controller:

```
[AcceptVerbs(HttpVerbs.Get)]
[Authorize]
public ActionResult Create()
{
    return View(new Message());
}
```

Note the use of the `Authorize` attribute; this prevents unauthorized access to the `Create` action, since we only want logged in (authorized) users to create messages. The code now compiles, and the test fails. We make a small change:

```
[AcceptVerbs(HttpVerbs.Get)]
[Authorize]
public ActionResult Create()
{
    ViewData["Title"] = "Create New Message";
    return View(new Message());
}
```

and now the test passes. Next, we want to make sure that an error is returned if the message's name is missing. First, we will change the `SetUp` method to instantiate an instance of the model with valid values:

```
[SetUp]
public void SetUp()
```

```
{
    controller = new MessageController();
    model = new Message()
            {
                Subject = "My newsletter subject",
                Name = "October newsletter",
                Text = "Hello subscriber",
                Html = "Hello <b>subscriber</b>"
            };
}
```

Then we write a test to validate that an error is returned if the name is missing:

```
[Test]
public void create_should_return_error_if_name_is_missing()
{
    model.Name = string.Empty;
    var result = controller.Create(model);
    var errorKey = "Name";
    var errorMessage = "Name is required";
    AssertCreateValidationError(result, errorKey, errorMessage);
}
```

The `AssertCreateValidationError` is a helper function that we will use to assert validation errors, the returned results, and the page title.

```
private void AssertCreateValidationError(ActionResult result,
                                         string errorKey,
                                         string errorMessage)
{
    //assert results
    Assert.IsNotNull(result);
    Assert.IsInstanceOfType(typeof(ViewResult), result);
    controller.ViewData.ModelState.AssertErrorMessage(errorKey, errorMessage);
    Assert.IsInstanceOfType(typeof(Message),
                            ((ViewResult)result).ViewData.Model);
    //assert that the ViewData.Model
    var outModel = (((ViewResult)result).ViewData.Model as Message);
    Assert.AreEqual(model.Subject, outModel.Subject);
    Assert.AreEqual(model.Name, outModel.Name);
    Assert.AreEqual(model.Text, outModel.Text);
    Assert.AreEqual("Create New Message", controller.ViewData["Title"],
                    "Page title is wrong");
}
```

Again, the code will not compile until we write the `Create` action method.

```
[AcceptVerbs(HttpVerbs.Post)]
public ActionResult Create(Message model)
{
    return View(model);
}
```

Make sure that the test fails, and then make the following changes until it passes. First, we need an instance of the `IMessageService` interface, so we add the following constructors and property to the `MessageController` class:

```csharp
public MessageController()
    : this(null)
{
}


[Inject]
public MessageController(IMessageService service)
{
    Service = service ?? new InMemoryMessageService();
}


public IMessageService Service { get; set; }
```

Then we implement the `Add` method to the service class:

```csharp
public int Add(Message message)
{
    var errors = ValidationRunner.Run(message);
    if (errors != null && errors.Count > 0)
    {
        throw new ValidationException(errors);
    }
    return 0;
}
```

The preceding code should throw a validation exception because the name is missing. This is because our `Message` class is defined as follows:

```csharp
public class Message
{
    [Required(ErrorMessage = "Name is required")]
    public string Name { get; set; }
    [Required(ErrorMessage = "Subject is required")]
    public string Subject { get; set; }
    public string Html { get; set; }
    [Required(ErrorMessage = "A plain text body is required")]
    public string Text { get; set; }
    public int Id { get; set; }
}
```

The test should now pass. We will repeat the same steps to test for the `Subject` property:

```csharp
[Test]
public void create_should_return_error_if_subject_is_missing()
{
    model.Subject = string.Empty;
    var result = controller.Create(model);
    var errorKey = "Subject";
    var errorMessage = "Subject is required";
```

```
        AssertCreateValidationError(result, errorKey, errorMessage);

}
```

Following is another test for the `Text` property:

```
[Test]
public void create_should_return_error_if_text_is_missing()
{
    model.Text = string.Empty;
    var result = controller.Create(model);
    var errorKey = "Text";
    var errorMessage = "A plain text body is required";
    AssertCreateValidationError(result, errorKey, errorMessage);
}
```

Next, we want to make sure that the message is added to the repository:

```
[Test]
public void create_should_add_message_to_repository()
{
    //mock the repo
    var mockRepo = new Mock<IMessageRepository>();
    //set expectations
    mockRepo.Expect(r => r.Add(model)).Returns(1);
    var mockValidationRunner = new Mock<IValidationRunner>();
    var service = new InMemoryMessageService(mockRepo.Object,
                                        mockValidationRunner.Object);
    controller = new MessageController(service);
    var result = controller.Create(model);
    mockRepo.VerifyAll();
}
```

This will fail since we are not calling the repository `Add` method. This is easily fixed by making the following change to the `Add` method in the service class:

```
public int Add(Message message)
{
    var errors = ValidationRunner.Run(message);
    if (errors != null && errors.Count > 0)
    {
        throw new ValidationException(errors);
    }
    return Repository.Add(message);
}
```

The full service class now looks like this:

```
public class MessageService : IMessageService
{
    private IValidationRunner ValidationRunner { get; set; }
    private IMessageRepository Repository { get; set; }

    public MessageService()
```

```
        : this(null, null)
    {
    }


    [Inject]
    public MessageService(IMessageRepository repository,
        IValidationRunner validationRunner)
    {
        ValidationRunner = validationRunner ?? new ValidationRunner();
        Repository = repository ?? new InMemoryMessageRepository();
    }


    public int Add(Message message)
    {
        var errors = ValidationRunner.Run(message);
        if (errors != null && errors.Count > 0)
        {
            throw new ValidationException(errors);
        }
        return Repository.Add(message);
    }
}
```

The `Repository` *class was created in Chapter 6.*

Now that we have most of the `Create` functionality set up, we should create a `View` to make sure that things are working as expected. This is not too different from what we have previously done with other views related to contacts and contact lists. The `View` is as follows:

```
<h2>
    Create New Message</h2>
<%= Html.ValidationSummary()%>
<%= Html.JQueryGenerator("createmessage", ViewData.Model) %>
<form id="createmessage" action="/message/create" method="post">
<div>
    <label for="name">
        Name</label>
    <br />
    <%=Html.TextBox("name") %>
    <br />
    <label for="subject">
        Subject</label>
    <br />
    <%=Html.TextBox("subject") %>
    <br />
    <label for="html">
        Html Body (optional)</label>
    <br />
    <%=Html.TextArea("html") %>
    <br />
    <label for="text">
        Text Body</label>
    <br />
```

```
        <%=Html.TextArea("text") %>
        <br />
        <input type="submit" value="Create Message" />
    </div>
    </form>
```

The form looks like Figure 10-1 if you try to submit it.

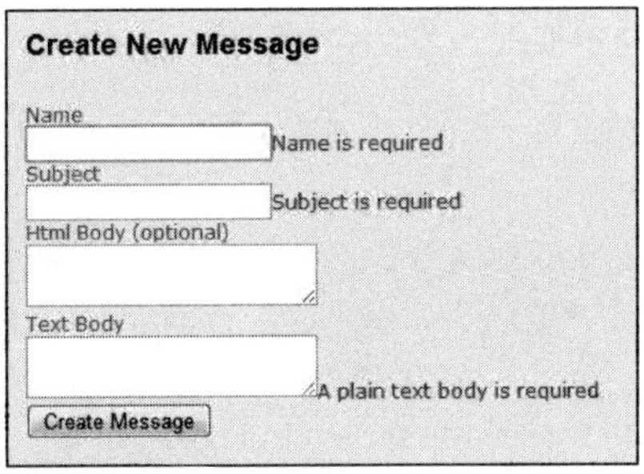

Create New Message
Name
Name is required
Subject
Subject is required
Html Body (optional)
Text Body
A plain text body is required
Create Message

Figure 10-1

After testing the preceding view, you will realize that we didn't add any notification to show that a save was successful. So let's go ahead and do that, starting with the following test:

```
[Test]
public void create_should_add_flash_message_if_save_is_successful()
{
    var mockService = new Mock<IMessageService>();
    mockService.Expect(s => s.Add(model)).Returns(1);
    controller = new MessageController(mockService.Object);
    var result = controller.Create(model);
    Assert.IsTrue(controller.ModelState.IsValid, "model state is invalid");
    Assert.Contains(controller.TempData,
                new KeyValuePair<string, object>
                    ("flash",
                     "Message successfully created"),
                "Flash message is missing");
    mockService.VerifyAll();
}
```

The following changes to the `Action` method are needed to pass the previous test:

```
[AcceptVerbs(HttpVerbs.Post)]
public ActionResult Create([Bind(Prefix = "", Exclude = "Id")]  Message model)
{
    ViewData["Title"] = "Create New Message";
    ViewData.Model = model;
    try
    {
        var id = Service.Add(model);
    }
    catch (ValidationException ex)
```

```
    {
        foreach (var error in ex.ValidationErrors)
        {
            ViewData.ModelState.AddModelError(
                error.PropertyName,
                error.ErrorMessage);
        }
    }

    if (!ViewData.ModelState.IsValid)
    {
        return View(model);
    }

    TempData["flash"] = "Message successfully created";
    return View(new Message());
}
```

Now, when a save is successful, we see the screen in Figure 10-2.

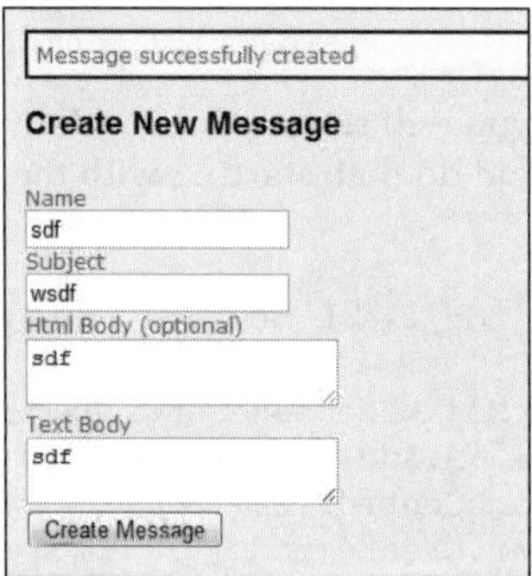

Figure 10-2

Eventually, we will change the code to redirect to the appropriate destination, for example, the Send page or a page containing a list of messages, or whatever is needed. We will just have to write the appropriate test.

The next step is editing an existing message, but before we do that, let's add a page to list all existing messages first. This way we will be able to click on the Edit link on a message and get to the Edit screen. First, let's make sure that the Create screen redirects to the Browse/List view. This is done with a simple test:

```
[Test]
public void create_should_redirect_to_list_view_after_successful_save()
{
    var mockService = new Mock<IMessageService>();
    mockService.Expect(s => s.Add(model)).Returns(1);
    controller = new MessageController(mockService.Object);
    var result = controller.Create(model);
    result.AssertRedirectToRouteResult("browse");
    mockService.VerifyAll();
}
```

A simple change to the return value of the `Action` method will pass the previous test:

```
return RedirectToAction("browse");
```

We now create the browse tests and code. This is very similar to what we have done before for the Contact Lists, so I will just go ahead and show you the end result. We will end up with these tests:

```
[Test]
public void browse_messages_should_retrieve_20_or_less_messages_at_once()
{
    PopulateRepository();
    var result = controller.Browse(null);
    Assert.IsInstanceOfType(typeof(PagedList<Message>),
                            controller.ViewData.Model,
                            "View data is the wrong type");
    Assert.LessThanOrEqualTo(((PagedList<Message>)controller.ViewData.Model).Count,
                            20, "Page size is wrong");
    result.AssertViewResult(controller, "Browse Messages", "browse");
}


[Test]
public void browse_contacts_should_retrieve_messages_for_loggedin_user_only()
{
    PopulateRepository();
    var result = controller.Browse(null);
    Assert.AreEqual(25,
                    ((PagedList<Message>)controller.ViewData.Model).TotalItemCount,
                    "Item count is wrong");
}
```

To get these tests to compile, we have to write some supporting code in the test class. First, we declare these class fields:

```
private string Username = "testusername";
private Guid UserId = Guid.NewGuid();
static StandardKernel kernel;

private Mock<MembershipProvider> MockMembership =
    new Mock<MembershipProvider>();
private Mock<MembershipUser> MockMembershipUser =
    new Mock<MembershipUser>();
private Mock<IPrincipal> user =
    new Mock<IPrincipal>();
private Mock<IIdentity> identity =
    new Mock<IIdentity>();
private Mock<HttpContextBase> httpContext =
    new Mock<HttpContextBase>();
private Mock<HttpRequestBase> request = new Mock<HttpRequestBase>();

private Mock<ControllerBase> controllerbase =
    new Mock<ControllerBase>();

private MessageController controller;
private Message model;
```

Update the `SetUp` method to initialize the controller and mock the appropriate objects:

```
[SetUp]
public void SetUp()
{
    MockMembership = new Mock<MembershipProvider>();
    MockMembershipUser = new Mock<MembershipUser>();
    user = new Mock<IPrincipal>();
    identity = new Mock<IIdentity>();
    httpContext = new Mock<HttpContextBase>();
    request = new Mock<HttpRequestBase>();
    controllerbase = new Mock<ControllerBase>();

    SetupMocks(Username, UserId);

    controller = GetController();

    model = new Message()
            {
                Subject = "My newsletter subject",
                Name = "October newsletter",
                Text = "Hello subscriber",
                Html = "Hello <b>subscriber</b>"
            };
}
```

Add a helper method to populate a test repository:

```
private void PopulateRepository()
{
    var anotherUsername = Username + 2;
    var anotherUserId = Guid.NewGuid();
    var repo = (IMessageRepository)kernel.Get(typeof(IMessageRepository));
    for (var i = 0; i < 50; i++)
    {
        repo.Add(
            new Message
                {
                    Html = "random <b>html</b> " + i,
                    Id = i,
                    Name = "Message " + i,
                    Subject = "Subject " + i,
                    Text = "random text " + i,
                    User = i % 2 == 0
                            ? new User
                            {
                                UserId = UserId,
                                Username = Username
                            }
                            :
                            new User
                            {
                                UserId = anotherUserId,
                                Username = anotherUsername
```

```
                                            }
                });
        }
}
```

You might have to add a `User` *property to the* `Message` *class. This property indicates the owner of the message and establishes the relationship between the two models.*

Add helper methods to instantiate the controller:

```
private MessageController GetController()
{
    kernel = GetIoCKernel();

    var messageController = (MessageController)kernel
        .Get(typeof(MessageController));
    messageController.ControllerContext = new ControllerContext(
        httpContext.Object,
        new RouteData(),
        controllerbase.Object);
    return messageController;
}

private StandardKernel GetIoCKernel()
{
    var modules = new IModule[]
                    {
                        new InlineModule(
                            new Action<InlineModule>[]
                            {
                                m => m.Bind<IMessageService>()
                                        .To<InMemoryMessageService>(),
                                m => m.Bind<IMessageRepository>()
                                        .To<InMemoryMessageRepository>()
                                        .Using<SingletonBehavior>(),
                                m => m.Bind<IValidationRunner>()
                                        .To<ValidationRunner>()
                            })
                    };
    return new StandardKernel(modules);
}
```

Set up the mock objects and their expectations:

```
private void SetupMocks(string username, Guid userid)
{
    identity.Expect(i => i.Name).Returns(username);
    user.Expect(u => u.Identity).Returns(identity.Object);
    httpContext.Expect(h => h.User).Returns(user.Object);
    httpContext.Expect(h => h.Request).Returns(request.Object);
    MockMembership.Expect(m => m.GetUser(username, false))
        .Returns(MockMembershipUser.Object);
    MockMembershipUser.Expect(u => u.ProviderUserKey)
```

```
            .Returns(userid);
    }
```

The `Browse` action itself is pretty simple and is as follows:

```
[AcceptVerbs(HttpVerbs.Get), Authorize]
public ActionResult Browse(int? page)
{
    ViewData["Title"] = "Browse Messages";

    page = page ?? 1;
    ViewData.Model = Service.GetPage(User.Identity.Name, page);
    return View("browse");
}
```

For this to compile, we make some changes to the service interface and class to add the `GetPage` method:

```
public PagedList<Message> GetPage(string username, int? page)
{
    page = page ?? 1;
    page = page < 1 ? 1 : page;
    return Repository.Get()
        .Where(c => c.User.Username.ToLower() == username.ToLower())
        .ToPagedList((int)(page - 1), 20);
}
```

I have skipped the sorting code here for the sake of clarity and simplification.

Lastly, let's put a `View` together to see if this works as expected:

```
<h2>
    Browse Messages</h2>
<table class="grid">
    <thead>
        <tr>
            <th>
                Name
            </th>
            <th>
                Actions
            </th>
        </tr>
    </thead>
    <tbody>
        <%
            foreach (var message in ViewData.Model)
            {%>
        <tr>
            <td>
                <%=message.Name%>
            </td>
            <td>
```

```
            <a href='/message/edit/<%=message.Id %>'>edit</a>
        </td>
    </tr>
    <%
        }%>
  </tbody>
</table>
<%
    Html.RenderPartial("pagination", new PaginationViewData
                            {
                            PageActionLink =
                                "/message/browse/{page}",
                            PageNumber = ViewData.Model.PageNumber,
                            PageSize = ViewData.Model.PageSize,
                            TotalItemCount = ViewData.Model.TotalItemCount,
                            PageCount = ViewData.Model.PageCount
                            });%>
```

If we navigate to the /message/browse URL, we will see an empty page because the repository is empty. So, just as we did with the Contact List, we will populate the in-memory repository with 50 messages, of which 25 are owned by the logged-in user. We basically add this code inside the loop that populates the repository:

```
messagerepo.Add(new Message
                {
                    Html = "random <b>html</b> " + i,
                    Name = "Message " + i,
                    Subject = "Subject " + i,
                    Text = "random text " + i,
                    User = i % 2 == 0
                            ? new User
                            {
                                UserId = (Guid)provider
                                            .GetUser("test", false)
                                            .ProviderUserKey,
                                Username = provider
                                    .GetUser("test", false)
                                    .UserName
                            }
                            :
                            new User
                            {
                                UserId = (Guid)provider
                                            .GetUser("test2", false)
                                            .ProviderUserKey,
                                Username = provider
                                            .GetUser("test2", false)
                                            .UserName
                            }
                });
```

Now, when we visit the Browse view, we should see the two pages of messages, the first page containing 20 messages (Figure 10-3) and the second page containing the remaining five (Figure 10-4).

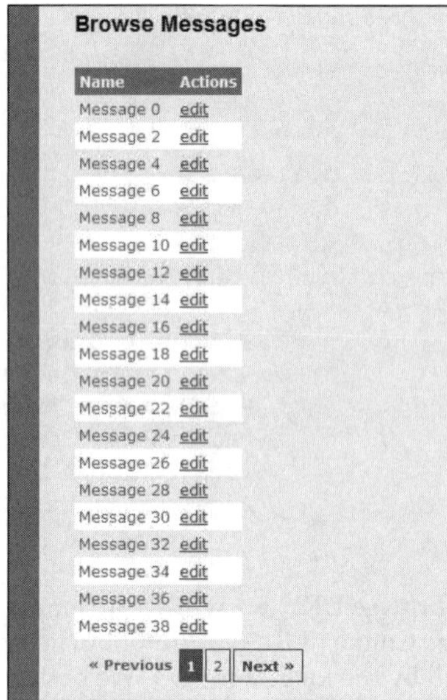

Figure 10-3

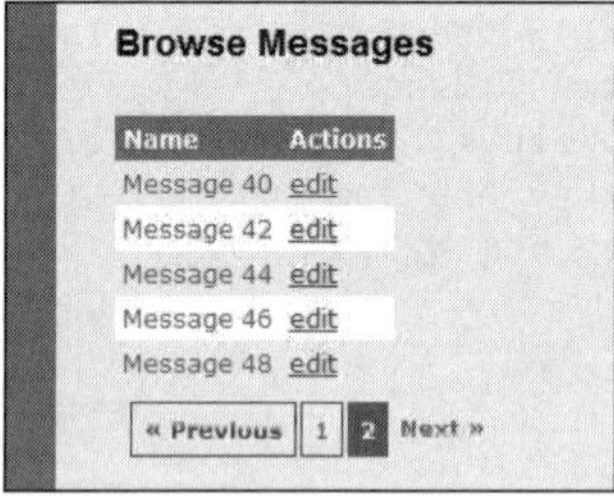

Figure 10-4

The next step is to code the edit functionality. This is very similar to what we previously did with the Contact Lists. The test is as follows:

```
[Test]
public void edit_message_should_return_view()
{
    PopulateRepository();
    var result = controller.Edit(1);
    result.AssertViewResult(controller, "Edit Message", "edit");
}
```

The Action method is as follows:

```
[AcceptVerbs(HttpVerbs.Get), Authorize]
[HandleError]
public ActionResult Edit(int id)
{
```

```
        ViewData["Title"] = "Edit Message";
        return View("edit");
    }
```

Next, we test that the requested message is returned:

```
    [Test]
    public void edit_message_should_get_requested_message()
    {
        PopulateRepository();
        var result = controller.Edit(1);
        Assert.IsInstanceOfType(typeof(Message), controller.ViewData.Model);
        Assert.AreEqual(1, ((Message)controller.ViewData.Model).Id);
        result.AssertViewResult(controller, "Edit Message", "edit");

    }
```

Then we just change the `Action` method to retrieve the requested message:

```
    [AcceptVerbs(HttpVerbs.Get), Authorize]
    [HandleError]
    public ActionResult Edit(int id)
    {
        ViewData["Title"] = "Edit Message";
        ViewData.Model = Service.Get(User.Identity.Name, id);
        return View("edit");
    }
```

In order for the code to compile, we have to implement the `Get` method on the service interface as follows:

```
    public Message Get(string username, int id)
    {

        return Repository.Get().Where(c =>
                            c.Id == id &&
                            c.User.Username.ToLower() == username.ToLower())
                    .SingleOrDefault();
    }
```

We also want to make sure that we return an appropriate error message if the requested message does not exist:

```
    [Test]
    public void edit_message_should_return_error_page_if_requested_message_not_found()
    {
        try
        {
            PopulateRepository();
            var result = controller.Edit(45789); //non-existing message
            Assert.Fail("Failed to throw exception");
        }
        catch (ArgumentException)
        {
```

```
                controller.TempData.AssertItem("error",
                                        "The message you requested could not be found");
        }
    }
```

For the test to pass, we change the `Edit` action method to:

```
[AcceptVerbs(HttpVerbs.Get), Authorize]
[HandleError]
public ActionResult Edit(int id)
{
    ViewData["Title"] = "Edit Message";
    ViewData.Model = Service.Get(User.Identity.Name, id);
    if (ViewData.Model == null)
    {
        TempData["error"] = "The message you requested could not be found";
        throw new ArgumentException();
    }
    return View("edit");
}
```

Another condition we need to test to is that the user can only see his or her messages; so if the requested message is owned by a different user, we should get an error message.

```
[Test]
public void edit_message_should_return_error_page_if_user_is_not_owner()
{
    var id = 2;
    try
    {
        PopulateRepository();
        var result = controller.Edit(id); //owned by another user
        Assert.Fail("Failed to throw exception");
    }
    catch (ArgumentException)
    {
        var repo = (IMessageRepository)kernel.Get(typeof(IMessageRepository));
        Assert.AreEqual(1, repo.Get().Count(c => c.Id == id));
        controller.TempData.AssertItem("error",
                                "The message you requested could not be found");
    }
}
```

This test will pass because our `Get` method filters the message by the username. Although the test passes, we should make sure that it is actually working; we can simply change the `Get` method as follows and make sure that the test fails:

```
public Message Get(string username, int id)
{

    return Repository.Get().Where(c =>
                            c.Id == id)
                        .SingleOrDefault();
}
```

Lastly, we want to make sure that we can save the changes to the repository. For the sake of brevity, I will not write all the test cases, but will just write enough to make the view work.

```
[Test]
public void edit_message_should_save_changes_to_repository()
{
    PopulateRepository();
    var repo = (IMessageRepository)kernel.Get(typeof(IMessageRepository));
    var oldMessage = repo.Get().SingleOrDefault(m => m.Id == 1);
    var oldName = oldMessage.Name;
    var newName = "New name";
    var newMessage = new Message
                        {
                            Name = newName,
                            Html = oldMessage.Html,
                            Id = oldMessage.Id,
                            Subject = oldMessage.Subject,
                            Text = oldMessage.Text,
                            User = oldMessage.User
                        };
    Assert.AreEqual(oldName, repo.Get().SingleOrDefault(m => m.Id == 1).Name);

    var result = controller.Edit(newMessage);

    Assert.AreEqual(newName, repo.Get().SingleOrDefault(m => m.Id == 1).Name);
}
```

The post `Edit` action is as follows:

```
[AcceptVerbs(HttpVerbs.Post), Authorize,HandleError]
public ActionResult Edit(Message message)
{
    ViewData["Title"] = "Edit Message";
    ViewData.Model = Service.Save(User.Identity.Name, message);
    TempData["flash"] = "Message successfully saved";
    return View("browse");
}
```

I have skipped several test cases because they are similar to what we have been doing before, and there is no need to repeat them again. You still have to write those tests, however; for example, you need to test that `Save` is validating the input, that only the owner of the message can save the changes, that all fields are correctly saved, and so on.

We can now create a `View` and see if things are working as they should:

```
<h2>
    Edit Message</h2>
<%= Html.ValidationSummary()%>
<%= Html.JQueryGenerator("editmessage", ViewData.Model) %>
<form id="editmessage" action="/message/edit" method="post">
<div>
    <label for="name">
        Name</label>
```

```
            <br />
            <%=Html.TextBox("name") %>
            <br />
            <label for="subject">
                Subject</label>
            <br />
            <%=Html.TextBox("subject") %>
            <br />
            <label for="html">
                Html Body (optional)</label>
            <br />
            <%=Html.TextArea("html") %>
            <br />
            <label for="text">
                Text Body</label>
            <br />
            <%=Html.TextArea("text") %>
            <br />
    <%=Html.Hidden("id", ViewData.Model.Id) %>
            <input type="submit" value="Save Message" />
    </div>
    </form>
```

If we go to the Browse page and click on the Edit link next to any message, we should see Figure 10-5.

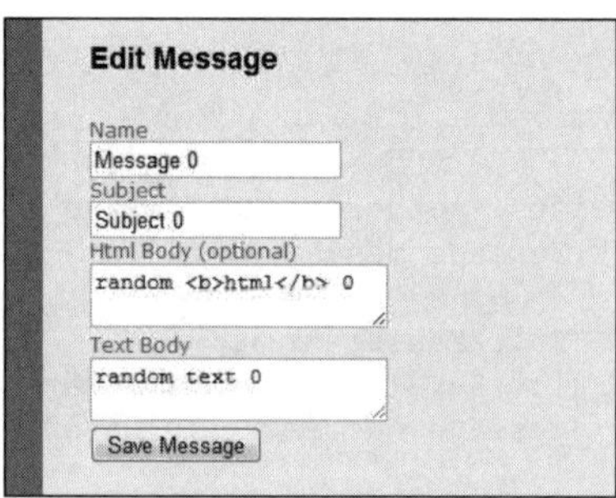

Figure 10-5

So far, so good. Click on the "Save Message" button, and you will see the error message shown in Figure 10-6.

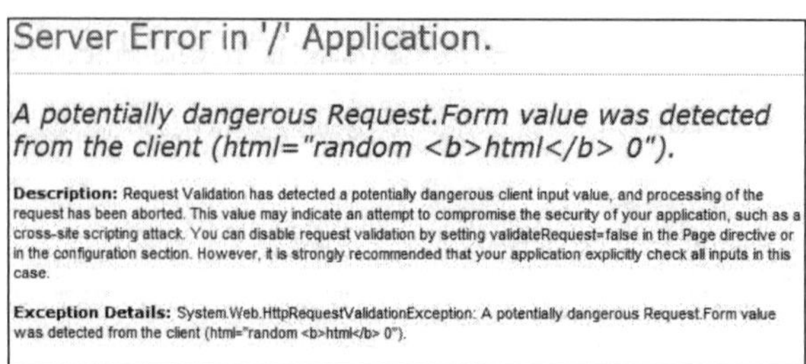

Figure 10-6

As you can see from the error message in Figure 10-6, this error is due to the fact that we are trying to post HTML code. This is because of something called *Request Validation*, which is a security feature meant to protect your application from cross-site script attacks.

Scripting Attacks

According to a white paper on ASP.NET at `www.asp.net/learn/whitepapers/request-validation`:

> *Many sites are not aware that they are open to simple script injection attacks. Whether the purpose of these attacks is to deface the site by displaying HTML, or to potentially execute client script to redirect the user to a hacker's site, script injection attacks are a problem that web developers must contend with.*
>
> *Script injection attacks are a concern of all web developers, whether they are using ASP.NET, ASP, or other web development technologies.*
>
> *The ASP.NET request validation feature proactively prevents these attacks by not allowing unencoded HTML content to be processed by the server unless the developer decides to allow that content.*

Despite what the error message says, the fix for this is different and can be done by simply decorating your post action with the attribute `[ValidateInput(false)]`. Once we make that change and try to change the message's name and save, we should get redirected to the Browse view, showing the changes shown in Figure 10-7.

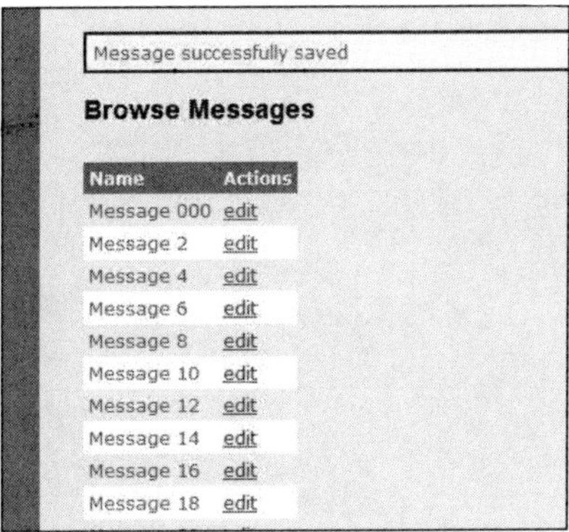

Figure 10-7

Summary

In this section, we wrote code that allows us to create and modify a message. As in the rest of the book, we have written our tests first and only written the code necessary to make our tests pass. This does not mean that our test suite is complete — several edge cases exist that should have tests written for them and then the necessary changes to the code should be made. An example of such is: What would happen if the user performs an HTTP POST to the Edit action using an ID that doesn't exist in the database? Currently the action would fail. Finding and handling edge cases such as this may be time-consuming, but in the long run, it increases the quality of your application greatly.

In the following chapters, we will increase the usefulness of the Editor screen we have created by supporting both HTML and WYSIWIG (What-You-See-Is-What-You-Get).

11

HTML WYSIWYG Editing

In Chapter 10, we developed basic message creation and editing. We will extend our work thus far to allow for a user-friendly HTML editor.

Problem

Although our application so far allows for adding and editing the HTML body of the message, it is not very friendly. It assumes that the user knows HTML and can simply design an HTML message using markup. This is not just user-unfriendly, but it is also tedious and error-prone. Almost all users will want to:

- ❏ Style the text using bold, italics, and so on.
- ❏ Easily add hyperlinks.
- ❏ Embed inline images.

We cannot expect them to do all this using markup and must provide a better way. Unfortunately, there is no standard HTML element that you can simply add to your web page to enable HTML editing. It would be nice to have been able to simply add an <htmleditor> tag and have a full-blown editor embedded in your web page.

Design

Although we cannot add an HTML element to our web page to enable rich text editing, there is an easy solution. Luckily, there are several HTML editors that are freely available for us to use. Some of them can be as easy as adding a simple tag or line of markup to your web page. Some of these editors use JavaScript, Flash, Java, ActiveX, and so on. Since it is always preferred not to assume that your users have a certain plug-in installed, we will only examine JavaScript-based editors.

Solution

There are several editors available online, but let's only examine a few of them. I want to objectively evaluate the selection, and, therefore, I will consider the following factors in my decision:

- ❑ Functionality/features
- ❑ Ease of use/implementation
- ❑ Community support
- ❑ Documentation

TinyMCE

```
http://tinymce.moxiecode.com/
```

Description

From the website:

> *TinyMCE is a platform independent web based Javascript HTML WYSIWYG editor control released as Open Source under LGPL by Moxiecode Systems AB. It has the ability to convert HTML TEXTAREA fields or other HTML elements to editor instances. TinyMCE is very easy to integrate into other Content Management Systems.*

Figure 11-1 is an example of a TinyMCE editor with some basic editing features turned on.

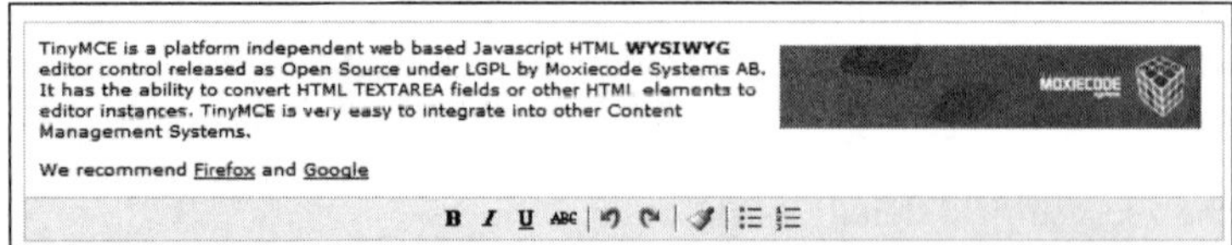

Figure 11-1

Use

```
<script type="text/javascript" src="/scripts/tiny_mce/tiny_mce.js"></script>
<script type="text/javascript">
tinyMCE.init({
 mode : "exact",
 elements: "html",
 theme : "simple"
});
</script>
```

Comments

This is a very capable editor and has a simple mode. I am not a big fan of its HTML editor and image gallery because they pop up a browser window rather than an AJAX dialog box.

WYMeditor

```
www.wymeditor.org/
```

Description

From the website:

> WYMeditor is a web-based WYSIWYM (What You See Is What You Mean) XHTML editor.
>
> WYMeditor's main concept is to leave details of the document's visual layout, and to concentrate on its structure and meaning, while trying to give the user as much comfort as possible (at least as WYSIWYG editors).
>
> WYMeditor has been created to generate perfectly structured XHTML strict code, to conform to the W3C XHTML specifications and to facilitate further processing by modern applications.
>
> With WYMeditor, the code can't be contaminated by visual informations like font styles and weights, borders, colors… The end-user defines content meaning, which will determine its aspect by the use of style sheets. The result is easy and quick maintenance of information.
>
> As the code is compliant to W3C XHTML specifications, you can for example process it using a XSLT (at the client or the server side), giving you a wide range of applications.

Figure 11-2 shows an example of a WYMeditor that shows how the editor displays the content wrapped in visual containers with the HTML tag displayed in the left-hand corner. Some might argue that this is not true WYSIWYG.

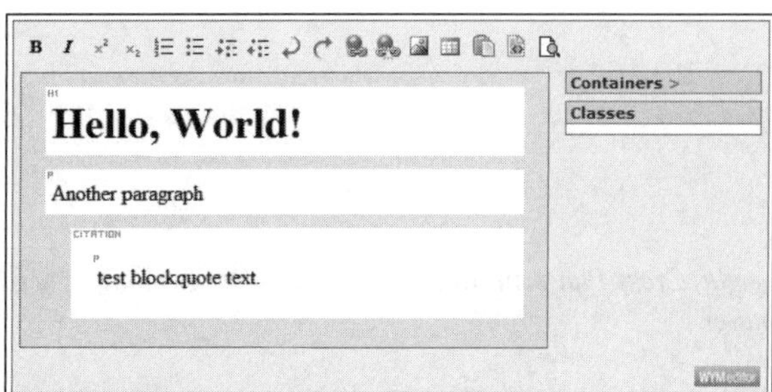

Figure 11-2

Use

```
<script type="text/javascript"
src="/scripts/wymeditor/jquery.wymeditor.pack.js"></script>
<script type="text/javascript">
$(function() {
    $('#html').wymeditor();
});
</script>
```

Comments

WYMeditor uses jQuery, which is a plus, since we will not have to depend on another JavaScript library. I love the visual editor and how it shows the container type (Figure 11-2). The HTML source code can be edited without any pop-ups (Figure 11-3), but adding an image or a table pops up a browser window.

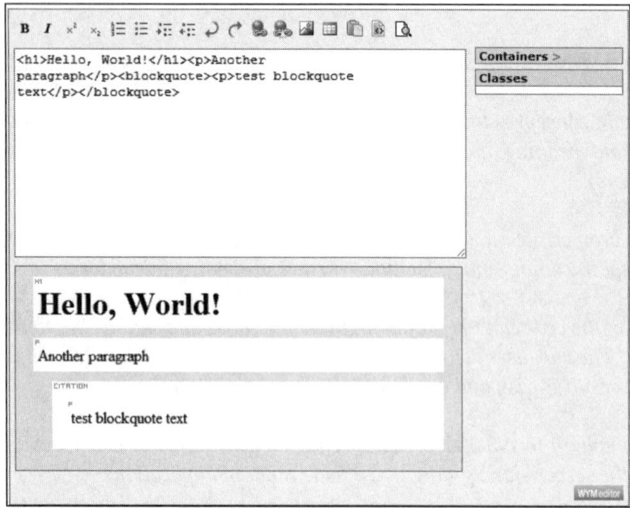

Figure 11-3

NicEdit

www.nicedit.com/

Description

From the website:

> *NicEdit is a Lightweight, Cross Platform, Inline Content Editor to allow easy editing of web site content on the fly in the browser.*

> *NicEdit Javascript integrates into any site in seconds to make any element/div editable or convert standard textareas to rich text editing.*

An example of NicEdit is shown in Figure 11-4. By now, you must have noticed that almost all these editors look very similar.

Figure 11-4

Use

```
<script type="text/javascript" src="http://js.nicedit.com/nicEdit-latest.js">
</script>
<script type="text/javascript">
//<![CDATA[
bkLib.onDomLoaded(function() { new nicEditor().panelInstance('html');});
//]]>
</script>
```

Comments

NicEdit doesn't use any pop-ups, and the image uploader is very functional and doesn't even cause a postback (Figure 11-5).

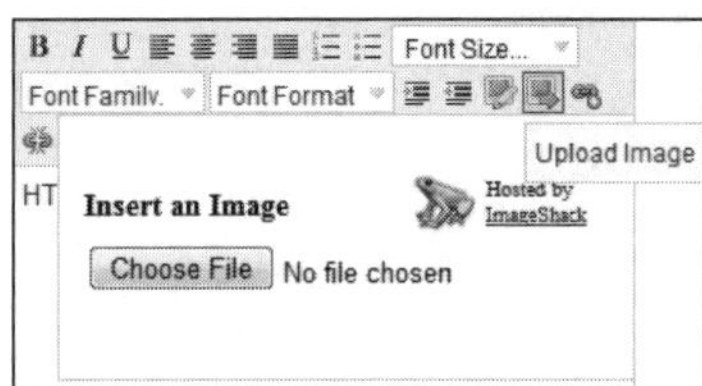

Figure 11-5

The HTML editor is also built in and doesn't pop up any windows (Figure 11-6).

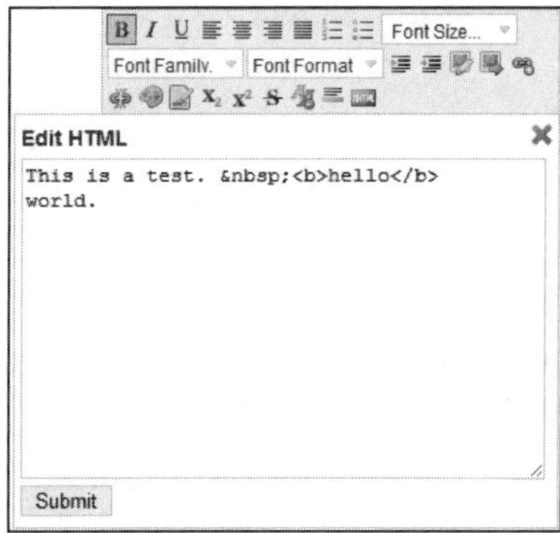

Figure 11-6

jWYSIWYG

```
http://projects.bundleweb.com.ar/jWYSIWYG/
```

Description

From the website:

> *This plugin is an inline content editor to allow editing rich HTML content on the fly. It's a simpler version of WYMeditor with much less features. With a small file size less than 26Kb total and only 18Kb of code and 7Kb packed, the main concept is to keep it simple, not all users need font coloring or create tables, just the basic.*

As you can see in Figure 11-7, this editor can be configured to be very simple. It has a minimalistic look and feel but meets all the requirements of a rich text editor.

Figure 11-7

Use

```
<script type="text/javascript" src="/scripts/jquery.wysiwyg.js"></script>
<script type="text/javascript">
$(function()
{
    $('#html').wysiwyg();
});
</script>
```

Comments

jWYSIWYG uses jQuery, so we will not have to include another JavaScript library. It is very simple and functional and doesn't pop up a window for source editing (Figure 11-8).

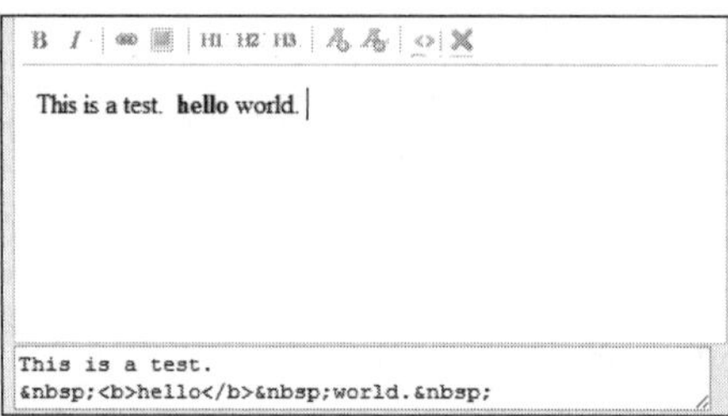

Figure 11-8

Others

As previously mentioned, there are several options for a WYSIWYG editor, and we have only looked at a few. One notable alternative is Yahoo's Rich Text Editor (http://developer.yahoo.com/yui/editor/). It is a great text editor but has dependencies on Yahoo's JavaScript library, also known as *YUI* (Yahoo! UI Library).

The Winner

There is really no *winner* per se, since they are all very comparable. With that said and for the sake of this application, we will go with simplicity and select jWYSIWYG. We are already using jQuery in our pages, so all we have to do is add a reference to the style sheet and to the JavaScript file itself.

```
<link href="/Scripts/jquery-wysiwyg/jquery.wysiwyg.css" rel="stylesheet"
type="text/css" />
<script src="/Scripts/jquery-wysiwyg/jquery.wysiwyg.js"
type="text/javascript"></script>
```

Then we simply add the following script at the bottom of the Create and Edit pages:

```
<script type="text/javascript">
    $(document).ready(function() {
        $("#html").wysiwyg();
    });
</script>
```

That's all we have to do to get rich text capability added. One thing to keep in mind is that the default settings for the editor don't include HTML source editing, but this is very easy to enable and can be done as follows:

```
<script type="text/javascript">
    $(document).ready(function() {
        $("#html").wysiwyg({
            controls: {
                html: { visible: true }
            }
        });
    });
</script>
```

We haven't really made any changes to the code, and there are no tests to add or run. We can simply validate our code by editing an existing message, modifying the HTML body, saving it, and then reloading it to make sure that everything works as advertised.

Summary

In this chapter, we reviewed and selected an HTML WYSIWYG editor and enhanced the new text field using that editor. Adding the new editor functionality was very simple, with no back-end code changes involved. The HTML editor provided us with a nice baseline of features for our users. For your own projects, try evaluating the features of various HTML editors and see which one best fits your requirements.

12

Image Hosting

In the last couple of chapters, we talked about creating and editing messages as well as using a rich (WYSIWYG) editor to edit the email content. One of the features of the editor is the ability to upload and insert images into the message body. In this chapter, we will discuss the details of implementing such a feature to allow us to upload and store the image as well as serve it to the end-user (the message recipient).

Problem

Other than formatting, the main reason our users would want to use HTML messages would be to include images. An image is not necessarily a picture of something (a car, a computer, or whatever); it could be a banner, a logo, a promotional badge, or even a "Sign Up Now" button. We need to give the users the ability to upload an image and use it within their email. This involves several problems/steps. First, we want to provide a way for the user to upload an image. Second, we want to give them a way to browse their "image gallery" and select the image to insert into the image. Third, we want to host and serve these images so that when the end-user reads the message, he or she will be able to see the images.

Design

We need to tackle these problems systematically. The first thing we need to do is to think about the process. The user will click a button on the WYSIWYG editor to insert an image. This will display a user interface (UI) where the user can upload a picture, insert a picture using a URL, or select previously uploaded pictures from his or her gallery. Once a picture is selected, we need to add the picture to the message editor.

The "Insert Image" button that comes included with the editor only allows for inserting a URL to an image as shown in Figure 12-1. This doesn't address our problems. We will have to implement our own custom solution.

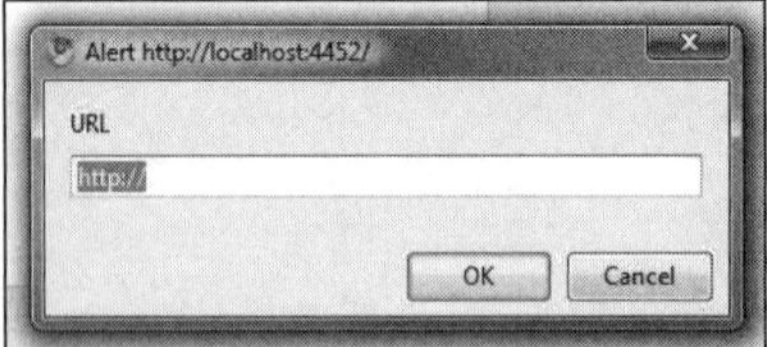

Figure 12-1

I will skip over some of the functionality of a full-fledged gallery for the sake of simplicity and because there are other solutions out there that you can use. A quick Google search for "jQuery image gallery" will turn up several Open Source and free alternatives. Let's make this simple.

Solution

If you use the out-of-the-box "Insert Image" button, you will get the dialog shown in Figure 12-1. If we insert a URL to a picture, we see something like Figure 12-2.

Figure 12-2

We can overwrite the default button behavior to execute custom JavaScript using the following code:

```
$("#html").wysiwyg({
    controls: {
        html: { visible: true },
        insertImage: {
            visible: true,
            exec: function() { alert("insert image button clicked"); }
        }
    }
});
```

This simply tells the editor to make the "Insert Image" button visible and to have it execute our custom code. If we click the button, we get the Alert box shown in Figure 12-3.

Now we have an entry point into our custom code. Instead of displaying an Alert box, we are going to display a modal JavaScript dialog box. We will use the jQuery UI library.

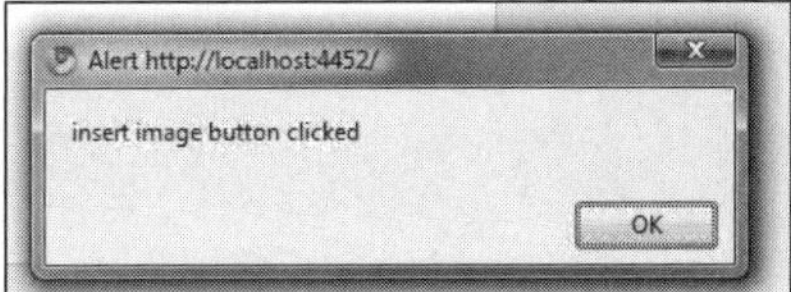

Figure 12-3

---

jQuery UI Library

jQuery UI is a widget and interaction library built on top of the jQuery JavaScript Library that you can use to build highly interactive web applications. One component of this library is a `Dialog` control that allows us to create JavaScript-based modal dialogs.

The library is located at `http://jqueryui.com` and has a configuration utility that customizes your download to include only the components that you need and that comes pre-built with several themes.

After downloading the customized jQuery UI Library and adding it to our project, we will add two links to our master page. One links to the style sheet and the other links to the JavaScript file; they should look as follows:

```
<link href="/Content/css/smoothness/jquery-ui-1.7.1.custom.css" rel="stylesheet"
type="text/css" />
<script src="/Scripts/ui/jquery-ui-1.7.1.custom.min.js"
type="text/javascript"></script>
```

We can now add a hidden layer (`div` element) to include the content of the dialog and use JavaScript to display it. A test dialog HTML is shown next:

```
<div id="dialog" title="Basic modal dialog" style="display: none">
    <p> Adding the modal overlay screen makes the dialog look more prominent
        because it dims out the page content.</p>
</div>
```

The JavaScript code to display this dialog is as follows:

```
<script type="text/javascript">
    $(document).ready(function() {
        $("#html").wysiwyg({
            controls: {
                html: { visible: true },
                insertImage: {
                    visible: true,
                    exec: function() { showImageDialog(); }
                }
            }
        });
    });
```

```
    function showImageDialog() {
        $("#dialog").dialog({
            modal: true
        });
    }
</script>
```

If we click on the "Insert Image" button, we see the screen shown in Figure 12-4.

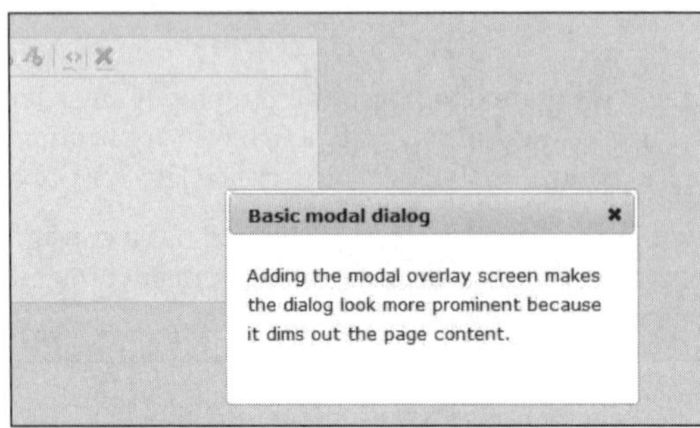

Figure 12-4

We now have the beginnings of our gallery interface. One of the gallery features is to upload a file. When a file is uploaded, it is posted to the server and can be accessed through the `Request.Files` collection. After performing some validation, we will save the file to storage.

Let's start with a test:

```
[Test]
public void upload_should_save_uploaded_file()
{
    //mock file
    var filename = "fish.jpg";
    var file1 = new Mock<HttpPostedFileBase>();
    file1.Expect(d => d.FileName).Returns(filename);
    var ms = new MemoryStream();
    Resources.Fish.Save(ms, ImageFormat.Jpeg);
    file1.Expect(d => d.InputStream).Returns(ms);
    MyMocks.Request.Expect(r => r.Files.Count).Returns(1);
    MyMocks.Request.Expect(r => r.Files[0]).Returns(file1.Object);

    //mock service
    var mockService = new Mock<IGalleryService>();
    mockService.Expect(s => s.Upload(username, filename, ms)).Returns(0);

    var con = new GalleryController(mockService.Object);
    con.SetFakeControllerContext();

    con.Upload();

    //verify mocks
```

```
        MyMocks.Request.VerifyAll();
        file1.VerifyAll();
        mockService.VerifyAll();
    }
```

There is a lot going on in the previous test, so let us take a look at it. First, we need to mock a file. I copied an image file called *fish.jpg* into the test project Resources. I did that by opening the project properties and clicking on the Resources tab, then clicking on "Add Existing File" in the menu (see Figure 12-5).

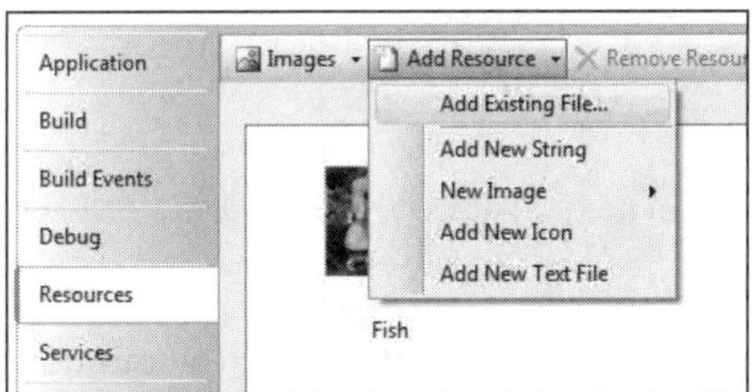

Figure 12-5

Mocking the file was straightforward. We basically mock the `Files` collection on the mock `Request` object. We mock it to return a count of 1, and we mock the first item in the collection to return the file-name and file stream.

Next, we mock the call to the service interface `Upload` method (we haven't created it yet). The rest of the test is similar to what we have been doing in previous chapters — set the controller's fake context, call the action, and verify the results.

As expected, the project doesn't compile. We first have to create our `GalleryController` class and its Upload action:

```
public class GalleryController : Controller
{
    public IGalleryService Service { get; set; }

    [Inject]
    public GalleryController(IGalleryService service)
    {
        Service = service;
    }

    [AcceptVerbs(HttpVerbs.Post)]
    [Authorize]
    public ActionResult Upload()
    {
        if(Request.Files.Count == 0)
            return null;

        var filename = Request.Files[0].FileName;
        var stream = Request.Files[0].InputStream;
```

```
        Service.Upload(User.Identity.Name, filename, stream);
        return null;
    }
}
```

The Upload action accepts only a post (that is how files are uploaded/posted to the server). It also requires the user to be logged in, since we need the username to properly associate the uploaded image with the user. I am returning `null` for the time being (just enough to get the code to compile and the test to pass).

Finally, we create our gallery service interface:

```
public interface IGalleryService
{
    int Upload(string username, string filename, Stream stream);
}
```

We will not worry about the interface implementation at the moment. Our test passes, which means that our file is being accessed properly and the right information (username, filename, and file stream) is passed to the `Upload` method from the service class.

Before we go any further, I want to make sure that this code works on the website. So, let's try it out. But before we can get it to work, we will have to do some plumbing, starting with the gallery service interface implementation. Of course, the following code should be preceded with tests, but we will skip this for the sake of brevity and to avoid repetition:

```
public class InMemoryGalleryService: IGalleryService
{
    private IGalleryRepository Repository { get; set; }

    public InMemoryGalleryService()
        : this(null)
    {
    }

    [Inject]
    public InMemoryGalleryService(IGalleryRepository repository)
    {
        Repository = repository ?? new InMemoryGalleryRepository();
    }

    public int Upload(string username, string filename, Stream stream)
    {
        return Repository.Upload(username, filename, stream);
    }
}
```

Create and implement the `IGalleryRepository` interface:

```
public interface IGalleryRepository
{
```

```
        int Upload(string username, string filename, Stream stream);
}

public class InMemoryGalleryRepository : IGalleryRepository
{
    private List<GalleryFile> GalleryFiles { get; set; }

    private List<Stream> Files { get; set; }

    public InMemoryGalleryRepository()
    {
        GalleryFiles = new List<GalleryFile>();
        Files = new List<Stream>();
    }


    private int _autoId;
    private int AutoId
    {
        get
        {
            _autoId += 1;
            return _autoId;
        }
    }

    public int Upload(string username, string filename, Stream stream)
    {
        var galleryFile = new GalleryFile
                        {
                            Id = AutoId,
                            Username = username,
                            OriginalFilename = filename,
                            Filename = Guid.NewGuid().ToString() +
                                    Path.GetExtension(filename)
                        };
        Files.Add(stream);
        GalleryFiles.Add(galleryFile);
        return galleryFile.Id;
    }
}
```

That was a simple implementation that stores the files in memory. A real-life implementation can store the file to a database, a filesystem, or cloud storage.

Do you remember how we previously created a modal dialog box that we were going to use for the gallery interface? Let's add a file upload to that dialog (Figure 12-6):

```
<div id="dialog" title="Image Gallery" style="display: none">
    <form id="frmImageUpload" enctype="multipart/form-data"
        action="/gallery/upload" method='post'>
```

```
            <input type="file" id='imageuploader' name='imageuploader'/>
            <input type="submit" value="Upload" />
        </form>
    </div>
```

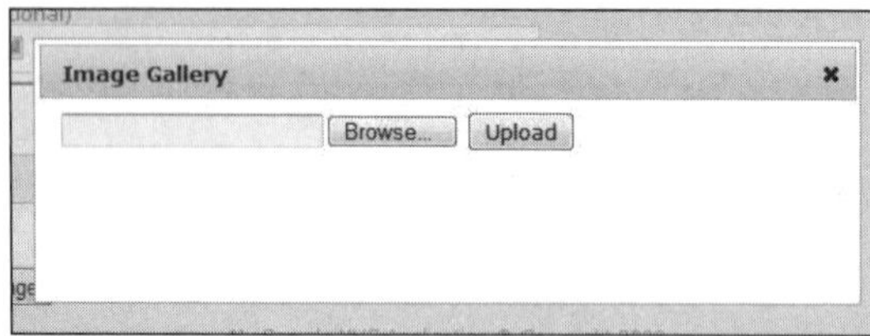

Figure 12-6

There a few things to note in the previous code. A file upload element (i.e., an `input` element with type `file`) must live inside a form, and that form must have its `enctype` set to `multipart/form-data`. It is also important to note that the above code will submit the form and refresh the page, which is not what we want. If the page refreshes, we will lose our form data and the dialog box will disappear. We want to use AJAX to submit the form. Luckily, there is an easy way to do this using jQuery:

```
$(document).ready(function() {
    $("#frmImageUpload").submit(function() {
        var f = $("#frmImageUpload");
        var action = f.attr("action");
        var serializedForm = f.serialize();
        $.post(action,
                serializedForm,
                function(result) {
                    alert(result.message);
                },
                "json");
        return false;
    });
});
```

The preceding code intercepts the form's `submit` event and uses jQuery's `post` method to submit the form's data using AJAX. We must return `false` to prevent the actual `submit` event from taking place, and that is how we avoid a page refresh. The third argument of the `post` method is a callback function that takes one parameter. For now, we are simply displaying an alert with the result's message. You are probably asking yourself what is the `result` variable and what is the `result.message`? The `result` variable is going to be a JSON object that is returned from the server that will have a `message` property with the appropriate value. Note that you can use other formats like text, xml, and so on; the format can be specified in the last argument (in this case, we specified `"json"`). Also note that you must specify the `id` and `name` attributes of the file `input` element or it will not work.

JSON

JSON (JavaScript Object Notation) is a lightweight data-interchange format. It is easy for humans to read and write and easy for machines to parse and generate. It is based on a subset of the JavaScript Programming Language, Standard ECMA-262, 3rd edition, December 1999.

JSON is a text format that is completely language-independent but uses conventions that are familiar to programmers of the C family of languages, including C, C++, C#, Java, JavaScript, Perl, Python, and many others. These properties make JSON an ideal data-interchange language.

Here is a JSON representation of an object:

```
{
    "firstName": "Bill",
    "lastName": "Gates",
    "address": {
        "streetAddress": "1234 Microsoft Way",
        "city": "Redmond",
        "state": "WA",
        "postalCode": 10000
    },
    "phoneNumbers": [
        "212 555-1234",
        "646 555-4567"
    ]
}
```

Luckily, ASP.NET MVC is very JSON-friendly, and it is very easy to serialize and de-serialize objects to and from JSON. To test the previous JavaScript code, we will change the Upload action to the following:

```
[AcceptVerbs(HttpVerbs.Post)]
[Authorize]
public ActionResult Upload()
{
    if (Request.Files.Count == 0)
        return Json(new {message="No files to upload"});

    var filename = Request.Files[0].FileName;
    var stream = Request.Files[0].InputStream;
    Service.Upload(User.Identity.Name, filename, stream);
    return Json(new { message = "File uploaded successfully" });
}
```

All we really did is change the return values. If we click on the Upload button without selecting a file, we will get the screen shown in Figure 12-7.

Figure 12-7

If we select a file and click Upload, we should see an Alert window telling us that the file was uploaded successfully. Instead, we see the same window shown in Figure 12-7. That is because our AJAX submit doesn't submit the file to the server. Fortunately, there are many jQuery plug-ins that enable AJAX uploads. They simply use a *hack* that submits the file through a dynamically created iframe, which, in turn, prevents any page refreshes. We could use one of these plug-ins, or we could create a simple iframe uploader.

```
<div id="dialog" title="Image Gallery" style="display: none">
    <iframe id='frameuploader' src="/gallery/uploader"
            style='width:100%;height:100%;' frameborder="0"></iframe>
</div>
```

The Uploader action simply returns a `View`:

```
[AcceptVerbs(HttpVerbs.Get)]
[Authorize]
public ActionResult Uploader()
{
    return View();
}
```

The `View` contains the upload form and will still look like Figure 12-6:

```
<form id="frmImageUpload" enctype="multipart/form-data" action="/gallery/upload"
    method='post'>
    <input type="file" id='imageuploader' name='imageuploader' />
    <input type="submit" value="Upload" />
    <%=Html.ValidationMessage("imageuploader") %>
</form>
```

We should also write new tests to test the new functionality that we are adding to the Upload action. We need to test that a validation error is added when no file is selected:

```
[Test]
public void upload_should_return_error_if_file_is_missing()
{
    //mock file
    var file1 = new Mock<HttpPostedFileBase>();
    MyMocks.Request.Expect(r => r.Files.Count).Returns(0);

    //mock service
```

```
        var mockService = new Mock<IGalleryService>();

        var con = new GalleryController(mockService.Object);
        con.SetFakeControllerContext();

        var result = con.Upload();

        result.AssertViewResult(con, null, "Uploader");
        con.ModelState.AssertErrorMessage("imageuploader", "No files to upload");

        //verify mocks
        MyMocks.Request.VerifyAll();
        file1.VerifyAll();
        mockService.VerifyAll();
    }
```

We then change the action to pass the test:

```
[AcceptVerbs(HttpVerbs.Post)]
[Authorize]
public ActionResult Upload()
{
    if (Request.Files.Count == 0 || Request.Files[0].ContentLength == 0)
    {
        ModelState.AddModelError("imageuploader", "No files to upload");
        return View("Uploader");
    }

    var filename = Request.Files[0].FileName;
    var stream = Request.Files[0].InputStream;

    return View("Uploader");
}
```

You will notice that these changes will break the first test (upload_should_save_uploaded_file).
The test can be modified as follows:

```
[Test]
public void upload_should_save_uploaded_file()
{
    //mock file
    var filename = "fish.jpg";
    var file1 = new Mock<HttpPostedFileBase>();
    file1.Expect(d => d.FileName).Returns(filename);
    file1.Expect(d => d.ContentLength).Returns(1);

    var ms = new MemoryStream();
    Resources.Fish.Save(ms, ImageFormat.Jpeg);
    file1.Expect(d => d.InputStream).Returns(ms);
    MyMocks.Request.Expect(r => r.Files.Count).Returns(1);
    MyMocks.Request.Expect(r => r.Files[0]).Returns(file1.Object);

    //mock service
```

```
var mockService = new Mock<IGalleryService>();
mockService.Expect(s => s.Upload(username, filename,
                                    ms)).Returns(0);

var con = new GalleryController(mockService.Object);
con.SetFakeControllerContext();

var result = con.Upload();

result.AssertViewResult(con, null, "Uploader");

//verify mocks
MyMocks.Request.VerifyAll();
file1.VerifyAll();
mockService.VerifyAll();
}
```

Now that both tests are passing, we can run the application and make sure that the file is uploaded correctly and that the validation error is displayed if no file exists, as in Figure 12-8.

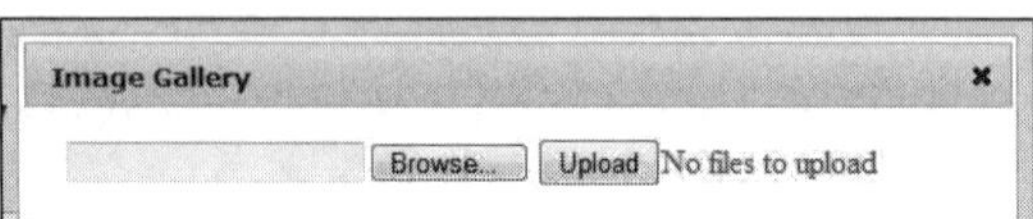

Figure 12-8

But we already knew that files were not uploading, so we need to test a successful upload. We need to display the list of images after a successful upload. The easiest way to do that is to use an AJAX call to get the images after the iframe refreshes. We can easily use jQuery to listen for the `load` event of the iframe as follows:

```
$("#frameuploader").load(function() {
    //retrieve images
});
```

Before we get into the details of the JavaScript, let's write a test for the action to retrieve images:

```
[Test]
public void getallimages_gets_list_of_uploaded_images()
{
    var mockService = new Mock<IGalleryService>();
    mockService.Expect(s => s.GetAllImages(username))
        .Returns(GetFakeListOfImages());

    var con = new GalleryController(mockService.Object);
    con.SetFakeControllerContext();

    var result = con.GetAllImages();

    Assert.IsInstanceOfType(typeof(JsonResult), result);
    var jsonResult = result as JsonResult;
    Assert.IsInstanceOfType(typeof(IList), jsonResult.Data);
```

```
        Assert.AreEqual(3, ((IList)jsonResult.Data).Count);
}
```

The previous test basically makes sure that we are returning a `JsonResult` and that it contains a list of the images. Since this is going to be an AJAX call, we will make it very simple and only return the image ID. The action method is as follows:

```
[AcceptVerbs(HttpVerbs.Get)]
[Authorize]
public ActionResult GetAllImages()
{
    var images = Service.GetAllImages(User.Identity.Name);
    return Json((from img in images select new {id = img.Id}).ToList());
}
```

The project will not compile until we add all the appropriate methods to the interfaces and implement them. That is similar to what we have been doing, so I am not going to get into the details here.

Let's talk about more interesting things, specifically, retrieving the list of images when the iframe loads and displaying the images. We first add a `div` element to hold the images:

```
<div id='galleryImages'></div>
```

The JavaScript is as follows:

```
$("#frameuploader").load(function() {
    $.get('/gallery/getallimages',
            null,
            function(data, textStatus) {
                $("#galleryImages").empty();
                $(data).each(function() {
                    $("#galleryImages")
                        .append("<img height='32px' src='/gallery/getimage/"
                            + this.id + "'/>");
                });
            },
            'json');
});
```

The previous JavaScript fires when the iframe is loaded and makes a call to the /gallery/getallimages action using the jQuery `get` method. When the request is completed, the callback function is called. We add code in the callback to clear the `div` containing the images, and then we loop through the returned data. If you recall, the returned data is a JSON array of image IDs. We then create an `image` element for each item in the array with the image source pointing to `/gallery/getimage/{id}`. The resulting HTML would look something like this:

```
<div id="galleryImages">
    <img height="32" src="/gallery/getimage/1"/>
    <img height="32" src="/gallery/getimage/2"/>
    <img height="32" src="/gallery/getimage/3"/>
</div>
```

We don't have an action to get the image, so let's write a test for that. The test should ensure that a `FileResult` is returned with the correct content type. The `FileResult` is a special `ActionResult` return type that can be used to stream any file back to the client, which is perfect for file downloads, dynamic images, or for retrieving images stored in a database or in the cloud.

```
[Test]
public void getimage_returns_image_as_a_file()
{
    var ms = new MemoryStream();
    Resources.Fish.Save(ms, ImageFormat.Jpeg);
    var bytes = new byte[ms.Length];
    ms.Read(bytes, 0, (int)ms.Length);

    var mockService = new Mock<IGalleryService>();
    mockService.Expect(s => s.GetImageBytes(username,1))
        .Returns(bytes);

    var con = new GalleryController(mockService.Object);
    con.SetFakeControllerContext();

    var result = con.GetImage(1);

    Assert.IsInstanceOfType(typeof(FileResult), result);
    var fileResult = result as FileResult;
    Assert.AreEqual("image/jpeg", fileResult.ContentType);
}
```

The `Action` method looks like this:

```
[AcceptVerbs(HttpVerbs.Get)]
public ActionResult GetImage(int id)
{
    var img = Service.GetImageBytes(User.Identity.Name, id);
    return File(img, "image/jpeg");
}
```

Again, I will not get into the details of implementing the service and repository since they are very similar to what we have been doing all along.

We can now test our `View`, upload some pictures, and see the list of existing images. You will notice that after each upload, the dialog box retrieves the new list to include the new image. You can see an example in Figure 12-9.

Figure 12-9

It is important to note that this is not a production-ready full implementation, and many of the details have been left out. In real life, you will want to retrieve thumbnails and not the full images. You will also want to paginate the list of images. I wanted to focus on the major pieces without distracting you with all the intricate details. I hope this gives you enough insight into what to do next.

We almost have a working image gallery. The next step is to select an image and have it inserted into our message body. This can be achieved with some JavaScript. We need to do two things: handle the `click` event on the image and insert the image into the WYSIWYG editor. We will rewrite our iframe `load` event handler as follows:

```
$("#frameuploader").load(function() {
    $.get('/gallery/getallimages',
            null,
            function(data, textStatus) {
                $("#galleryImages").empty();
                $(data).each(function() {
                    var imgid = this.id;
                    var img = $("<img height='32px' src='/gallery/getimage/"
                        + imgid + "'/>");
                    img.click(function() {
                        $("#html").wysiwyg("insertImage",
                                "http://localhost:4452/gallery/getimage/" + imgid);
                        $myDialog.dialog("close");
                    });
                    $("#galleryImages")
                        .append(img);
                });
            },
            'json');
});
```

The big difference here is that we create the image as a jQuery object and then wire its `click` event to insert the image into the editor and then close the dialog. We should end up with something like the screen shown in Figure 12-10.

You shouldn't hard-code the base URL into your JavaScript. Instead, you should dynamically generate it from the `Request.Url` *property.*

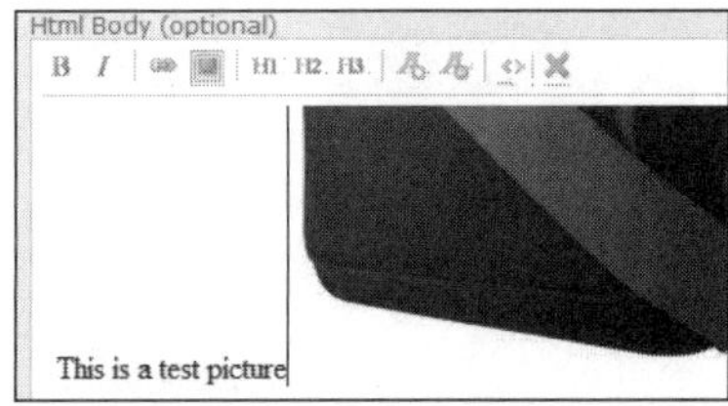

Figure 12-10

Summary

In this chapter, we got our hands dirty with some cool jQuery. We were able to quickly implement a WYSIWYG editor and customize it with AJAX file uploads to enable image insertion. We were also able to dynamically generate content and load files using AJAX without refreshing the browser. By now, you should be able to realize the power and, more importantly, the simplicity of jQuery.

We also used new features of the MVC framework, specifically its very simple JSON serialization and de-serialization as well as its byte streaming capabilities that allowed us to return images dynamically through a URL.

13

Message Templating

We have covered message creation including simple text and rich text messages as well as image hosting. All these features give users the capabilities they need to create a message that looks exactly the way they want. But all these steps have to be done manually. We need to give them a starting point so that they can get up and running quickly. In this chapter, we will create a templating system that provides a list of pre-made templates that will allow our users to instantly create a professional-looking email.

Problem

Even with the WYSIWYG editor, designing a message from scratch is time-consuming and repetitive. We need a way to provide users a pre-made template to use for their message. We also want to give them the ability to save their favorite designs as a template to be reused in future messages.

Design

There are two types of templates. There are pre-made templates that can be used by anyone, and there are user-made templates that are only available for that user. The pre-made templates are simply HTML files that can be read from a file or database and used as the starting body of the message. Figure 13-1 is an example of a template for a newsletter.

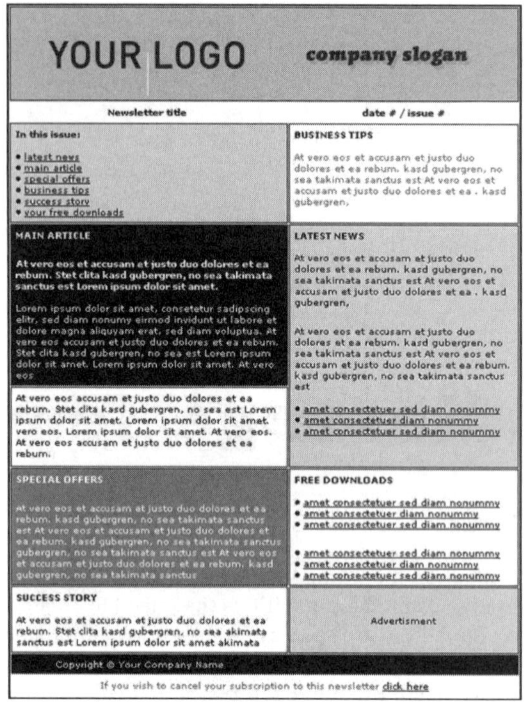

Figure 13-1

I am not going to show you the HTML for this template because it is too long, but Figure 13-2 is a screenshot of the HTML with the style and body tags collapsed.

```
<!DOCTYPE HTML PUBLIC "-//W3C//DTD HTML 4.01 Transitional//EN"
"http://www.w3.org/TR/html4/loose.dtd">
<html>
<head>
<title>Your Newsletter</title>
<meta http-equiv="Content-Type" content="text/html; charset=iso-8859-1" />
<style>...</style>
</head>
<body>...</body>
</html>
```

Figure 13-2

There are tons of free templates that you can find online and use to create your library of templates.

Once we create our library of templates, we can then display a list of templates to the user during message creation. When the user clicks on a template, we will read the template's HTML and add it into the WYSIWYG editor. The user can then make changes to the template and fill in the body with actual content.

> **Template Images. Caution!!!**
>
> Most templates will include some images whether they are images for a border, a separator, a custom background, or anything in between. Make sure that these images are referenced using the full URL and not relative or absolute URLs because they are going to be viewed in the user's email box and not on your website.
>
> For example, if you are using an image as a separator between sections, then it should be referenced like this:
>
> ```
> <img
>     src='http://acme.com/content/templates/images/t1_sep.gif'/>
> ```
>
> These will *not* work in the user's inbox:
>
> ```
> <img src=' /content/templates/images/t1_sep.gif'/>
> <img src='images/t1_sep.gif'/>
> ```

Solution

We will start off with a simple test to get the list of system templates. We will mock the call to the service class to return some `Template` objects:

```
[Test]
public void list_returns_system_templates()
{
    var mockSer = new Mock<ITemplateService>();
    mockSer.Expect(s => s.Get()).Returns(new List<Template>
                                    {
                                        new Template(),
                                        new Template()
                                    });
    var con = new TemplateController(mockSer.Object);
    var result = con.List();
    Assert.IsNotNull(result);
    result.AssertViewResult(con, null, "list");
    Assert.IsInstanceOfType(typeof(IList<Template>), con.ViewData.Model);
    Assert.AreEqual(4, (con.ViewData.Model as IList<Template>).Count);

}
```

Next step, let's make the solution compile. Create the controller with our List action as follows:

```
public class TemplateController : Controller
{
    [AcceptVerbs(HttpVerbs.Get)]
    [Authorize]
    public ActionResult List()
    {
```

```
            return null;
        }
    }
```

Create the model class `Template`:

```
    public class Template
    {
    }
```

Let's add the extra plumbing to make it pass the test. Add and initialize the template service with the `TemplateController` constructor:

```
    public ITemplateService Service { get; set; }

    public TemplateController():this(null)
    {

    }

    public TemplateController(ITemplateService service)
    {
        Service = service;
    }
```

The test should now pass. It is a good idea to see how things are looking with a view to make sure that things are working. Let's create a test for the service class. We will go ahead and mock the repository interface:

```
    [Test]
    public void get_should_return_list_of_templates()
    {
        var mockRepo = new Mock<ITemplateRepository>();
        mockRepo.Expect(r => r.Get()).Returns(new List<Template>
                                    {
                                        new Template(),
                                        new Template()
                                    }.AsQueryable());
        ITemplateService service = new InMemoryTemplateService(mockRepo.Object);
        var templates = service.Get();
        Assert.IsNotNull(templates);
        Assert.AreEqual(2, templates.Count);
    }
```

The project will not compile until we make a few changes. First, we need to implement the `ITemplateService` interface:

```
    public class InMemoryTemplateService : ITemplateService
    {
        public ITemplateRepository Repository { get; set; }

        public InMemoryTemplateService()
            : this(null)
        {
```

```
        }

        [Inject]
        public InMemoryTemplateService(ITemplateRepository repository)
        {
            Repository = repository;
        }

        public IList<Template> Get()
        {
            return null;
        }
    }
```

The test will still fail until we make a change to call the repository's `Get` method:

```
public IList<Template> Get()
{
    return Repository.Get().ToList();
}
```

We have a few more things to do before we can start creating a view to exercise all these methods. The next step is to implement the `Repository` interface. We will make this very simple and just hard-coded with some test data.

```
public class InMemoryTemplateRepository : ITemplateRepository
{
    public IQueryable<Template> Get()
    {
        return new List<Template>
                {
                    new Template
                        {
                            Path = "/content/templates/template1.htm",
                            Thumbnail = "/content/templates/images/template1.jpg"
                        },
                    new Template
                        {
                            Path = "/content/templates/template2.htm",
                            Thumbnail = "/content/templates/images/template2.jpg"
                        },
                    new Template
                        {
                            Path = "/content/templates/template3.htm",
                            Thumbnail = "/content/templates/images/template3.jpg"
                        },
                    new Template
                        {
                            Path = "/content/templates/template4.htm",
                            Thumbnail = "/content/templates/images/template4.jpg"
                        }
                }.AsQueryable();
    }
}
```

The model class, `Template`, is now starting to take some shape:

```csharp
public class Template
{
    public string Path { get; set; }
    public string Thumbnail { get; set; }
}
```

One last step to wire all these together is to register the interfaces for dependency injection with Ninject:

```csharp
Bind<ITemplateService>().To<InMemoryTemplateService>();
Bind<ITemplateRepository>().To<InMemoryTemplateRepository>()
    .Using<SingletonBehavior>();
```

Now it's time to visualize all this with a `View`. We will just add a simple list of template thumbnails on the message creation page for the user to choose from. I want to display this `View` in the message creation page, so I will go ahead and create a strongly typed partial view. We will keep it very simple for now and just display the thumbnails:

```
<%@ Control Language="C#"
            Inherits="System.Web.Mvc.ViewUserControl<IList<Template>>" %>
<% foreach (var template in Model)
    {%>
<img src='<%=template.Thumbnail %>' />
<%} %>
```

In the message create view, we will render the template gallery as follows:

```
<div id='templatesContainer'>
    <%Html.RenderPartial("/views/template/list.ascx", ViewData["templates"]); %>
</div>
```

This code will not work, and if we try to navigate to the create message screen, we will see the screen that appears in Figure 13-3.

Server Error in '/' Application.

The model item passed into the dictionary is of type 'MvcBookApplication.Data.Models.Message' but this dictionary requires a model item of type 'System.Collections.Generic.IList`1[MvcBookApplication.Data.Models.Template]'.

Description: An unhandled exception occurred during the execution of the current web request. Please review the stack trace for more information about the error and where it originated in the code.

Exception Details: System.InvalidOperationException: The model item passed into the dictionary is of type 'MvcBookApplication.Data.Models.Message' but this dictionary requires a model item of type 'System.Collections.Generic.IList`1[MvcBookApplication.Data.Models.Template]'.

Source Error:

```
Line 45:        </div>
Line 46: <div id='templatesContainer'>
Line 47:        <%Html.RenderPartial("/views/template/list.ascx", ViewData["templates"]); %>
Line 48: </div>
Line 49:
```

Source File: t:\projects\MvcBookApplication\MvcBookApplication\Views\Message\Create.aspx   **Line:** 47

Figure 13-3

The problem is that the Create action doesn't set the `ViewData["templates"]`. Before we can fix this, let's first create a test for it:

```
[Test]
public void create_should_set_templates_in_viewdata_on_get_requests()
{
    var mockSer = new Mock<ITemplateService>();
    mockSer.Expect(s => s.Get()).Returns(new List<Template>
                                 {
                                     new Template(),
                                     new Template()
                                 });

    controller.TemplateService = mockSer.Object;
    controller.Create();

    mockSer.VerifyAll();
    Assert.IsInstanceOfType(typeof(IList<Template>),
        controller.ViewData["templates"]);
    var templates = controller.ViewData["templates"] as IList<Template>;
    Assert.IsNotNull(templates);
    Assert.AreEqual(2, templates.Count);
}
```

We are basically testing that the `ViewData` contains an item for the templates and that it is of the correct type, not null, and has four templates. The test should fail. We will get the list of templates by adding the following line to the Create action:

```
ViewData["templates"] = TemplateService.Get();
```

Then we have to create the `TemplateService` property and initialize it:

```
public MessageController()
    : this(null,null)
{
}

[Inject]
public MessageController(IMessageService service,ITemplateService templateService)
{
    TemplateService = templateService ?? new InMemoryTemplateService();
    Service = service ?? new InMemoryMessageService();
}

public ITemplateService TemplateService { get; set; }
```

Owing to the constructor changes, some of our `MessageController` tests fail, so we have to go back and fix those tests and make sure they are still passing. Isn't Test Driven Development (TDD) great? Once all these errors are fixed, our test should pass.

The `View` should now work, and we should see something like Figure 13-4.

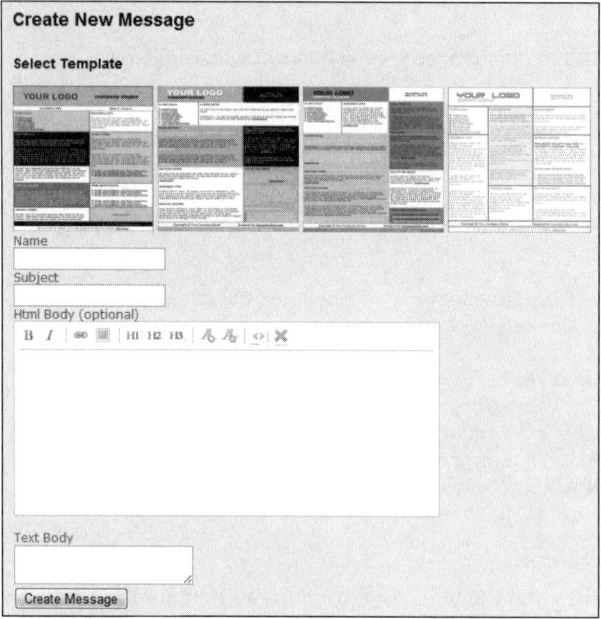

Figure 13-4

Let's add some JavaScript magic to apply the template to the WYSIWYG editor. First, we will wrap the thumbnails with a link as follows:

```
<a href='<%=template.Path %>' class='templatelink'>
    <img src='<%=template.Thumbnail %>' />
</a>
```

Then we add a `click` event handler for all links with the class `'templatelink'` and tell it to load the template file from the path and insert into the WYSIWYG editor:

```
$(".templatelink").click(function() {
    $.get($(this).attr("href"), null, function(data) {
        $("#html").wysiwyg('setContent', data);
    });
    return false;
});
```

If you try to click on one of the thumbnails, the WYSIWYG editor gets populated with the content of the HTML file and is ready for the user to customize. You can see that in Figure 13-5.

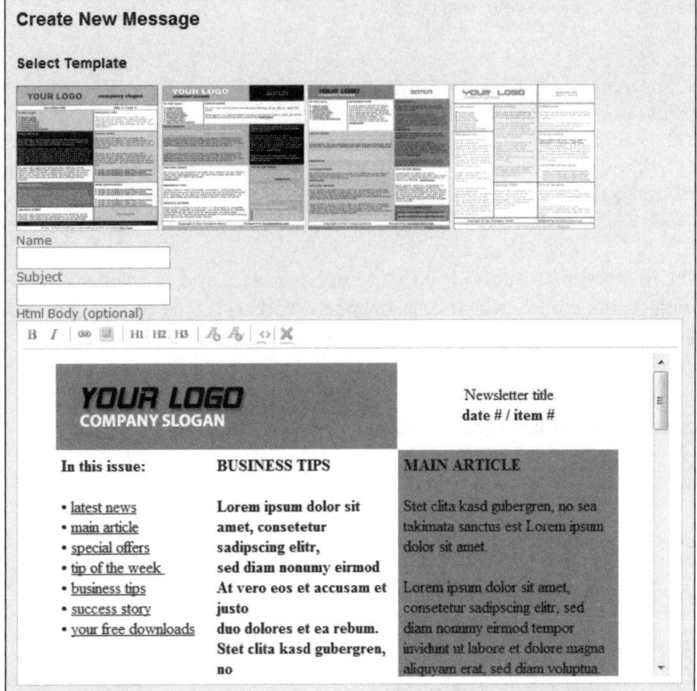

Figure 13-5

My Templates

Now that we have the logic for displaying the templates, selecting a template, and updating the editor with the template's code in place, let's work on giving the user the ability to save his or her own templates for later reuse.

We want our save functionality to use AJAX so that we won't have to leave the message create page to save the template. The first test is as follows:

```
[Test]
public void save_saves_user_template()
{
    var template = new Template();
    var username = "test";
    var mockSer = new Mock<ITemplateService>();
    mockSer.Expect(s => s.Save(username, template)).Returns(1);
    var con = new TemplateController(mockSer.Object);
    con.SetFakeControllerContext();
```

```
var result = con.Save(template);

mockSer.VerifyAll();
Assert.IsInstanceOfType(typeof(JsonResult), result);
var jsonResult = result as JsonResult;
Assert.IsInstanceOfType(typeof(JsonData), jsonResult.Data);
Assert.IsTrue(((JsonData)jsonResult.Data).success);
Assert.AreEqual(1, ((JsonData)jsonResult.Data).id);
}
```

The previous test calls the Save method with a template object and then checks the results. The expected result is a JSON object that contains a success property and an ID property. This code will not compile until we add the Save method to the service interface and controller and create the JsonData class. We also have to set up the fake context on the controller since we will be calling the User.Identity.Name property.

The service interface method is shown next:

```
int Save(string username, Template template);
```

The JsonData class is as follows:

```
public class JsonData
{
    public int id { get; set; }
    public bool success { get; set; }
}
```

And the Save controller action looks like this:

```
[AcceptVerbs(HttpVerbs.Post)]
[Authorize]
public ActionResult Save(Template template)
{
    return null;
}
```

The test will obviously fail. We need to call the Save method on the service interface and return JsonResult with an instance of JsonData. It looks like this:

```
[AcceptVerbs(HttpVerbs.Post)]
[Authorize]
public ActionResult Save(Template template)
{
    var id = Service.Save(User.Identity.Name, template);
    return Json(new JsonData()
                    {
                        success = true,
                        id = id
                    });
}
```

Let's implement the `Save` method on the service class and write a test for it:

```
[Test]
public void save_should_save_to_repository_and_return_id()
{
    var template = new Template();
    var username = "test";
    var mockRepo = new Mock<ITemplateRepository>();
    mockRepo.Expect(r => r.Save(username, template)).Returns(1);

    ITemplateService service = new InMemoryTemplateService(mockRepo.Object);
    var id = service.Save(username, template);

    mockRepo.VerifyAll();
    Assert.AreEqual(1,id);
}
```

We have to write the `Save` method on the repository, which looks identical to the one we just wrote for the service class:

```
int Save(string username, Template template);
```

There are several conditions that I am not testing here but that should be tested in a real-world application. Here is a list of possible tests you can run:

- Test for model validation
- Test that username is not missing
- Test error conditions and messages

Naturally, the next step is to test this code in the `View`, but before we do so, let us implement the functionality to retrieve user templates. We can write another method for listing the user templates, but instead I will overload the `List`/`Get` methods. The test is as follows:

```
[Test]
public void list_returns_user_templates()
{
    var username = "test";
    var mockSer = new Mock<ITemplateService>();
    mockSer.Expect(s => s.Get(username)).Returns(new List<Template>
                                {
                                    new Template(),
                                    new Template(),
                                    new Template()
                                });
    var con = new TemplateController(mockSer.Object);
    var result = con.List(username);
    Assert.IsNotNull(result);
    result.AssertViewResult(con, null, "list");
    Assert.IsInstanceOfType(typeof(IList<Template>), con.ViewData.Model);
    Assert.AreEqual(3, (con.ViewData.Model as IList<Template>).Count);
}
```

Compiling the project requires overloading the `Get` method on the service class:

```
IList<Template> Get(string username);
```

as well as changing the signature of the List action to the following:

```
[AcceptVerbs(HttpVerbs.Get)]
[Authorize]
public ActionResult List(string username)
{
    if(string.IsNullOrEmpty(username))
        return View("list", Service.Get());
    else
        return View("list", Service.Get(username));
}
```

These changes will break tests that call the List action without a parameter but that can be changed to `controller.List(null)` instead of `controller.List()`.

I am going to skip the next steps to avoid repetitiveness. These steps involve implementing the service and repository tests and code necessary to retrieve the user templates. Remember that these templates could be stored on the filesystem or database, but for testing purposes, we are using a repository that stores in memory. We can always swap the repository out and replace it with a database or filesystem-backed repository.

Once all this is in place, we will go ahead and make sure that things are working as they should in the `View`. In our `View`, we will add this snippet of code that will display thumbnails of `"my templates"` if there are any.

```
<% if ((ViewData["mytemplates"] as IList) != null &&
        (ViewData["mytemplates"] as IList).Count > 0)
   {%>
    <h3>My Templates</h3>

    <div id='myTemplates'>
        <% Html.RenderPartial("/views/template/list.ascx",
                            ViewData["mytemplates"]);%>
    </div>
<%}%>
```

We need to add this line of code to our Create message action:

```
ViewData["mytemplates"] = TemplateService.Get(User.Identity.Name);
```

Just as we did previously for the templates, we should write a test to ensure that the `"mytemplates"` data is set correctly:

```
[Test]
public void create_should_set_mytemplates_in_viewdata_on_get_requests()
{
    var mockSer = new Mock<ITemplateService>();
    mockSer.Expect(s => s.Get(Username)).Returns(new List<Template>
```

```
                                              {
                                                  new Template(),
                                                  new Template(),
                                                  new Template()
                                              });

        controller.TemplateService = mockSer.Object;
        controller.Create();

        mockSer.VerifyAll();
        Assert.IsInstanceOfType(typeof(IList<Template>),
            controller.ViewData["mytemplates"]);
        var templates = controller.ViewData["mytemplates"] as IList<Template>;
        Assert.IsNotNull(templates);
        Assert.AreEqual(3, templates.Count);
    }
```

Our `View` will not display anything since we haven't saved any templates. So let's do that. We want to add a toolbar button to the WYSIWYG editor to save the current content of the editor as an HTML template. Saving a template will require two values — the HTML content and the template name. This clearly shows that our initial code for the Save action will not work. Our Save action needs to change from `public ActionResult Save(Template template)` to `public ActionResult Save(string name, string content)`. Luckily, we have tests to ensure that we don't break anything. I will not detail all the changes since there is really nothing new that needs to be learned here.

We can add a toolbar to the WYSIWYG editor as follows:

```javascript
$("#html").wysiwyg({
    controls: {
        html: { visible: true },
        insertImage: {
            visible: true,
            exec: function() { showImageDialog(); }
        },
        saveTemplate: {
            visible: true,
            exec: function() { saveTemplate(); }
        }
    }
});
```

Then we can write the method `saveTemplate` to perform the actual saving as follows:

```javascript
function saveTemplate() {
    var content = $("#html").wysiwyg('getContent').html();
    var name = prompt("What is the name of the template?");
    $.ajax({
        type: "POST",
        url: "/template/save",
        dataType: 'json',
        data: { name: name, content: content },
        success: function(data) {
            if (data.success == true)
```

```
            alert("Template saved");
        else
            alert("Error saving");
    }
  });
}
```

The previous JavaScript method retrieves the content of the editor and prompts the user for a template name, then makes an AJAX POST request to the Save action in the template controller passing the appropriate data. You will also notice that we parse the returned data by calling its success property, which is set in the action using the `JsonResult` return type with a `JsonData` object.

I did not write code to dynamically generate the thumbnail for the templates and simply hard-coded some of the thumbnails.

There is also other functionality that we did not get into because it would be simply repeating many of the things with which we are already familiar. This functionality includes things like deleting an existing template, validating template filenames, generating thumbnails, and so on.

Summary

We have extended our message creation and WYSIWYG capabilities by giving the user the ability to create a message from a template. The templates are simply pre-made content pieces that populate the WYSIWYG editor. We defined some system/global templates that would be accessible to all users, but we also created the framework to enable users to create and reuse their own templates.

We did all this using some neat jQuery tricks and again have shown the power that is available to us through jQuery as well as the usefulness of a full suite of automated unit tests.

14

Billing and Subscriptions

Ultimately, we want to generate revenue from our application. There are many approaches to generate revenue from your web applications, and one of them is to charge a subscription fee for your services. We want our users to choose among several subscription plans that fit their needs and be able to click on a button to enter their payment information and get automatically billed every month.

Problem

We need to process credit card payments and automatically charge the monthly subscription fee to the user. We want our application to be flexible enough to allow us to switch our payment gateway with minimal impact on the overall application.

Design

There are several payment gateways readily available for us to use to process the payments and automate the subscription billing process. For the sake of this book, we will use PayPal as our payment processor of choice, but we will design our application to allow for easy switching to a different payment processor.

We will abstract our payment processor implementation using an interface that will enable us to write tests against mock implementations as well as easily add new implementations of the interface. Almost every payment processing system follows a similar process, in which they notify your application of the transaction information through an HTTP post to a *callback* or *notification* URL. We want to be able to receive this POST request, parse the data, and apply our business logic. Most payment gateways expect to receive a confirmation from your application that you received the callback — a *handshake*.

The interface for our payment service is very simple, as shown below and in Figure 14-1.

Figure 14-1

```
public interface IPaymentService
{
    void ProcessPayment(NameValueCollection formCollection);
    void PerformHandShake(HttpRequestBase Request);
}
```

Solution

We will start by creating a new test fixture called `PayControllerTests` as well as create a controller called PayController. Our callback action will not be rendering a view; it will simply accept the posted data from the payment processor (in this case, PayPal), perform the handshake, and process the data. Our first test will make sure that we are not returning any views:

```
[Test]
public void callback_should_return_null()
{
    var con = new PayController();
    var result = con.Callback();
    Assert.IsNull(result);
}
```

This test will fail until we add the following code to our PayController:

```
[AcceptVerbs(HttpVerbs.Post)]
public ActionResult Callback()
{
    return null;
}
```

For the next test, we want to verify that the callback method performs the handshake:

```
[Test]
public void callback_should_perform_hand_shake()
{
    var mockService = new Mock<IPaymentService>();
    mockService
        .Expect(s => s.PerformHandShake(MyMocks.Request.Object));

    var con = new PayController(mockService.Object);
    con.SetFakeControllerContext();
```

```
        con.Callback();

        mockService.VerifyAll();
    }
```

The test mocks the payment service and sets an expectation that the `PerformHandShake` must be called using the `Request` object of the controller. We will reuse the mocks and helper methods we already created in our project and then set the fake context on the controller to use them.

This test causes a cascade of code changes. First, we want to be able to compile the code and need to add an overloaded constructor to accept an instance of `IPaymentService`:

```
public IPaymentService PaymentService { get; set; }

public PayController()
    : this(null)
{
}

[Inject]
public PayController(IPaymentService paymentService)
{
    PaymentService = paymentService;
}
```

Run the test and you will see it fail because the expectation is not met. Then change the callback action as follows and rerun the test to make sure it passes:

```
[AcceptVerbs(HttpVerbs.Post)]
public ActionResult Callback()
{
    PaymentService.PerformHandShake(Request);
    return null;
}
```

Applying the same logic, we will test that the callback action calls the process payment method:

```
[Test]
public void callback_should_process_payment()
{
    var mockService = new Mock<IPaymentService>();
    mockService
        .Expect(s => s.ProcessPayment(MyMocks.Request.Object.Form));

    var con = new PayController(mockService.Object);
    con.SetFakeControllerContext();

    con.Callback();

    mockService.VerifyAll();
}
```

The final action is shown next:

```
[AcceptVerbs(HttpVerbs.Post)]
public ActionResult Callback()
{
    PaymentService.PerformHandShake(Request);
    PaymentService.ProcessPayment(Request.Form);
    return null;
}
```

That is all that our callback method needs to do. Of course, you will need to add some logging and exception-handling code. For example, you might want to send an email to an administrator if the payment processing fails.

PayPal Implementation

So far, we have done our testing with a mock payment service, but we will need a concrete implementation, and as previously mentioned, we will use PayPal as our payment processor.

First, let us examine the handshake process. The following steps need to be performed to create a successful handshake for PayPal:

1.   Get the values posted by PayPal.

2.   Create a new request to PayPal and send the same data appended with `"&cmd=_notify-validate"`. We are basically asking PayPal to verify the data that we received.

3.   PayPal responds, telling us whether the data is valid or not.

The handshake code follows next, but please note that I took out logging and exception handling for the sake of clarity:

```
public void PerformHandShake(HttpRequestBase Request)
{
    //Read the PayPals' Instant Pay Notification (IPN) POST
    var strFormValues = Encoding.ASCII
        .GetString(Request.BinaryRead(Request.ContentLength));

    // Create the request back
    var req = WebRequest
        .Create("https://www.paypal.com/cgi-bin/webscr");

    // Set values for the request back
    req.Method = "POST";
    req.ContentType = "application/x-www-form-urlencoded";
    var strNewValue = strFormValues + "&cmd=_notify-validate";
    req.ContentLength = strNewValue.Length;

    // Write the request back IPN strings
    var stOut = new StreamWriter(req.GetRequestStream(), Encoding.ASCII);
    stOut.Write(strNewValue);
    stOut.Close();
```

```csharp
            //send the request, read the response
            var strResponse = req.GetResponse();
            var IPNResponseStream = strResponse.GetResponseStream();
            var encode = System.Text.Encoding.GetEncoding("utf-8");
            var readStream = new StreamReader(IPNResponseStream, encode);


            var read = new char[256];
            var count = readStream.Read(read, 0, 256);
            string IPNResponse = new string(read, 0, count);
            if (IPNResponse == "VERIFIED")
            {
                //IPN is valid
            }
            else
            {
                //IPN is INVALID
            }

            //tidy up, close streams
            if (readStream != null) readStream.Close();
            if (strResponse != null) strResponse.Close();
        }
```

The problem with the previous code is that it is hard to test. We need to refactor it so that we can mock the requests and responses. We need to mock the creation of the `WebRequest`, so we will refactor out that code into an interface as follows:

```csharp
    public interface IPayPalServiceHelper
    {
        WebRequest CreateRequest(string url);
    }
```

Then we implement the interface as shown next:

```csharp
    public class PayPalServiceHelper : IPayPalServiceHelper
    {
        public WebRequest CreateRequest(string url)
        {
            return WebRequest.Create(url);
        }
    }
```

We then need to add a constructor to our class to take in a helper instance:

```csharp
    public IPayPalServiceHelper PayPalServiceHelper { get; set; }

    [Inject]
    public PayPalService(IPayPalServiceHelper payPalServiceHelper)
    {
        PayPalServiceHelper = payPalServiceHelper;
    }
```

Now we can change the line where we create the `WebRequest` to the following:

```
var req = PayPalServiceHelper
    .CreateRequest("https://www.paypal.com/cgi-bin/webscr");
```

We can now write a test to verify that the request is created and its properties correctly set. This is shown in the following test:

```
[Test]
public void handshake_should_create_request_to_paypal()
{
    var url = "https://www.paypal.com/cgi-bin/webscr";

    //mock the paypal response
    var mockPaypalResponse = new Mock<WebResponse>();
    mockPaypalResponse.Expect(r => r.GetResponseStream())
        .Returns(new MemoryStream());

    //mock the request to paypal
    var mockPaypalRequest = new Mock<WebRequest>();
    mockPaypalRequest.Expect(r => r.GetRequestStream())
        .Returns(new MemoryStream());
    mockPaypalRequest.Expect(r => r.GetResponse())
        .Returns(mockPaypalResponse.Object);

    //mock the service helper
    var mockHelper = new Mock<IPayPalServiceHelper>();
    mockHelper.Expect(h => h.CreateRequest(url))
        .Returns( mockPaypalRequest.Object);

    var requestcontent = "five";
    MyMocks.Request
        .Expect(r => r.ContentLength).Returns(requestcontent.Length);
    MyMocks.Request
        .Expect(r => r.BinaryRead(requestcontent.Length))
        .Returns((new ASCIIEncoding()).GetBytes(requestcontent));
    var service = new PayPalService(mockHelper.Object);
    service.PerformHandShake(MyMocks.Request.Object);

    //verify mocks
    long length = (requestcontent + "&cmd=_notify-validate").Length;
    mockPaypalRequest.VerifySet(r=> r.Method,"POST");
    mockPaypalRequest.VerifySet(r => r.ContentType,
                                "application/x-www-form-urlencoded");
    mockPaypalRequest.VerifySet(r => r.ContentLength, length);
    mockPaypalRequest.VerifyAll();
    mockHelper.VerifyAll();
}
```

Payment Processing

We have verified that the POST request we received is valid and is from PayPal, so we can go ahead and process the payment. There are two events we want to handle: subscription and cancellation.

PayPal passes this information in the form collection. An example of a new subscription data might look as follows:

```
txn_type=subscr_signup&subscr_id=S-
3BN760482J751000N&last_name=User&option_selection1=testsite&residence_country=US
&mc_currency=USD&item_name=Personal+Plan&amount1=0.00&business=paypal_1227363488
_biz%40dotnetfactory.com&amount3=10.00&recurring=1&verify_sign=
Afk7dIEf1cCYHX9Cs2tsYImOIL4QA46mcwPz-PuS2G9Gl6EI.VmIbAfO&payer_status=
verified&test_ipn=1&payer_email=paypal_1227363521_per%40dotnetfactory.com
&first_name=Test&receiver_email=paypal_1227363488_biz%40dotnetfactory.com
&payer_id=VSE7RKLHAZJ7J&option_name1=Site+Url&reattempt=1&item_number=2001
&subscr_date=08%3a53%3a33+Nov+22%2c+2008+PST&btn_id=8399&charset=windows-
1252&notify_version=2.5&period1=1+M&mc_amount1=0.00&period3=1+M&mc_amount3=10.00
```

The important values that we will need are:

- `txn_type`
- `payer_email`
- `item_name`

These values will tell us the transaction type, that is, subscribe or cancel; the payer's email; and the item name. The item name can be used to differentiate between different subscription plans, for example, Personal, Power, and Pro plans. Our first test makes sure that the repository save method is called with the correct information:

```csharp
[Test]
public void proccesspayment_should_call_repository_save_when_subscribing()
{
    var email = "payer@test.com";
    var plan = "Personal Plan";
    var mockRepo = new Mock<ISubscriptionPlanRepository>();
    mockRepo.Expect(s => s.Save(email, plan))
        .Returns(1);

    var service = new PayPalService(mockRepo.Object, null);
    var formCollection = new NameValueCollection
                            {
                                {"txn_type", "subscr_signup"},
                                {"payer_email", email},
                                {"item_name", plan}
                            };

    service.ProcessPayment(formCollection);
    mockRepo.VerifyAll();
}
```

For the previous code to compile, we have to create the `ISubscriptionPlanRepository` interface with a `Save` method:

```csharp
public interface ISubscriptionPlanRepository
{
    int Save(string email, string plan);
}
```

Then we need to change the PayPalService constructor to take an instance of the repository:

```
public ISubscriptionPlanRepository SubscriptionPlanRepository { get; set; }
public IPayPalServiceHelper PayPalServiceHelper { get; set; }

[Inject]
public PayPalService(ISubscriptionPlanRepository subscriptionPlanRepository,
IPayPalServiceHelper payPalServiceHelper)
{
    SubscriptionPlanRepository = subscriptionPlanRepository;
    PayPalServiceHelper = payPalServiceHelper;
}
```

The project will compile and the test will fail until we write the ProcessPayment method shown next:

```
public void ProcessPayment(NameValueCollection formCollection)
{
    //subscribe site
    var payerEmail = "";
    if (formCollection.AllKeys.Contains("payer_email"))
    {
        payerEmail = formCollection["payer_email"];
    }
    var txn_type = "";
    if (formCollection.AllKeys.Contains("txn_type"))
    {
        txn_type = formCollection["txn_type"];
    }
    var itemName = "";
    if (formCollection.AllKeys.Contains("item_name"))
    {
        itemName = formCollection["item_name"];
    }

    SubscriptionPlanRepository.Save(payerEmail, itemName);
}
```

Next, we test the case when the user is unsubscribing, as follows:

```
[Test]
public void
processpayment_should_call_repositor_save_when_unsubscribing_with_free_plan()
{
    var email = "payer@test.com";
    var plan = "Free Plan";
    var mockRepo = new Mock<ISubscriptionPlanRepository>();
    mockRepo.Expect(s => s.Save(email, plan))
        .Returns(1);

    var service = new PayPalService(mockRepo.Object, null);
    var formCollection = new NameValueCollection
                    {
                        {"txn_type", "subscr_cancel"},
                        {"payer_email", email}
```

```
            };

        service.ProcessPayment(formCollection);
        mockRepo.VerifyAll();
    }
```

The test will fail until we update the `ProcessPayment` as follows:

```
public void ProcessPayment(NameValueCollection formCollection)
{
    //subscribe site
    var payerEmail = "";
    if (formCollection.AllKeys.Contains("payer_email"))
    {
        payerEmail = formCollection["payer_email"];
    }
    var txn_type = "";
    if (formCollection.AllKeys.Contains("txn_type"))
    {
        txn_type = formCollection["txn_type"];
    }
    var itemName = "";
    if (formCollection.AllKeys.Contains("item_name"))
    {
        itemName = formCollection["item_name"];
    }

    if (txn_type == "subscr_cancel")
    {
        SubscriptionPlanRepository.Save(payerEmail, "Free Plan");

    }
    else if (txn_type == "subscr_signup")
    {
        SubscriptionPlanRepository.Save(payerEmail, itemName);
    }
}
```

Again, for the sake of clarity, I have not included exception handling, but the final solution should properly handle errors in processing payments.

Putting It All Together

Let's create a view to make sure that everything is working properly. First off, we need a view for the user to subscribe. We start with the following test:

```
[Test]
public void subscribe_should_return_view()
{
    var controller = new PayController();
    var result = controller.Subscribe();
    result.AssertViewResult(controller, "Subscribe", "subscribe");
}
```

The action simply sets the title and returns the view:

```
[AcceptVerbs(HttpVerbs.Get)]
public ActionResult Subscribe()
{
    ViewData["Title"] = "Subscribe";
    return View("subscribe");
}
```

This view will contain the "Subscribe Now" button. To create this button, do the following:

1. Log in to PayPal's Developer sandbox.

2. Create a subscription button.

3. Copy the button code from PayPal.

4. Paste it in the view.

The PayPal button code will look something like this:

```
<form action="https://www.paypal.com/cgi-bin/webscr" method="post">
<input type="hidden" name="cmd" value="_s-xclick">
<input type="hidden" name="hosted_button_id" value="1234567">
<table>
<tr><td><input type="hidden" name="on0" value="Site Url">Site
Url</td></tr><tr><td><input type="text" name="os0" maxlength="60">
</table>
<input type="image" src="https://www.paypal.com/en_US/i/btn/btn_subscribeCC_LG.gif"
border="0" name="submit" alt="">
<img alt="" border="0" src="https://www.paypal.com/en_US/i/scr/pixel.gif" width="1"
height="1">
</form>
```

This will create a button similar to the one shown in Figure 14-2.

Figure 14-2

PayPal's Developer sandbox allows you to create fully working buttons that go through the entire payment process but without actually processing any money. This is great for testing your application and making sure all the code works correctly without having to actually pay any money.

Once you click on the Subscribe button, you will be taken to the PayPal website to complete the transaction and then returned to your website. Once the payment is processed, PayPal will post the transaction information to the callback URL you specified when creating the button. In our test case, it will be `http://localhost:3451/pay/callback`. If you place a breakpoint in the callback action, the application will break when PayPal posts its data. You can then step through it and make sure that everything works correctly.

To test the unsubscription code, after you subscribe, log in to your PayPal sandbox account and cancel the subscription. This will cause PayPal to cancel the subscription and post the transaction detail to the callback method again.

For the view to actually work, we need to do a few things. First, we have to configure Ninject to inject the new interfaces. We need to add the following code to the dependency injection configuration:

```
Bind<IPaymentService>().To<PayPalService>();
Bind<IPayPalServiceHelper>().To<PayPalServiceHelper>();
Bind<ISubscriptionPlanRepository>().To<InMemorySubscriptionPlanRepository>();
```

We also have to create the repository implementation. We will use the same pattern we previously used for the contact and message repositories.

```
public class InMemorySubscriptionPlanRepository :ISubscriptionPlanRepository
{
    private List<SubscriptionPlan> SubscriptionPlans { get; set; }

    public InMemorySubscriptionPlanRepository()
    {
        SubscriptionPlans = new List<SubscriptionPlan>();
    }

    private int _autoId;
    private int AutoId
    {
        get
        {
            _autoId += 1;
            return _autoId;
        }
    }

    public int Save(string email, string plan)
    {
        var subscriptionPlan = SubscriptionPlans.SingleOrDefault(
            p => p.Email == email);
        if(subscriptionPlan == null)
        {
            subscriptionPlan = new SubscriptionPlan();
            subscriptionPlan.Id = AutoId;
            SubscriptionPlans.Add(subscriptionPlan);
        }
        subscriptionPlan.Email = email;
        subscriptionPlan.Plan = plan;
        return subscriptionPlan.Id;
    }
}
```

The SubscriptionPlan model is as follows:

```
class SubscriptionPlan
{
    public int Id { get; set; }
    public string Email { get; set; }
    public string Plan { get; set; }
}
```

Summary

In this chapter, we created a way for our users to subscribe to our services. We have designed our payment handling framework generically enough to enable us to use any payment processor. We also created a concrete implementation to illustrate the entire process using PayPal.

It is important to note that there are several alternatives to PayPal and some are just as easy to implement. I used PayPal to illustrate the concepts because of its ease of use, popularity, and my prior personal experience with it.

Implementing a payment processing service is an excellent candidate for mocking. We are able to mock a payment without actually creating a payment. This allows us to create simple tests that are not coupled to a specific web service or vendor.

15

Usage Tracking

Our customers have created messages and newsletters and have sent them to their clients. They want to be able to track the success of their campaign and see if their customers are opening their emails or responding to their communications.

Problem

We need to track and collect some metrics on the messages sent. Specifically, we want to know how many people opened the message, that is, read the email; how many clicked on links and which links were clicked; as well as who clicked which links.

There are two problems that we have to solve here. The first problem is figuring out how to track if the user opened the email. We cannot run JavaScript on the recipient's email client because most email clients (if not all) do not allow script execution. The second problem is figuring out how to track hyperlinks to know who clicked a link and what link they clicked.

Some of these metrics can only be measured if the email sent is in HTML format, so we will not get 100 percent reporting, but since most people receive HTML-formatted email, the missing data should be insignificant.

Design

The two problems mentioned previously need to be addressed differently. The first issue with tracking — who opened the email message — can be solved by using an interesting trick. Since we cannot run any client scripts, how do we tell if a message was opened? Surprisingly, there is a simple solution to this problem — we use an invisible image (a 1 pixel × 1 pixel white image). When the user opens the email message, the invisible image will be loaded, and by using a dynamically generated image, we can determine who opened the email. For example, here is a regular HTML tag for an image:

```
<img src='http://eventcontact.com/someinvisibleimage.jpg' />
```

Instead, we can dynamically generate the image link and pass parameters to the query string that will allow us to identify the user. We can do something like this:

```
<img src='http://acme.com/tracker/dynamicimage?email=abc@abc.com&messageid=1' />
```

The URL will be routed to the tracker controller, which will parse the query string and record the information in the database and then return to the client a 1 pixel × 1 pixel image. Since this URL will only be requested when the user views the email message, we are able to detect a successful view.

The second problem of tracking links is somewhat similar in concept. The idea is to use a link redirector so we can record the link click and then redirect the user to the requested link. For example, if there is a link in the message that takes the user to the order page — `http://acme.com/order` — the HTML for the link would look like this:

```
<a href='http://acme.com/order'>http://acme.com/order</a>
```

We can easily enable tracking by changing the `href` attribute to use our link redirector, so it could look something like this:

```
<a href='http://acme.com/tracker/link?url=http%3A%2F%2Facme.com%2Forder
            &email=abc@abc.com&messageid=1'>http://acme.com/order</a>
```

Now, the user clicks the link and is taken to our tracker controller's redirect action, which simply records the click and redirects the user to the requested URL.

Solution

Let's go ahead and create a controller with two actions:

```
public class TrackerController : Controller
{
    [AcceptVerbs(HttpVerbs.Get)]
    public ActionResult DynamicImage(string email, int? messageId)
    {
        return null;
    }

    [AcceptVerbs(HttpVerbs.Get)]
    public ActionResult Link(string url, string email, int? messageId)
    {
        return null;
    }
}
```

We will start our solution by creating a test to make sure that an image is returned even if no parameters are defined. This will ensure that the users don't get a broken image in their email. Here is the test:

```
[Test]
public void dynamicimage_should_return_image_even_when_no_parameters_defined()
{
    var con = new TrackerController();
    var result = con.DynamicImage(null);
    Assert.IsNotNull(result,"Result is null");
    Assert.IsInstanceOfType(typeof(FileContentResult), result,
                            "Wrong type returned");
    var fileContent = result as FileContentResult;
    Assert.AreEqual("tracker.jpg", fileContent.FileDownloadName,
                    "Wrong file name");
    Assert.AreEqual("image/jpeg", fileContent.ContentType, "Wrong content type");
}
```

This test basically calls the `DynamicImage` action and makes sure that the returned value is of type `FileContent` and that the filename and file content type are correct. In order to pass this test, we create an action in the `TrackerController` class as follows:

```
public class TrackerController : Controller
{
    [AcceptVerbs(HttpVerbs.Get)]
    public ActionResult DynamicImage(MessageAudit messageAudit)
    {
        var content = System.IO.File.ReadAllBytes
                            (Server.MapPath("~/content/tracker.jpg"));
        return File(content, "image/jpeg", "tracker.jpg");
    }
}
```

Make sure that you create a 1 pixel × 1 pixel JPEG image with your favorite image editor and save it in the content folder with the name *tracker.jpg*.

This test will still fail because the `Server` object is not initialized; we have to mock the call. We are also going to define a constant in the test fixture class to point to the location of the content folder on the computer:

```
private const string CONTENT_PATH =
    @"L:\projects\MvcBookApplication\MvcBookApplication\Content\";

[Test]
public void dynamicimage_should_return_image_when_no_parameters_defined()
{
    var con = new TrackerController();
    con.SetFakeControllerContext();
    MyMocks.Server.Expect(s => s.MapPath("~/content/tracker.jpg"))
        .Returns(CONTENT_PATH + "tracker.jpg");

    var result = con.DynamicImage(null);

    Assert.IsNotNull(result, "Result is null");
```

```
Assert.IsInstanceOfType(typeof(FileContentResult), result,
                        "Wrong type returned");
var fileContent = result as FileContentResult;
Assert.AreEqual("tracker.jpg", fileContent.FileDownloadName,
                "Wrong file name");
Assert.AreEqual("image/jpeg", fileContent.ContentType,
                "Wrong content type");
MyMocks.Server.VerifyAll();
}
```

The test simply mocks the call to the server's `MapPath` method and returns the path to the image using the hard-coded constant. One last thing we need to do before the project compiles and the test passes is to create the model `MessageAudit` as follows:

```
public class MessageAudit
{
    public int Id { get; set; }
    public int MessageId { get; set; }
    public string Email { get; set; }
    public string Action { get; set; }
    public DateTime CreatedOn { get; set; }
}
```

With our next test, we want to make sure that the View action gets recorded in the database (repository). Here is our test:

```
[Test]
public void dynamicimage_should_record_access_of_image()
{
    var messageAudit = new MessageAudit
                        {
                            Action = "View",
                            CreatedOn = DateTime.Now,
                            Email = "test@test.com",
                            MessageId = 2
                        };
    var mockService = new Mock<IMessageAuditService>();
    mockService.Expect(s => s.Add(messageAudit)).Returns(1);

    var con = new TrackerController(mockService.Object);
    con.SetFakeControllerContext();
    MyMocks.Server.Expect(s => s.MapPath("~/content/tracker.jpg"))
        .Returns(CONTENT_PATH + "tracker.jpg");

    var result = con.DynamicImage(messageAudit);
    Assert.IsNotNull(result, "Result is null");
    Assert.IsInstanceOfType(typeof(FileContentResult), result,
                            "Wrong type returned");
    var fileContent = result as FileContentResult;
    Assert.AreEqual("tracker.jpg", fileContent.FileDownloadName,
                    "Wrong file name");
    Assert.AreEqual("image/jpeg", fileContent.ContentType,
```

```
                    "Wrong content type");
        MyMocks.Server.VerifyAll();
        mockService.VerifyAll();
    }
```

The main objective of this test is to make sure that the `DynamicImage` action calls the `Add` method on the service class. This is enforced with the `mockService.VerifyalAll();` call at the end of the test.

Obviously, the project will not compile since we are missing the service interface. We are going to go ahead and use the same patterns we have been using throughout the book and create a repository and service interfaces as follows:

```
public interface IMessageAuditRepository
{
    int Add(MessageAudit messageAudit);
}


public interface IMessageAuditService
{
    int Add(MessageAudit messageAudit);
}
```

Then we will update the `TrackerController` class to take an instance of the `IMessageAuditService` interface through injection. Here are the changes to the `TrackerController` class:

```
public IMessageAuditService MessageAuditService { get; set; }

public TrackerController()
    : this(null)
{

}

[Inject]
public TrackerController(IMessageAuditService messageAuditService)
{
    MessageAuditService = messageAuditService ?? new InMemoryMessageAuditService();
}
```

Everything looks good now and the project compiles; we just have to make the test pass by changing the action to call the `Add` method on the service class:

```
[AcceptVerbs(HttpVerbs.Get)]
public ActionResult DynamicImage(MessageAudit messageAudit)
{
    if (messageAudit != null)
        MessageAuditService.Add(messageAudit);

    var content = System.IO.File.ReadAllBytes
                        (Server.MapPath("~/content/tracker.jpg"));
    return File(content, "image/jpeg", "tracker.jpg");
}
```

We cannot track whether a user opened an email message properly unless we have the user's email address and the message ID. With that said, let's create a test to make sure that we don't save anything to the database unless the email address is present. Here is the test:

```
[Test]
public void dynamicimage_should_record_access_only_if_email_is_present()
{
    var messageAudit = new MessageAudit
                        {
                            Action = "View",
                            CreatedOn = DateTime.Now,
                            Email = null,
                            MessageId = 2
                        };

    var con = new TrackerController(null);
    con.SetFakeControllerContext();
    MyMocks.Server.Expect(s => s.MapPath("~/content/tracker.jpg"))
        .Returns(CONTENT_PATH + "tracker.jpg");

    var result = con.DynamicImage(messageAudit);

    Assert.IsNotNull(result, "Result is null");
    Assert.IsInstanceOfType(typeof(FileContentResult), result,
                        "Wrong type returned");
    var fileContent = result as FileContentResult;
    Assert.AreEqual("tracker.jpg", fileContent.FileDownloadName,
                "Wrong file name");
    Assert.AreEqual("image/jpeg", fileContent.ContentType,
                "Wrong content type");
    MyMocks.Server.VerifyAll();
}
```

This test passes a null service instance to the `TrackerController`, so any call to the `Add` method on the service class will throw an exception. The test can be made to pass by simply adding another condition in the action to test for a missing email address; here is the action:

```
[AcceptVerbs(HttpVerbs.Get)]
public ActionResult DynamicImage(MessageAudit messageAudit)
{
    if (messageAudit != null && !string.IsNullOrEmpty(messageAudit.Email))
    {

        MessageAuditService.Add(messageAudit);

    }

    var content = System.IO.File.ReadAllBytes
                        (Server.MapPath("~/content/tracker.jpg"));
    return File(content, "image/jpeg", "tracker.jpg");
}
```

We will do the same thing by testing for the presence of a message ID and ensuring that we don't save if it is missing:

```
[Test]
public void dynamicimage_should_record_access_only_if_message_id_is_present()
{
    var messageAudit = new MessageAudit
    {
        Action = "View",
        CreatedOn = DateTime.Now,
        Email = "test@test.com"
    };

    var con = new TrackerController(null);
    con.SetFakeControllerContext();
    MyMocks.Server.Expect(s => s.MapPath("~/content/tracker.jpg"))
        .Returns(CONTENT_PATH + "tracker.jpg");

    var result = con.DynamicImage(messageAudit);

    Assert.IsNotNull(result, "Result is null");
    Assert.IsInstanceOfType(typeof(FileContentResult), result,
                        "Wrong type returned");
    var fileContent = result as FileContentResult;
    Assert.AreEqual("tracker.jpg", fileContent.FileDownloadName,
                "Wrong file name");
    Assert.AreEqual("image/jpeg", fileContent.ContentType,
                "Wrong content type");
    MyMocks.Server.VerifyAll();
}
```

Again, passing this test is a simple change to the action to test if the message ID is greater than zero.

```
[AcceptVerbs(HttpVerbs.Get)]
public ActionResult DynamicImage(MessageAudit messageAudit)
{
    if (messageAudit != null &&
        !string.IsNullOrEmpty(messageAudit.Email) &&
        messageAudit.MessageId > 0)
    {

        MessageAuditService.Add(messageAudit);

    }

    var content = System.IO.File.ReadAllBytes
                    (Server.MapPath("~/content/tracker.jpg"));
    return File(content, "image/jpeg", "tracker.jpg");
}
```

We want to be able to track the type of action being performed by the user. This is tracked by the `Action` property on the `MessageAudit` class. Don't let the name confuse you: `MessageAudit.Action` is just a property that will map to a column in the database and will contain the type of action such as "View", "Link", and so on. A call to DynamicImage means that the user has viewed the email message, so we want to make sure that it sets the type of action performed to "View". Here is the test for that:

```csharp
[Test]
public void dynamicimage_should_set_action_view()
{
    var messageAudit = new MessageAudit
    {
        CreatedOn = DateTime.Now,
        Email = "test@test.com",
        MessageId = 2
    };
    var mockService = new Mock<IMessageAuditService>();
    mockService.Expect(s => s.Add(messageAudit)).Returns(1);

    var con = new TrackerController(mockService.Object);
    con.SetFakeControllerContext();
    MyMocks.Server.Expect(s => s.MapPath("~/content/tracker.jpg"))
        .Returns(CONTENT_PATH + "tracker.jpg");

    var result = con.DynamicImage(messageAudit);

    Assert.AreEqual("View", messageAudit.Action);
    MyMocks.Server.VerifyAll();
    mockService.VerifyAll();
}
```

We are simply passing in an instance of MessageAudit that doesn't have the Action property set, and then we check to make sure that it gets set to "View" after a call to DynamicImage. Here are the changes to DynamicImage to make the test pass:

```csharp
[AcceptVerbs(HttpVerbs.Get)]
public ActionResult DynamicImage(MessageAudit messageAudit)
{
    if (messageAudit != null &&
        !string.IsNullOrEmpty(messageAudit.Email) &&
        messageAudit.MessageId > 0)
    {
        messageAudit.Action = "View";
        MessageAuditService.Add(messageAudit);

    }

    var content = System.IO.File.ReadAllBytes
                        (Server.MapPath("~/content/tracker.jpg"));
    return File(content, "image/jpeg", "tracker.jpg");
}
```

That covers the DynamicImage method and the tracking of an email message view. Let's test the next action we want to track — clicked links. Since we want to be able to report the links clicked by the user, we will have to add another property to the MessageAudit model to store the link. Let's call it URL. Here is the new model class:

```csharp
public class MessageAudit
{
    public int Id { get; set; }
    public int MessageId { get; set; }
    public string Email { get; set; }
    public string Action { get; set; }
    public string Url { get; set; }
    public DateTime CreatedOn { get; set; }
}
```

Our first test will make sure that the link action redirects to the URL:

```csharp
[Test]
public void link_should_redirect_to_url()
{
    var messageAudit = new MessageAudit
    {
        Url = "http://test.com"
    };

    var con = new TrackerController();
    con.SetFakeControllerContext();

    var result = con.Link(messageAudit);
    Assert.IsNotNull(result, "Result is null");
    Assert.IsInstanceOfType(typeof(RedirectResult), result,
                            "Wrong type returned");
    var redirectResult = result as RedirectResult;
    Assert.AreEqual(messageAudit.Url, redirectResult.Url);
}
```

We are basically calling a Link action on the controller and making sure that we are getting back a `RedirectResult` and that the redirect URL is the same as the one specified in the `MessageAudit` instance. We can easily pass this test by adding the following action to the `TrackController` class:

```csharp
[AcceptVerbs(HttpVerbs.Get)]
public ActionResult Link(MessageAudit messageAudit)
{
    return Redirect(messageAudit.Url);
}
```

Our next test makes sure that we are recording the event to the database by verifying that the Add method of the service class is getting called.

```csharp
[Test]
public void link_should_record_redirect()
{
    var messageAudit = new MessageAudit
```

```
    {
        Url = "http://test.com",
        Email = "test@test.com",
        MessageId = 2
    };
    var mockService = new Mock<IMessageAuditService>();
    mockService.Expect(s => s.Add(messageAudit)).Returns(1);

    var con = new TrackerController(mockService.Object);

    var result = con.Link(messageAudit);

    mockService.VerifyAll();
}
```

To pass this test, we simply call the Add method as follows:

```
[AcceptVerbs(HttpVerbs.Get)]
public ActionResult Link(MessageAudit messageAudit)
{
    MessageAuditService.Add(messageAudit);
    return Redirect(messageAudit.Url);
}
```

Similar to what we did with the DynamicImage method, we only want to save to the database if the message ID is present, so we create the following test:

```
[Test]
public void link_should_record_redirect_only_if_messageid_is_present()
{
    var messageAudit = new MessageAudit
    {
        Url = "http://test.com",
        Email = "test@test.com"
    };

    var con = new TrackerController();

    var result = con.Link(messageAudit);

    var redirectResult = result as RedirectResult;
    Assert.AreEqual(messageAudit.Url, redirectResult.Url);
}
```

We then add a condition in our Link method to test that MessageId is greater than zero before calling the Add method:

```
[AcceptVerbs(HttpVerbs.Get)]
public ActionResult Link(MessageAudit messageAudit)
{
    if(messageAudit.MessageId > 0)
    {
        MessageAuditService.Add(messageAudit);
```

```
        }
        return Redirect(messageAudit.Url);
    }
```

If for some reason the URL parameter is missing, then we want to make sure that we redirect some-where and not throw an error. For now, we will just redirect to our home page (the index action on our home controller). Here is our test:

```
[Test]
public void link_should_redirect_to_homepage_if_url_is_missing()
{
    var messageAudit = new MessageAudit
                            {
                                Email = "test@test.com",
                                MessageId = 2
                            };

    var con = new TrackerController();

    var result = con.Link(messageAudit);
    Assert.IsInstanceOfType(typeof (RedirectToRouteResult), result,
                        "Wrong result type");
    result.AssertRedirectToRouteResult("index", "home");
}
```

We will pass this test by redirecting to the Index action on the home controller if the URL is missing. Here are the changes to the Link action:

```
[AcceptVerbs(HttpVerbs.Get)]
public ActionResult Link(MessageAudit messageAudit)
{
    if (messageAudit == null || string.IsNullOrEmpty(messageAudit.Url))
    {
        return RedirectToAction("index", "home");
    }
    if(messageAudit.MessageId > 0)
    {
        MessageAuditService.Add(messageAudit);
    }

    return Redirect(messageAudit.Url);
}
```

Finally, we want to make sure that the type of the action being audited is correctly set. In this case, it needs to be set to "Click". The test is as follows:

```
[Test]
public void link_should_set_action_to_click()
{
    var messageAudit = new MessageAudit
    {
        Url = "http://test.com",
        Email = "test@test.com",
```

```
        MessageId = 2
    };
    var mockService = new Mock<IMessageAuditService>();
    mockService.Expect(s => s.Add(messageAudit)).Returns(1);

    var con = new TrackerController(mockService.Object);

    var result = con.Link(messageAudit);

    var redirectResult = result as RedirectResult;
    Assert.AreEqual(messageAudit.Url, redirectResult.Url);
    Assert.AreEqual("Click", messageAudit.Action);
    mockService.VerifyAll();
}
```

The test passes by setting the `Action` property to `"Click"` right before we call the `Add` method as follows:

```
[AcceptVerbs(HttpVerbs.Get)]
public ActionResult Link(MessageAudit messageAudit)
{
    if (messageAudit == null || string.IsNullOrEmpty(messageAudit.Url))
    {
        return RedirectToAction("index", "home");
    }
    if(messageAudit.MessageId > 0)
    {
        messageAudit.Action = "Click";
        MessageAuditService.Add(messageAudit);
    }

    return Redirect(messageAudit.Url);
}
```

Summary

In this chapter, we solved two problems related to tracking actions by our email message readers. We used a hidden tracking image to track the viewing of an image. We did that by adding a tiny, almost invisible image to the email message that points to a dynamically generated image. The URL to the dynamic image contains information about the message and the user that allows us to record the fact that the user has opened the email message and viewed it.

We also track hyperlinks in the email message by changing them to use our tracker controller. The links are changed to point to a Link action to the tracker controller that will use URL parameters to identify the message and the recipient, record the information to the database, and then redirect the user to the requested link.

16

Fill In the Blanks

So far, the previous chapters covered a lot of ground, but there were many blanks intentionally left unfilled. Creating a full, production quality application requires more detail than the pages of this book can hold. This chapter will sum things up and discuss how you can fill in the blanks for your application.

Problem

There are several things you have to do before you can release this application into the wild. You need to look at website styling, code refactoring, code optimization, and application scaling, among a few other things.

Design

Since this chapter discusses several topics, I will break it into subtopics so that it will be easier to follow. You can read the whole design topic, or you can just read the subtopic you are interested in and then jump to the related solution section.

User Interface

Creating a consistent style, look, and feel for your application is crucial and requires a lot of effort. There is no substitute for a professional designer, but using a standard UI library can help both developer and designer communicate efficiently. There are several UI libraries that are freely available, and most are Open Source. My personal favorite, which also happens to work well for us here since we are using jQuery, is the jQuery UI — `http://jqueryui.com`.

Refactor and Optimize

One of the many benefits of Test Driven Development (TDD) is that it allows you to make changes with the comfort of knowing that the tests will catch any mistakes. This makes refactoring many times easier. You refactor, run your tests, and make sure that all tests pass. If they don't, then the refactoring broke something.

With that in mind, we will go ahead and refactor and optimize our application. It's important to note that this section doesn't only apply to your server code. There is a lot of optimization to perform on the client side as well that will make pages download and run faster.

Scaling

This is a good problem to have. It means that your application is a hit and there are more users using it. On the flip side, you have to maintain an acceptable level of performance; otherwise, your users will start flocking to your competitors. We need to easily scale our application to accommodate our new users and increased demand.

Solution

User Interface

The jQuery UI is a very powerful and consistent user interface library. It also has an excellent online theme designer called ThemeRoller that lets you design your own theme online and then download it and use it within your website. You can see jQuery's ThemeRoller in Figure 16-1.

Figure 16-1

The library not only comes with styles and icons (Figure 16-2), but also contains several useful UI controls.

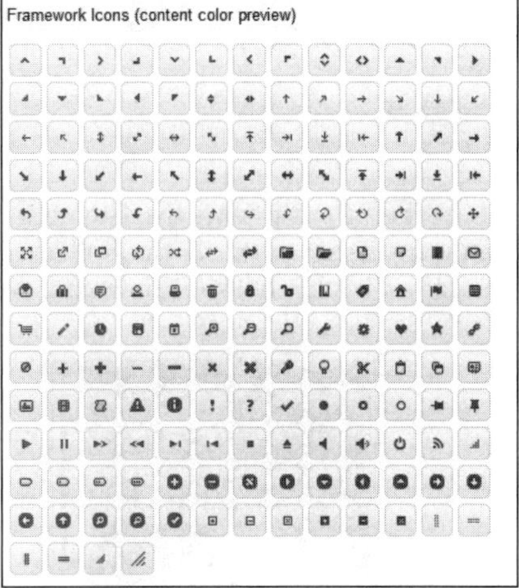

Figure 16-2

Some of the notable UI controls included are the Accordion (Figure 16-3), the Date Picker (Figure 16-4), and the Tabs (Figure 16-5).

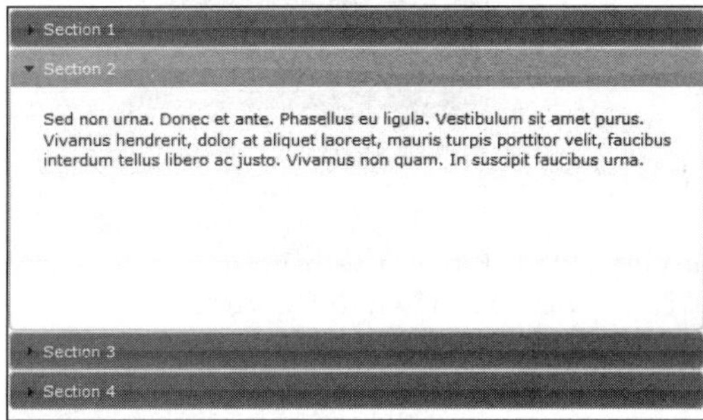

Figure 16-3

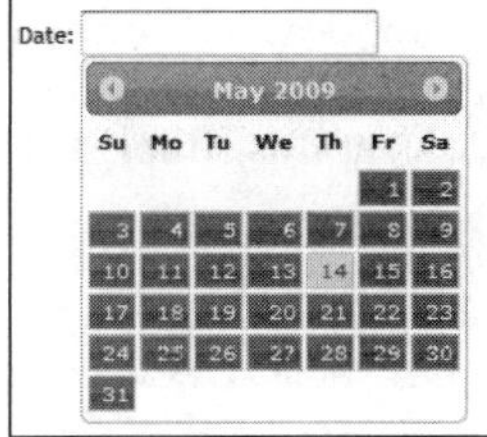

Figure 16-4

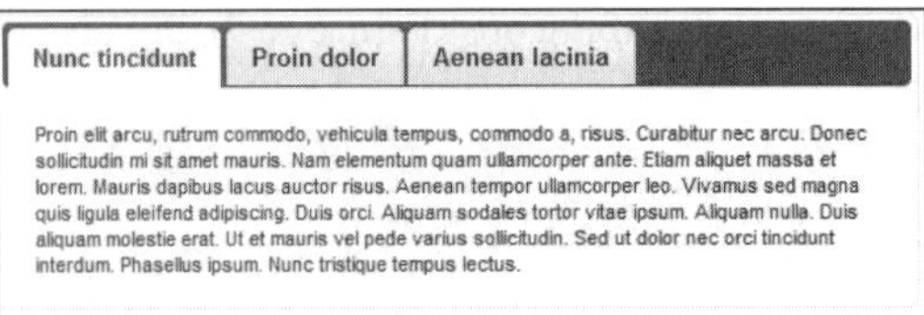

Figure 16-5

Another really useful feature of the theme designer is the ThemeRoller Firefox Bookmarklet (Figure 16-6). This will launch a mini-version of the ThemeRoller right on your website and let you try different themes and modify the colors on the fly to see how your website will look.

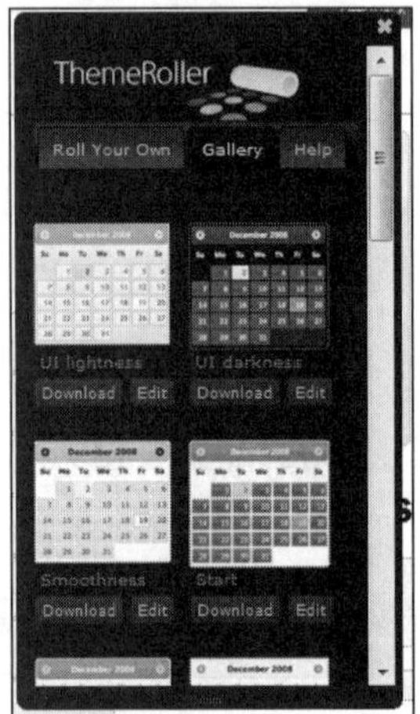

Figure 16-6

Once you have created the perfect look for your website, you can customize the download so that you only download the features you want, as shown in Figure 16-7.

In order to fully reap the benefits of the jQuery UI library, you must understand and use their conventions. By following these conventions, you will be able to switch themes instantly without any work. You can even provide your users the option to select their own themes. The library includes a robust CSS Framework that includes classes that cover a wide array of UI needs and can be manipulated with the jQuery UI ThemeRoller. There are several CSS classes that are designed to be applied to UI elements to achieve visual consistency across the application. You can find a detailed description of all the classes online at `http://jqueryui.com`, so I will not discuss all of them here. I will just mention a few, to give you an idea of how they work. Take a look at this simple HTML:

```
<div style='width: 400px'>
    <div>
        My Header</div>
    <div >
        This is my content. Lorem Ipsum is simply dummy text of the printing and
typesetting industry. Lorem Ipsum has been the industry's standard dummy text ever
since the 1500s, when an unknown printer took a galley of type and scrambled it to
make a type specimen book. It has survived not only five centuries, but also the
```

```
leap into electronic typesetting, remaining essentially unchanged. It was
popularised in the 1960s with the release of Letraset sheets containing Lorem
Ipsum passages, and more recently with desktop publishing software like Aldus
PageMaker including versions of Lorem Ipsum.
    </div>
</div>
```

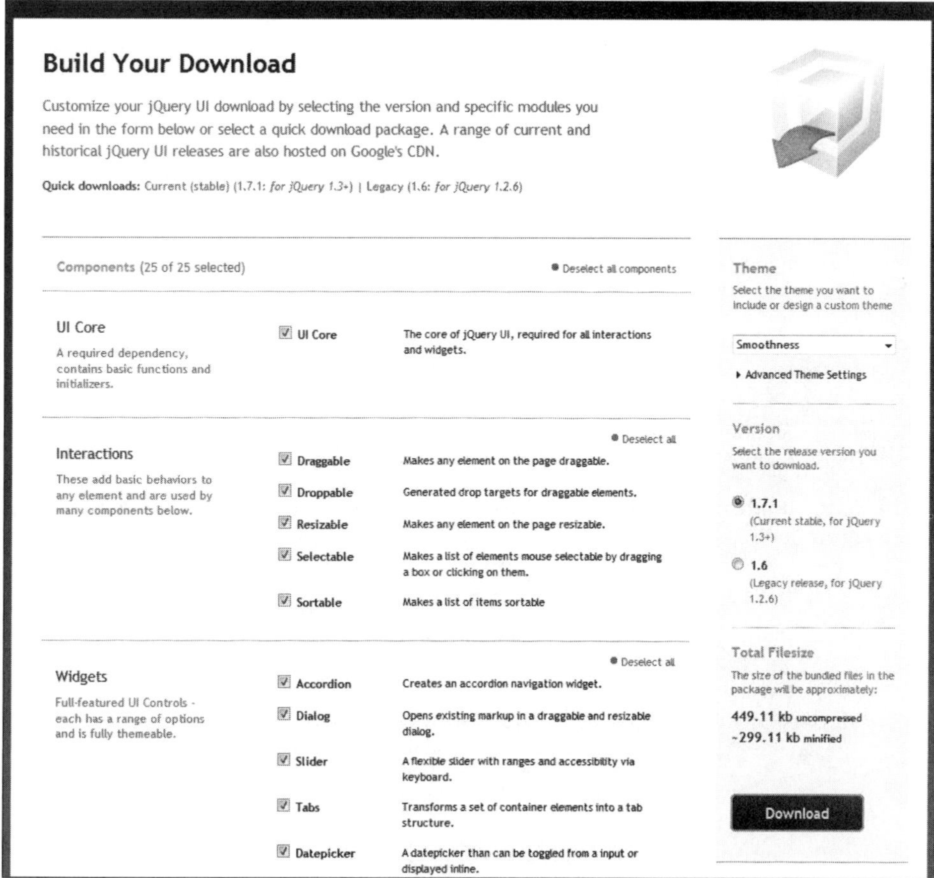

Figure 16-7

The previous HTML will render the web page shown in Figure 16-8.

My Header
This is my content. Lorem Ipsum is simply dummy text of the printing and typesetting industry. Lorem Ipsum has been the industry's standard dummy text ever since the 1500s, when an unknown printer took a galley of type and scrambled it to make a type specimen book. It has survived not only five centuries, but also the leap into electronic typesetting, remaining essentially unchanged. It was popularised in the 1960s with the release of Letraset sheets containing Lorem Ipsum passages, and more recently with desktop publishing software like Aldus PageMaker including versions of Lorem Ipsum.

Figure 16-8

We can use the following three classes defined in the CSS Framework to apply styling and theme support to our application:

- `.ui-widget` — Class to be applied on outer container of all widgets
- `.ui-widget-header` — Class to be applied to header containers
- `.ui-widget-content` — Class to be applied to content containers

The resulting markup is as follows:

```
<div class='ui-widget' style='width: 400px'>
    <div class='ui-widget-header'>
        My Header</div>
    <div class='ui-widget-content'>
        This is my content. Lorem Ipsum is simply dummy text of the printing and
typesetting industry. Lorem Ipsum has been the industry's standard dummy text ever
since the 1500s, when an unknown printer took a galley of type and scrambled it to
make a type specimen book. It has survived not only five centuries, but also the
leap into electronic typesetting, remaining essentially unchanged. It was
popularised in the 1960s with the release of Letraset sheets containing Lorem
Ipsum passages, and more recently with desktop publishing software like Aldus
PageMaker including versions of Lorem Ipsum.
    </div>
</div>
```

Using the Redmond theme from jQuery's extensive list of predefined themes, we render the page shown in Figure 16-9.

Figure 16-9

You might not see all the details shown in Figure 16-9 on paper, but on screen the difference is significant. The header has a beautiful blue background image, and there are distinct style and size differences between container, header, and content.

The best part about this is that we can switch themes instantly, and using ThemeRoller Firefox Bookmarklet, we can even see the changes on the fly. Take a look at the web page shown in Figure 16-10 with the "UI darkness" theme applied.

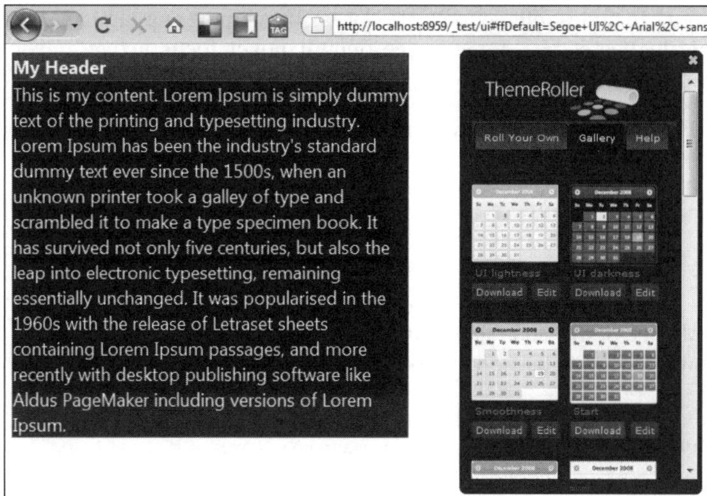

Figure 16-10

Figure 16-11 shows another example of a web page with the Black Tie theme applied. Note the stripes in the header's background.

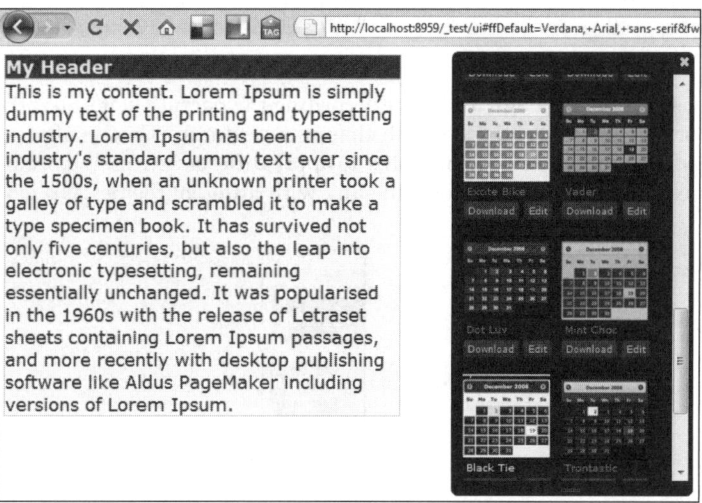

Figure 16-11

Following is another example in which we apply styles to the simple link `<a href='#'>Submit</a>` that will render the link shown in Figure 16-12.

Submit

Figure 16-12

The CSS Framework includes interaction state classes that can be applied to elements such as buttons and links to indicate their state — for example, default, hover, focus, active, and so on. The following code shows the link markup after applying a style to it. The rendered link is shown in Figure 16-13.

```
<a href='#' class='ui-state-default' style='padding: 4px;margin:4px;'>Submit</a>
```

Figure 16-13

We can even apply one of the icons shown in Figure 16-2 to the link by adding the appropriate class to a span indicating which icon to use. The markup is as follows:

```
<a href='#' class='ui-state-default'
   style='padding: 4px 4px 4px 18px; margin: 4px;'>
  <span class='ui-icon ui-icon-disk'
        style='position: absolute;margin: 2px 0 0 4px;'></span>Submit
</a>
```

The previous markup renders Figure 16-14.

Figure 16-14

The `ui-icon` class is smart enough to change according the parent's state. So if the link is in hover, active, default, or whatever state, the icon will change accordingly. This results in a visually consistent experience. Again, we can use the ThemeRoller to apply different styles and see how each one will affect our stylized link. Figure 16-15 shows the link with different themes applied to it.

Figure 16-15

Refactor and Optimize

When optimizing my code, I like to start with the low hanging fruit, the tweaks that give you the most bang for your buck. These are simple changes that can be easily applied and result in significant improvements to your application.

Minify JavaScript and CSS

Minification is the process of removing unnecessary characters from code to reduce its size. This results in a smaller file size, which, in turn, improves load time. For example, take a look at the following JavaScript code:

```
// this is my foo function
function foo() {
    var x = 2; //some variable
    alert(x); //display alert
    return false;
}
```

The previous code block when minified will look something like this:

```
function foo(){var x = 2;alert(x);return false;}
```

The savings in size and load times will be significant for a larger file. A good real-life example is jQuery itself. The development version of the library is 120 KB, and the production version, which is minified, is 56 KB. That is a reduction of more than half the size of the file.

gzip Components

gzip is the most popular compression method at this time. It was developed by the GNU project. gzipping generally reduces the response size by about 70 percent, and approximately 90 percent of today's browsers support gzip. Web browsers indicate support for compression with the Accept-Encoding header in HTTP requests.

```
Accept-Encoding: gzip, deflate
```

It is worthwhile to gzip HTML documents, scripts, and style sheets. It is also good to gzip any text response including XML and JSON, but avoid gzipping images and PDF files because they are already compressed and gzipping them wastes CPU power and time and could potentially increase the file size.

Other Front-End Optimization Tips

Put style sheets at the top of the page in the document HEAD. This allows browsers to render pages progressively and improves the *perceived performance* of the page. The user will start to see content as it is downloaded — for example, the logo, header, navigation, and so on. If the style sheet is at the bottom, some browsers will block until the entire page is downloaded, which will leave your users staring at a blank page.

Don't use a bigger image and scale it down using HTML. If you want a 60 × 60 image, then use a 60 × 60 image. Don't use a 400 × 400 image and scale it down in HTML using `<img width='60' height='60' src='myimage.jpg'/>`.

Use a favicon.ico, and make it small and cacheable. This is an image that is located in the root of the server and is used by the browser in the toolbar, address bar, bookmarks, and so on (see Figure 16-16). Unfortunately, it is requested whether you have it or not, and your server will respond with a 404 Not

Found if you don't have it. Make the image small, preferably under 1K, and set its Expires header a few months in the future so that it gets cached by the client.

Figure 16-16

Use GET for AJAX requests because a POST is implemented as a two-step process. A POST will send the headers first and then the data, but a GET will take one packet. It also makes semantic sense to use GET to retrieve data.

Output Caching

ASP.NET has an incredibly useful technique for caching content — output caching. This is also available to us in ASP.NET MVC and has the added bonus of caching controller actions using the `OutputCache` attribute.

```
[OutputCache(Duration = 60)]
public ActionResult SomeAction()
{
    return View();
}
```

The previous code will cache the action. The `OutputCache` attribute has parameters similar to the `<%@ OutputCache %>` directive. So you can vary the caching by a parameter, encoding, and so on, and set the cache location. The following code caches the action for 60 seconds and varies it by the `userName` parameter:

```
[OutputCache(VaryByParam = "userName", Duration = 60)]
public ActionResult Profile(string userName)
{
    return View();
}
```

Code Refactor

Code refactoring as defined in Wikipedia is the process of changing a computer program's internal structure without modifying its external functional behavior or existing functionality. This is usually done to improve code readability; simplify code structure; and improve maintainability, performance, and extensibility.

It is important to note that code refactoring doesn't only apply to the application code but also to your tests. For example, if we have multiple tests that perform similar steps, these common steps can be refactored into a method. To elaborate, imagine we have several test cases that need to assert the view results with the following lines of code:

```
var result = controller.SomeAction();
Assert.IsNotNull(result);
```

```
    Assert.IsInstanceOfType(typeof(ViewResult), result);
    Assert.IsEmpty(((ViewResult)result).ViewName);
    Assert.AreEqual("Some Title", controller.ViewData["Title"], "Page title is wrong");
```

Instead of rewriting the previous four lines of code inside several tests, we could refactor those into a method. The following code is an extension method that performs the same functionality:

```
public static void AssertViewResult(this ActionResult result,
                                    Controller controller,
                                    string title)
{
    Assert.IsNotNull(result);
    Assert.IsInstanceOfType(typeof(ViewResult), result);
    Assert.IsEmpty(((ViewResult)result).ViewName);
    Assert.AreEqual(title, controller.ViewData["Title"], "Page title is wrong");
}
```

Now our tests can simply perform the same functionality by calling this method as follows:

```
[Test]
public void SomeAction_Should_Return_View_With_Correct_Title()
{
    var result = controller.SomeAction();
    result.AssertViewResult(controller, "Some Title");
}
```

If we refactored this out of 20 tests, then we have eliminated 60 lines of code, but more importantly, we now have one place to maintain.

It is important to understand that refactoring does not fix bugs or add or remove functionality. It is the process of improving the source code without changing the overall results.

The beauty of using test-driven development is that we have the safety net of our tests to ensure that our refactoring did not break anything, that is, the end result has not changed.

Scaling

No matter how much you improve, optimize, and refactor the code, you will eventually get to a point where you just need more physical resources — be it more memory, a faster server, or multiple servers. Fortunately, we have several options at our disposal.

Scale Up (Scale Vertically)

Scaling up means adding more resources to (upgrading) your servers. This typically means adding more and/or faster CPUs, memory, hard drives, and so on to a server.

Scale Out (Scale Horizontally)

Eventually, even the fastest server will not be fast enough, and you will probably achieve better performance and for less money by scaling out. *Scale out* means adding more machines to your infrastructure. These machines are usually load-balanced using a software or hardware load balancer. A load balancer simply ensures that the workload is balanced across the machines, so that no one machine is overworked.

Cloud Computing

There are now several available options to allow you to host your application in the cloud and have the ability to get Internet Scale very easily and quickly and without breaking the bank. There are several solutions available for ASP.NET applications:

❑   Amazon Elastic Computer Cloud (EC2)

❑   Microsoft Windows Azure

❑   GoGrid

Both EC2 and GoGrid enable you to create virtual machines in the cloud whenever you need them, and you are charged per usage. This gives you the flexibility to launch 10 servers one day, and if demand increases, you can launch more, or if it decreases, you can delete unneeded machines to save money. These virtual machines are individual computers that are accessible just like regular machines.

Microsoft Windows Azure is a little different in that there are really no machines. It is more of a platform or a cloud operating system. You simply deploy your application into the cloud and set parameters to tell it how to scale up and down. Everything else is handled by the "operating system."

My personal favorite is GoGrid (Figure 16-17). It comes with free load balancing, and you can easily deploy web servers and database servers; you also have access to cloud storage.

Figure 16-17

Although this is not scientific, I have found that I received the best performance by combining cloud hosting for web servers with dedicated hosting for database servers. This is mostly because database servers require frequent I/O (disk) access, which is normally a lot slower in a virtual machine than in a dedicated machine. I believe that this sort of hybrid solution provides the best of both worlds and the benefit of instant scalability at an affordable price.

Summary

In this chapter, I tried to fill in some of the gaps in the overall application that we have overlooked in earlier chapters. It is important to note that each one of the topics discussed here can be a book of its own and this is in no way a thorough examination of these topics. It was simply an eye opener, a summary if you like, that will hopefully point you in the right direction and get you thinking about where to go next.

Index

C

caching

images, 257–258

output caching, 258

callbacks

payment processing and, 225

verifying performance by callback method, 226–228

campaign report, reports and stats design, 5

Cascading Style Sheets (CSS)

in jQuery UI Library, 252–256

minification of, 257

classes

ASP.NET MVC model, 7

defining user class, 122

`click` **events, images, 209**

client-side validation, 87–92

benefits of, 73

options for, 87–88

test class for, 88–92

validating contact view, 115–116

cloud computing, 260

code coverage, 19–20

code refactoring. See refactoring code

ComplexModelBinder, 69

composing messages

adding instance of `IMessageService`, 170

`Authorize` attribute for controlling access to message creation, 168

coding edit functionality, 180–181

creating message controller, 168

design process, 167

helper methods for populating repository, 176–177

listing existing messages, 174–175

overview of, 167

populating repository with messages, 179–180

problem statement, 167

Request Validation and, 185

returning error message if requested message does not exist, 181–182

saving changes to repository, 183

summary, 185–186

testing if user can see messages, 182

testing that message is added to repository, 171–172

validating message name, 168–169

views of, 172–173, 178–179, 183–184

compression, gzip for, 257

constructor parameters, dependency injection and, 103, 106–107

Contact Lists, 110

contact management

browsing contacts. See browsing contacts

checking validity of contact information (email, date of birth), 114–116

contact defined, 111

controller for, 112–113

`Create` action, 113–114, 119

creating contacts, 111

deleting contacts, 111, 143–144

design, 110–111

editing contacts. See editing contacts

establishing relationship between user and contact, 121–122

high-level design for, 32–33

importing contacts. See importing contacts

instantiating controller using dependency injection, 123–125

notification of successful creation of contact, 119–120

overview of, 3–5, 109

Q

queue-monitoring service, 31

R

RAD (Rapid Application Development), 7
range attribute, validation attributes, 84
Rapid Application Development (RAD), 7
read action, CRUD operations, 31
`RedirectToRouteResult` **value, 39**
Redmond theme, 254
refactoring code, 65–72
  assertions and, 70–72
  design, 66, 250
  generic assertions and, 66–67
  mocking and, 67–68
  model binders and, 69–70
  optimizing code and, 258–259
  overview of, 65
  PayPal implementation, 229
  problem statement, 65–66
  setup method running for every test, 67
  summary, 72
Register action tests
  error returned if email invalid, 45–47
  error returned if email missing, 43–44
  error returned if username invalid, 47–52
  error returned if username missing, 42–43
  getting to register view, 37–38
  redirects to home index on success,
      40–42, 52–53
  successfully registration of new
      user, 39–40
registration (signup) process
  action tests. See Register action tests
  forms authentication, 54–55
  login process, 27–28

overview of, 35–36
password confirmation, 27
problem, 35
reset password process, 28–29
user registration, 25–26
regular expression attribute, validation
    attributes, 84
reports and stats, viewing, 5
repositories
  adding contacts to, 159–161
  adding message to, 171
  creating for usage tracking, 240–241
  helper function for populating test
      repository, 176
  `IContactRepository`, 121
  `IGalleryRepository`, 200–201
  `IMessageRepository`. *See*
      `IMessageRepository`
  `IRespository` pattern as alternative to
      testing, 93
  for PayPal service, 235
  `PopulateRepository` method, 126–127
  populating with messages, 179
  repository pattern, 15
  saving changes to, 183
Request Validation, 185
`Request.Files`, **148, 198**
`Request.Url` **property, 209**
required attribute, validation attributes, 84
requirements
  aspect-oriented programming (AOP), 12–13
  code coverage, 19–20
  contact management design, 3–5
  design, 1–2
  IoC containers, 21
  JavaScript libraries, 19
  message management design, 2–3

View state, master page, 60–63

`ViewData`

  ASP.NET MVC, 8–9

  `ModelState` property, 10

  `TempData` vs., 9–10 

  testing for template item, 217

  testing `mytemplates` data, 222–223

viewing, compared with editing, 4

`ViewPage`, **ASP.NET MVC, 7**

Views folder, 56

`ViewUserControl`, **7**

virtual machines, cloud solutions and, 260

Visual Studio 2008, 7

W

W3C XHTML specification, 189

Web references

  free test runner, 34

  ReSharper, 34

WebForms model, ASP.NET

  defined, 6

  strengths of, 7

`WebRequest`, **mocking creation of, 229–230**

Windows Azure, Microsoft, 260

WYMeditor, 189–190

WYSIWYG (what you see is what you get) editors

  adding template to, 218–219

  design, 187 

  factors in choosing, 188

  jWYSIWYG, 192–193

  NicEdit, 190–191

  problem statement, 187 

  saving content as HTML template, 223–224

  TinyMCE, 188

  WYMeditor, 189–190

WYSIWYM (what you see is what you mean) editors, 189

X

XHTML, 189

Y

YAGNI (you ain't gonna need it) principle, 15

YUI (Yahoo! User Interface Library)

  Rich Text Editor and, 193

  using, 20